THE COMPLETE BOOK OF
GARDENING

THE COMPLETE BOOK OF
GARDENING

NEW
BURLINGTON
BOOKS

A QUINTET BOOK

Published by New Burlington Books
6 Blundell Street
London N7 9BH
Exclusive to Coles in Canada

ISBN 1-85348-351-6

This book was designed and produced by
Quintet Publishing Limited
6 Blundell Street
London N7 9BH

Designer: Melanie Williams (H J & Co.)
Project Editor: Emma Callery

Typeset in Great Britain by Typestyles, Essex
Manufactured in Singapore by Chroma Graphics Limited
Printed in Hong Kong by Leefung-Asco Printers Limited

CONTENTS

———— ✦ ————

Understanding your garden

chapter one

UNDERSTANDING YOUR GARDEN

The schedule of work in the garden will often depend on weather conditions, particularly in winter if the soil is frozen or too wet or covered in snow. Autumn jobs may spill over into winter, but if they have not been carried out by mid-winter, they may have to wait until spring. Spring gradually becomes very busy; early summer is moderately demanding and late summmer is comparatively quiet. However, within the seasons much variation of conditions can occur. In town gardens and, to a lesser extent, suburban gardens, the changes in the weather are mellowed by the surrounding buildings, but in country gardens a day-to-day awareness is as necessary as it is to a farmer. But wherever the garden, it pays to listen to the weather forecasts and to pick your time for doing various jobs. For instance, attempting to cultivate heavy soil that is very wet is damaging and hard work. The same applies when soil is really dry. Wait for a dry period or a drying wind in the first case and some gentle steady rain in the second.

Do not try to plant in autumn or winter when frost or snow are forecast and be very wary of planting during droughts. When spring fever overcomes you, do not rush out into the garden, even if the weather suddenly seems suitable. General seed-sowing time is better left until the weather is more stable and less likely to adversely affect germination. It is advisable not to plant tender species like bedding plants, dahlias and half-hardy annuals outdoors until the warm weather has begun — apart from the risk of night frosts, the soil itself is often still too cold for plants to start well. At the end of summer, be ready at short notice to take tender plants indoors and to cover up others such as dahlias, which will die given one or two sudden, early frosts. The seasons rarely start at the same time each year, and gardening jobs should be arranged accordingly: when the soil is in the right condition and the plants have reached a stage at which they need the next treatment.

7

Bright splashes of colour in your garden provide areas of tremendous impact.

The right environment

Before you set about choosing and acquiring plants, it is important to establish the type of environment your garden provides, particularly in terms of soil and climate. Matching the right plants with the right environment is a large part of garden survival. Heathers, for example, grow on windswept highlands and hillsides where there are more rocks than soil, and the soil itself is peaty and acid. Planting heathers in a flowerbed sheltered from wind in a deep, fertile soil will only result in excessively leafy plants, practically without flowers, which will be frequently infected with fungal diseases. Heathers should be planted in a rock garden where the soil is quick-draining and sparse, or in a site open to wind and sky, where the soil is sandy and stony.

Other factors are also important. Is your garden 'warm' or 'cold'? Is the rainfall heavy in your area? How windy is it? How much sunlight does your garden receive? These conditions may also vary considerably within the garden — areas which receive sunlight at different times of the day or not at all, areas which are sheltered from the wind or exposed to the elements. The micro-climate and particular conditions of a specific position are just as important for a plant's welfare as the conditions which pertain to the garden.

Although this may sound daunting, it is worth carrying out a thorough analysis of the resources in your garden before acquiring new plants. Proper consideration will save you money, time and inconvenience.

Garden planning

Whether you are dealing with a bare area of soil surrounding a new house, or a garden which is already established but new to you, or a garden which has been in your care for some time, you can increase the plants' chances of survival and improve their health if you consider the needs you want the garden to fulfil. In the same way that the rooms of your house should make provision for a wide range of activities and requirements, a yard might need to accommodate not only a range of plants but also provide space for pets, children, crops, recreation and utilities.

If you are a garden enthusiast but have children or pets, do not expect choice plants to survive if you do not provide open spaces for the children or animals to work off their energy. Shrubs are less vulnerable

Azaleas in raised container beds brighten a corner of a city garden. By varying the height of the beds and selecting the plants with care, the problems of gardening on such a small scale have been overcome. Lack of space is not the only problem a city gardener will have to tackle. In urban areas, the soil is often poor, pests are numerous and there may be excessive shade. Taking the existing conditions into account is a vital part of designing a successful garden, appropriate to the setting.

A *garden should reflect its setting and careful choice of plants is a key consideration. In this sub-tropical garden, cacti and exotic native species are effectively combined with a lawn and less spectacular garden plants (far left). The imposing façade of this colonial house is perfectly complemented by the formal flowerbeds, neat box hedges and expanse of immaculate turf (below). The classic English country garden is a colourful blend of cottage flowers, herbs and shrubs, informal yet controlled (left).*

9

than herbaceous flowering plants; trees are likely to be climbed or scratched but can stand these attacks when well established — both shrubs and trees will need guards in their early years. Prickly plants will discourage onslaughts. Paths which lead directly to open areas without the possibility of cutting corners over beds or through young hedges are to be preferred.

Areas which are likely to take a lot of traffic, for instance around washing lines, garbage cans, shed, compost pile, frames, garage, drive, carport, and so on, obviously need to be surfaced with hard wearing materials; any grass mixture should be blended accordingly. Plants used to screen utility areas should be both pretty and tough — they are likely to be overlooked and neglected and these areas are likely to be located where draughts, shade, wind and cold are prevalent.

The amount of time you have, or wish, to spend on the garden is an important consideration. Some groups of plants are time-consuming,

others cover the ground beautifully year in, year out, without much extra help. If you have little time, but a passion for bedding plants and roses, or a perfect lawn, you are bound to be disappointed unless you restrict the area concerned. Crops, particularly vegetables, are very time-consuming, and beds of herbaceous perennials always need attention. The solution is either to design your garden around plants which do not require a great deal of time spent on their upkeep or to reconcile yourself to spending more time in the garden.

If the overall appearance is your prime consideration, you will have to be more selective in your choice of plants and more careful in positioning so that differences in height, shades of colours, leaf shapes and architectural form are well displayed. If different plants are grouped to create a particular effect, ensure that all require the same conditions for growth and that they grow at roughly the same rate.

Features that provide a design focal point include a pool, herb garden, paved sun-trap, arbour, rock garden or pergola. Making a plan before you start planting will enable you to choose the species and varieties most appropriate for these features. Draw the plan to scale on graph paper to give you an idea of proportions and relative size. If you have any artistic skill at all, try to turn the flat plan into a three-dimensional sketch, perhaps in colour. This will help you to discover unexpected juxtapositions of colour, and will reveal tall plants that hide window views and footpaths that take the longest way around the

garden. These hitches are inimical to your plants' good health and may only be discovered by advanced planning.

Many gardening enthusiasts, however, advocate gardens that 'just grow'; a good argument can be made that the best gardens are loosely planned and do not have a rigid, preconceived structure but accommodate needs and purposes as they arise. The plants that like the conditions will settle down and spread, and those that find them disagreeable will diminish and fade away.

Choosing plants

Before acquiring or buying new plants for your garden, it makes sense to engage in some research. Visiting gardens and nurseries not only helps you to make up your mind about what you like, it also enables you to assess the type of plants most suitable to your circumstances — position and soil type.

Space is important. If you crowd plants, particularly the large ones like shrubs and trees, they are doomed to dwindling growth, with only a few flowers or fruits and an early death. Visit places where you can see

Herbaceous borders should be a blend of perennials with attractive flowers and foliage (left). National garden exhibitions often include show-case gardens, which incorporate the latest accessories (above). Public gardens may also be a source of ideas, such as suitable plants for wooded areas (right), or creating an effective pool area (far right).

10

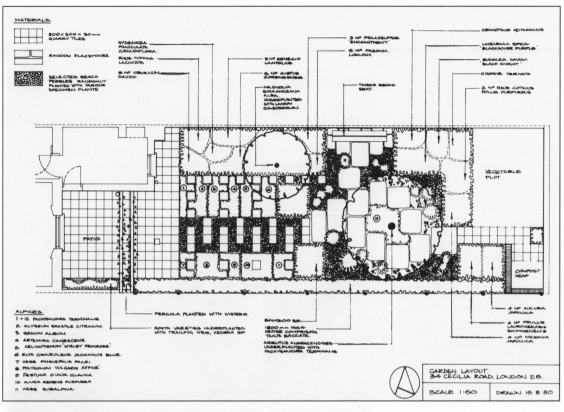

MATERIALS.

300 x 300 x 30 mm
QUARRY TILES

RANDOM FLAGSTONES

SELECTED BEACH
PEBBLES RANDOMLY
PLANTED WITH VARIOUS
SPECIMEN PLANTS

HYDRANGEA
PANICULATA
GRANDIFLORA.

RHUS TYPHINA
LACINIATA.

3 N° VIBURNUM
DAVIDII.

3 N° SENECIO
LAXIFOLIUS.

6 N° CISTUS
CORBARIENSIS.

MAGNOLIA
SOULANGEANA
ALBA,
UNDERPLANTED
WITH LAMIUM
GALEOBDOLON.

2 N° PHILADELPHUS
'ENCHANTMENT'.

2 N° PAEONIA
LUTEA.

TIMBER BENCH
SEAT.

CEANOTHUS VEITCHIANUS

LAVENDULA SPICA-
BLACKHOUSE PURPLE.

BUDDLEIA DAVIDII
'BLACK KNIGHT'

CHOISYA TERNATA

2 N° RHUS COTINUS
FOLIIS PURPUREUS

VEGETABLE
PLOT

COMPOST
HEAP

PATIO.

ALPINES.
1 + 12. PACHYSANDRA TERMINALIS.
2. ALYSSUM SAXATILE CITRINUM.
3. SEDUM ALBUM.
4. ARTEMISIA CANESCENS.
5. HELIANTHEMUM 'WISLEY PRIMROSE'.
6. RUTA GRAVEOLENS 'JACKMANS BLUE'.
7. HEBE PINGUIFOLIA PAGEI.
8. POLYGONUM VULGARE AFFINE.
9. FESTUCA OVINA GLAUCA.
10. AJUGA REPENS PURPUREA.
11. HEBE SUBALPINA.

PERGOLA PLANTED WITH WISTERIA.

HOSTA VARIETIES UNDERPLANTED
WITH TRAILING IVIES, HEDERA SP.

BAMBOO SP.

1800 mm HIGH
HEDGE COMPRISING
TAXUS BACCATA.

ARBUTUS UNEDO
UNDERPLANTED WITH
PACHYSANDRA TERMINALIS.

4 N° AUCUBA
JAPONICA.

2 N° PRUNUS
LAUROCERASUS
'SCHIPKAENSIS'

4 N° MAHONIA
JAPONICA.

GARDEN LAYOUT.
34 CECILIA ROAD, LONDON E8.

SCALE 1:50 | DRAWN 15.8.80

Left: *Once you have established what sort of plants and design would suit your garden, try making a more detailed plan. Choosing a wide selection of alpines and border plants must be done carefully, so that the maximum effect of colour can be achieved throughout the year. Plants are not the only feature of the garden, however, trees may also be a focal point. Take care to allow enough space for their branches and choose suitable plants to grow under them. Allow space for an open area of terrace or lawn, so that the garden does not become overcrowded. Other practical areas should be provided for a compost pile, and a vegetable plot if required.*

plants actually growing before you start to plant, to get an idea of their size and growth. Local gardens or parks will furnish ideas for plants and for garden design. Neighbourhood nurseries and garden centres often have a display garden showing plants available for sale, and assistants will be able to suggest suitable varieties for your conditions. Gardening society shows and exhibitions are also valuable, not least because they demonstrate a high standard of plant health as well as choice. Specialist societies, in particular, mount exhibits of plants which are seldom seen but which nonetheless make good garden plants.

If you cannot manage a visit to any of these sources of living plants, it often helps to look at the catalogues produced by the national nurseries and seedsmen. Many are profusely illustrated in colour and are true to the originals; the shape of the flowers is also shown. Size, time of flowering, other characteristics and cultivation needs will often be given. Browse through the numerous specialist gardening magazines which are available and, finally, look at your neighbours' gardens, if only to help you decide what not to grow!

Take a notebook with you when you go 'plant hunting', preferably one arranged alphabetically. Whatever else you may write, such as the height, colour and conditions, note the botanical name of the plant you like — you may forget it.

Acquiring plants

Plants are available from a wide variety of sources; most places where they can be viewed will also sell them. When you wish to purchase common plants, chain stores and garden centres will be adequate, but for rare and unusual plants, and for good ranges of specialist flowers such as chrysanthemums, delphiniums, carnations, lilies or whatever, you will have to apply to specialist societies. Stalls at country fairs and markets or your local garden centre may have an enterprising owner specialising in a group of plants, and there are private seed-lists available which cater solely for the out-of-the-ordinary. Friends' gardens should also be considered as helpful sources of plants, cuttings and seeds.

Wherever you get your plants, make sure that they are as strong, healthy and free of pest and disease as possible. If you are buying container-grown plants from a garden centre, avoid plants which have one or two thick roots protruding from the drainage hole of the container, or which are tightly packed throughout the soil-ball and coil around at the base. Even if they have been fed, their growth will have been restricted by the cramped container conditions. Choose plants whose top growth — leaves and shoots — is well-balanced, evenly growing from around the plant, undamaged and a good positive colour.

The best source of garden plants are reputable nurseries and garden centres. The dahlia exhibit is a typical nursery display showing the latest varieties (above). Many nurseries have extensive outdoor beds of plants for sale, such as this pansy garden (left). Plants from such places are likely to be healthy and disease-resistant. For specific types of plant, such as alpines, specialist nurseries provide a wide variety from which to choose (right).

12

whether green or variegated. You can buy plants in flowerbud, although it is better to plant them when they are only forming leaves and shoot extensions. It is not advisable, however, to ask a plant which is flowering to establish itself with new roots at the same time. It will do so, but slowly, and the flowers and buds will drop rapidly — it may not even flower the following year. In any case, it will need extra time and attention for either watering, feeding or protection so that it settles in place happily.

Plants whose stems or branches are broken or badly placed, with missing or damaged leaves, and with dangling or fading flowers should be avoided. Also watch out for those infested with pests and disease — aphids, caterpillars, red spider mites, white patches of mildew, grey mould, brown or black leaf spot — and any plants which are wilting or

whose compost is dry. The compost may have dried out several times already, and the plant can only be weakened as a result.

Plants bought by mail-order should be packed so that they are not damaged in transit, and so that the roots do not dry out — moist peat and a plastic sheet help to prevent this. You cannot know in advance whether the nursery will ensure their good survival with good packing, but advance research should establish which are the more careful nurseries. It is particularly important that shrub and tree roots remain moist, especially evergreens.

Many chain stores sell plants, including roses, shrubs and various climbers, wrapped in plastic sleeves in winter. Unfortunately, the warmth of the store after a few days encourages these normally dormant plants to break into leaf and start new root growth. Planting them in this state only leads to damage and, if cold and frost follow a few days later, can even mean the end of the plant. Buy plants which are still dormant from these sources, and accustom them gradually over a few days to the colder temperatures of the garden. Leave them outside for a few hours and gradually build up the time.

Plants acquired from friends may suffer from pests and fungal diseases, but a less apparent affliction is virus infection, sometimes only detectable by the stunting and small size of the plants. It is particularly important to make sure that any plant you obtain from a friend is clean and healthy.

Seeds from seedsmen have to conform to guarantees with regard to germination rates and purity. Seeds acquired from friends will not, of course, be guaranteed in this way and you will have to be prepared for the risk of non-germination, or plants which prove to be not all you expected or wanted. If you save your own seeds, keep them in dark, cool (40-45°F/4-7°C), completely airtight conditions. Put some silica gel in a container in advance to absorb moisture, then replace with fresh gel when you put in the seeds.

After all your care and consideration, if your chosen plant eventually does badly in the site where you have placed it, do not hesitate to dig it up and put it somewhere else. Most gardens have no room for sick, lingering plants; and often the disturbance of the move may stimulate the plant into action, regardless of whether the new position is better or not. After replanting, cut off the parts which are dead or dying, protect the plant from wind and cold, and make sure that it is securely supported, if that is necessary. Do not feed it. After heavy rain, carefully make holes in the soil around the plant to aerate the soil.

Care in choosing plants and time spent planning and designing will go a long way to ensuring the survival of your garden. Problems will not only be easier to solve when they occur, but many will also be prevented.

13

No garden has perfect soil and it takes experience to recognise a good type. A good soil needs to be well aerated. This will depend on the type of soil particles present and their quantity. Clay particles are tiny and packed tightly and closely together; grains of sand are comparatively large, loosely combined and spaced further apart. All soils are composed of some particles of each type, but a good one, such as loam, contains all types in the right proportion to ensure the required drainage and aeration.

Another important ingredient is humus, a black, finely divided substance which results from the breakdown of organic matter. Without it, a soil's structure will deteriorate, so that plant roots are unable to breathe, absorb moisture and thereby take in part of their food. Humus is spongy and has the ability to retain the water needed by sandy, stony or gravely soils, but can also provide the spaces needed for air that are lacking in any of the sticky clays or silty soils.

Any rotting vegetative and animal remains will supply humus. Farm manure is still considered to be the best, provided it is really well rotted, preferably under cover. A good substitute can be made in the garden by collecting together all the debris from ornamentals, crop plants and weeds, piling them into a heap and leaving them to rot. A container will prevent mess and will keep the material closely packed, thus ensuring that the heap heats up quickly and well. The rotting process will be speedier and, with a good high temperature, weed seeds will be killed together with any pests and diseases, providing the gardener with an excellent supply of garden manure for future feeding and fertilizer dressings.

The decay of compost pile materials is due to the action of bacteria, worms, fungi and insects on them, the bacteria having most effect. For all these to live and multiply they need oxygen, moisture and nutrients. In effect a compost pile is like a bonfire, which burns better with a good draught from below. It should be arranged on a base of crossed sticks, alternating bricks, large stones or blocks of wood, or anything that provides a space beneath the pile for air. To heat up sufficiently, piles should be at least 4×4ft (1.2×1.2m). They can be wider, but any higher would be inconvenient. Soft vegetation can be used in layers about 6in (15cm) deep, alternating with a layer of sprinkled lime or proprietary compost-maker. For even better results, a thin layer of rotted animal manure can be added occasionally. Layers of soil are sometimes advocated as well, but so much is added naturally, attached to the plants, that it seems unnecessary to do this.

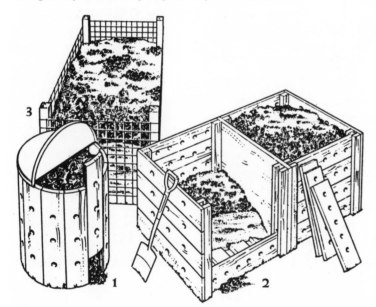

Above: *Compost bins are essential pieces of equipment. Every garden should have one, whether it is bought or homemade. Make sure that homemade ones have holes drilled in the sides to allow air to circulate and aid decomposition. There are a number of different models that may be used: a plastic bin with moveable slats (1); a* *wooden box with drilled holes (2) and an open wire netting type for the preparation of leaf mould (3). While the compost is rotting it is advisable to cover the pile with plastic sheeting to preserve warmth and moisture. Two compost piles are preferable, with one in use and one in the rotting process.*

Right: *Knowing what type of soil you are dealing with is essential to the successful growth of your plants. The best method of testing the soil is to mix some topsoil and water in a jar and leave it to settle overnight. If the level of sand is larger than any other layer, then your soil is sandy. The gritty material indicates the quantity of loam. If this constitutes 40 percent, the soil is considered a good loam. If the layer of clay is equal to the other two layers, the soil is clay-based.*

Organic matter

Water

Clay

Gritty material

Sand

14

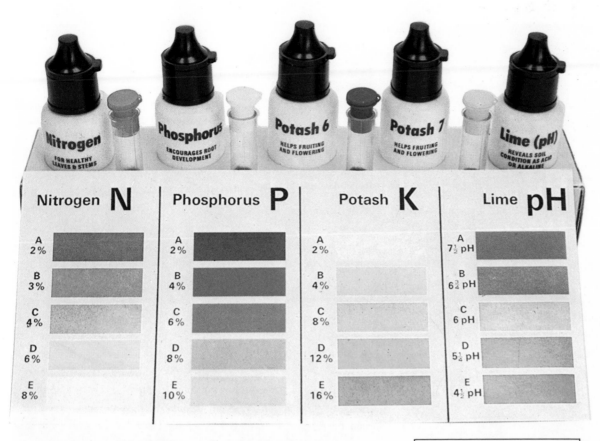

The chemical level of the soil can be measured with a soil testing kit. This kit contains colour charts and various solutions, which will determine the percentage level of nutrients contained in your soil (left). Take samples of soil from all parts of the yard, leaving them to dry out and removing any foreign bodies. Then crumble the soils with a tool, making sure not to touch the soil with your fingers, as this could affect the results. Quarter fill separate test-tubes with each of the samples (below, left). According to the particular substance for which you are testing, add a few drops of the appropriate solution to the the soil samples. Wait until the soil has settled, before matching it up with the corresponding colour chart (below, right). The result will then determine which fertilizer is necessary to improve the chemical balance.

The material will be ready for use when of a crumbly, dark brown-black consistency. If it is soil-like, it has been left too long and will have lost much of its goodness; if the shapes of leaves or stems can still be recognised, it has not been left long enough. Time to break down varies between six weeks and several months, depending on the weather, how quickly and how well the pile is built and your own expertise. In winter, it will hardly change and an autumn-built pile will not be ready for use until late spring.

THE pH LEVEL

Soil is said to be acid or alkaline (limey) and the degree of either is measured by a scale called the pH scale. Figures below 7.0 on this scale indicate acidity, increasing by 10 times for each figure; those above show alkalinity. There are a number of plants which will not grow at all in alkaline soil or which do much better in an acid one. Test kits can be bought at garden shops to determine this aspect of your soil. As the tests are quite simple and quick to do, it is easy to discover the state of various parts of the garden. The kits will also supply a table giving the quantities of lime that need to be added or not, depending on what reaction the soil provides. You may find that different areas of the garden give different results, and, in this case, should be treated accordingly.

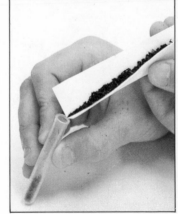

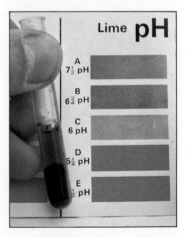

16

chapter two

BASIC CARE

The area surrounding most houses is usually covered with many types of plants and vegetation, which will inevitably need some attention. The task of organizing and maintaining this area needs to be approached in a systematic way that will ensure a healthy garden, yet fall within the bounds of the gardener's capabilities.

17

Maintaining a well-kept garden need not be time consuming once everything is established.

Bulbs

The routine care of bulbs is minimal. Most thrive if planted in a light, sandy or stony soil and a sunny place and continue to flower for many years without any problems. These include tulips, irises, hyacinths, grape hyacinths and narcissi. Some bulbs, mainly daffodils, produce offsets so freely however, that they become grassy, which means there are lots of leaves but practically no flowers, because the plants are crowded and are short of food. The remedy is to dig them up after flowering, discard all but the largest, and then replant these in a shallow hole in a sheltered place and leave them to ripen for the summer, letting the leaves die off naturally. Remember to mark the spot and then replant in early autumn in the normal way, at twice the depth of the bulb. This method of heeling in can also be used when the place where the bulbs have been flowering is wanted for a summer display of bedding plants.

The main point to remember about bulbs is to plant them at the right depth. They are often not put in deeply enough, so a good guide to follow is the one advised for daffodils, making sure that the depth of the soil above the tip of the bulb is at least equal to its length. Planting time is early to mid-autumn for spring-flowering bulbs except tulips, which can be bedded in late autumn; *Iris reticulata* should be planted towards the end of summer for flowering in winter, and summer-flowering bulbs can be put in at the beginning of spring. A few flower in autumn — nerine, crocus, crinum, colchicum — and these will need to be planted in mid-summer.

Bulbs should be planted to a depth equivalent to twice their height and placed in the soil with the point facing upward (left). Spring-flowering bulbs should not be stored until their leaves have died. This often means that they have to finish their growing period in another bed, to make way for other plants, or they can be placed in trays of peat (right). They should be laid out in rows of deep, moist peat.

The crocosmia comes from tropical and southern Africa, and grows from a corm, which produces 3ft (90cm) stems (left). The corms can be left in the ground during winter but in cold areas, liable to frost, they should be lifted and stored. The bluebell is a native of Britain, and grows from a bulb, which has no outer skin (below). This means that storage conditions should not be too damp or too dry, otherwise the bulbs will shrivel and die.

Annuals and biennials

These are short-lived plants, which are grown from seed. Annuals die within a year; biennials do not flower until their second growing season, and then die. Although temporary, they are quick to flower and cover the bare patches until other perennial plants can take over. Good results are due mainly to good seed-bed preparation. This starts a few months before by digging to at least one spade's depth, clearing out weeds, large stones and other rubbish, and then leaving the ground fallow, so that weeds can germinate and be hoed out as they are germinating. This is important: weed seedlings will grow more strongly than the ornamentals and can be difficult to control before the annuals get well established, and without harming the annuals. About a week before sowing, scatter a general compound fertilizer on the soil surface.

On the day chosen for sowing, which should be calm and mild, with rain to come, fork the soil to break up the lumps, firm it be treading evenly and level the surface by raking. At the same time rake out rubbish and break the soil down finely into breadcrumb-like particles. Sow the seeds thinly and evenly in the pattern decided on and rake a light covering of fine soil over them. By mid-spring, the soil should have started to warm up and germination should be within about a fortnight in most cases. However, seeds must have moisture to germinate and as the surface of a seed bed dries out quickly, watering will be necessary if no rain occurs within a day or two of sowing.

If there is a possibility that, in spite of all your care, weed seedlings are likely to appear, there are special weedkillers which can be used on seed beds which will not harm the cultivated seedlings. Non-appearance of seedlings can be due to birds, especially pigeons, taking the seed or sparrows making dust-baths in the seed bed. Seed treated against birds is available or you put up protection, such as netting, thread or tin foil. Another defence is to cover the bed with a slitted plastic sheet, which allows air and moisture to get to the seedlings and is light enough to rise with the seedlings as they grow, at the same time keeping them warm. This type of sheet needs to be weighted down at the edges with stones.

Once they have begun to grow, annuals should be thinned when small enough to handle, to roughly alternate spacing, and again when they start touching for final spacing. Lack of time or foresight in doing this will mean crowded, weak plants and a dull display — they may even

19

Iberis sempervirens *is a heavily flowering, low-growing plant, suitable for rock gardens* (left). *To encourage this healthy blooming, some cutting back must be carried out. The plants will need* *attention as soon as the flower heads start to fade* (above, left). *At this stage deadheading should also be performed* (above, right).

die because of damping-off disease. The taller plants will need staking. If the hardier ones were sown in autumn, make sure they do not become covered in leaves in late autumn, as slugs will eat them, hidden from sight. Sowing in autumn will result in much earlier flowering.

Biennials can be sown where they are going to flower, but the site will remain unattractive for about a year until they bloom, and it is more usual to sow them in a nursery bed, thin them there and then transplant to their flowering place. Early summer is the usual time for sowing biennials and final planting time is autumn.

20

Linums are prolific bloomers throughout the summer, and brighten up any border (above). Tagetes patula (French marigold) was originally a native of Mexico, but may now be seen in many gardens, flowering from the beginning of summer until the first frosts (left). Marigolds are known for their vibrant colours (below).

Above and right Salpiglossis, a native of Chile, is an unusual and attractive plant. It may be grown in annual or mixed borders, in a rich soil and sunny position. The annuals need some supporting during their life to ensure healthy, upright growth.

These flowering plants live from year to year, in some cases for many years. Most species die down to ground level in autumn, though the roots survive the winter in a dormant state, but some are evergreen and even flower in winter, for instance the hellebores. Many of these perennials grow so tall that they can be blown down by wind or become so top-heavy with summer rain that they break; delphiniums, lupins, rudbeckias are a few. To avoid this damage, either obtain plants which grow tall but are sturdy enough to stay upright, or support them.

Perennials are beautiful in flower, but some species will need deadheading through the season as the flower heads droop and die.

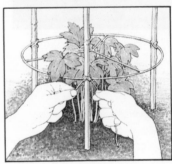

Solidagos are excellent plants for herbaceous borders or rock gardens (top). Their brilliantly coloured clusters of yellow flowers are also suitable for cutting. Rudbeckias are natives of North America, and are another easily grown herbaceous border plant (above). They thrive in any well-cultivated and well-drained garden soil, and prefer an open, sunny site. Herbaceous perennials require regular deadheading, especially if they are for border decoration.

Delphiniums are a good example of a tall-growing plant, which will need to be staked from an early stage. Use sticks and twine (top) and, as the plants grow taller, add another piece of wire. The adult plants will still need support and several pieces of twine will be required (left). A plastic ring can be used in place of the wire, and adjusted in height as the plant grows taller (above).

Deadheading has the advantage, too, of conserving the plant's energy, so that it sometimes goes into a second flowering, or new vegetative growth, instead of fruiting and setting seed. If seed is wanted for increase, deadheading should be ignored.

In autumn the top growth will gradually turn brown and die off. Since this is unsightly, many gardeners prefer to cut it right down to the crown, maintaining that this prevents fungal diseases from overwintering and takes away cover for pests. On the other hand, there are those who prefer to leave the top growth for protection of the crowns through the winter, so that it will rot naturally into the soil and thus maintain soil fertility. If the plants were heavily diseased, it is usually better to remove the dead growth and burn it rather than compost it.

22

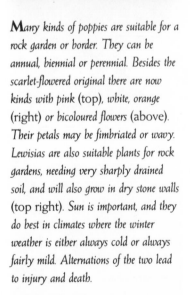

Many kinds of poppies are suitable for a rock garden or border. They can be annual, biennial or perennial. Besides the scarlet-flowered original there are now kinds with pink (top), white, orange (right) or bicoloured flowers (above). Their petals may be fimbriated or wavy. Lewisias are also suitable plants for rock gardens, needing very sharply drained soil, and will also grow in dry stone walls (top right). Sun is important, and they do best in climates where the winter weather is either always cold or always fairly mild. Alternations of the two lead to injury and death.

Perennials tend to deteriorate after a few years, but there is no need to discard them completely. It is the central part which flowers badly and grows weak because it is the oldest, so dig the plants up early in spring, break off the outside pieces, making sure they have roots attached, and then replant; the old woody centre should be discarded. Put the sections at the same level in the soil as before and whether you are planting, transplanting or increasing as here, provide a hole which is large enough to spread out the roots in; then crumble the soil back over the roots and firm them down.

A border of herbaceous perennials that is left to itself, will become rather jungly, weedy and flowerless. Borders should be thick and luxuriant, colourful all season and free from weeds. To ensure this healthy state, clear off the rubbish and weeds in autumn, spreading a compound fertilizer dressing on the soil surface around the plants if the soil is light, and fork it in, thus opening up the soil at the same time and helping drainage and aeration. In spring, a further light tidying after winter will be necessary, hoeing to remove any further weeds and, later, staking as required, finishing with mulching.

Basic care

Shrubs

Most shrubs grow into large plants, several feet high and wide, and go on growing, so that it becomes a problem trying to keep them under control. If they are neglected they will not flower and will grow as uniform masses of greenery, taking up too much room, overhanging the lawn and obstructing the mower. However, with only a little attention during the year, shrubs can be more rewarding than perennials.

Pruning is the main requirement, which means cutting back sensibly, instead of hacking the shoots and branches indiscriminately. Part of the space problem lies in the fact that the size of shrubs when fully grown is not always considered. This is an understandable error

because they are so small when planted that all the bare soil around them looks unattractive. However, it is preferable to know in advance exactly what size they will grow to — in a moist and well broken-down, heavy soil, they will grow much larger than expected — plant accordingly and fill in the gaps temporarily with annuals, bedding plants or quick-growing, but short-lived shrubs like tree lupins.

While young shrubs are growing, pruning will mostly be a matter of encouraging balanced growth and removing the few flowers that appear. Balancing the growth involves cutting off any shoot that is stronger than the rest and cutting off three quarters of short, weak shoots with thin stems. When the plants are adult, any formal cutting that is required can start, although there is no set time in the plant's life for this procedure and it can gradually be blended in with the minimal cutting of the earliest days. In general, flowering shrubs which bloom in spring and early summer are pruned as soon as flowering has finished; those which flower later in the summer and autumn are dealt with in spring, just as growth is starting, and those which are slow-growing or winter-flowering are dealt with in midspring.

The reasons for these different timings are that the earlier flowering kinds produce their blooms on the shoots they grew in the previous summer so if cut back in summer, all the growth that would flower the following season will have been removed. Those that flower later in the summer do so on the shoots that have grown that year — those which started to elongate in the spring immediately preceding the summer in which they are flowering. If a shrub is cut back early because it is overgrowing the path or blocking the front door the best of the flowering growth will have been removed and it will no longer be ornamental. Winter bloomers follow the same pattern; the slow-growing kinds hardly need formal pruning — they seem to flower without this help.

Cornus alba 'Elegantissima' is grown specifically for its bark and foliage (above). It is best if it is grown as an isolated specimen and not in a group. Pruning is an essential requirement of this species, in particular, otherwise the foliage will look dull and unimpressive (right). The colour of the bark and leaves will be greatly improved if the shrub is cut hard in early spring.

Right: Viburnum opulus is a native of Europe. It is a tall (up to 15ft/ 4.5m), bushy, deciduous shrub, flowering in late spring/early summer and producing its red berries in autumn. It is an adaptable shrub and able to grow in most reasonable garden soils. No regular pruning is required, although some thinning out may be necessary after flowering.

23

When pruning, cut off the shoots which have flowered, making the cut either just above a good new shoot which is already growing, or just above a bud which has begun to sprout, or at a point of origin of the shoot. Clear out dead growth as well, which will be brown and leafless and may be a whole shoot or branch or only the tip of a shoot; cut away completely the short, thin shoots; remove those which are awkwardly placed and growing into the bush's centre or crossing other better shoots. All this will help to let sunlight and air into the growth, but if it still seems slightly crowded thin it out a little.

When making the cut, try to position them just above a bud or shoot at an angle sloping away from the bud. One of the problems with pruning is that cut shoots often die — if dead they turn brown and break easily — from the cut down the stem, because the cut was made in the wrong place or in the wrong way. If the cut is too far away from the sideshoot, leaf-cluster or dormant bud, the snag left can easily be infected; if it is too close, the bud may die or be knocked off and the

growth of the adjacent shoot or leaf-cluster may be affected. If cut straight across, it will collect moisture; if cut sloping towards the bud or shoot, rain will be directed into the bud, and if cut raggedly, it provides even more of an opportunity for fungal rotting.

To help you avoid cutting off flower- or fruit-buds, remember that these are round and fat; vegetative buds, which only produce a shoot with leaves, are pointed and comparatively long and narrow. There are times when you may have to cut halfway down a flowering or leafy shoot, so you will know from this how much potential flowering growth is being removed. Cutting off part of such growth has the effect of stimulating some of the remaining buds into producing shoots instead of flowers. The reasons for this are complicated, but are connected with the balance of hormones and other biochemicals.

If a shrub is flowering badly, has lots of dead tips to the shoots, grows slowly and always seems to be infested with aphids, clear out all the extraneous growth, fork the soil around it carefully so as not to disturb or injure roots too much, sprinkle a light dressing of a phosphatic fertilizer onto the surface and water it in and then mulch with rotted compost or manure. The forking, feeding and mulching should be carried out inside a circle at least 2ft (60cm) in diameter around the plant, with the most suitable time being the spring.

Weigela (below) needs to have its stems cut back after flowering. Pieris formosa 'Forestii' (right) needs to have any faded flower heads removed and straggling shoots cut back. It is important to make the cut at a strong shoot and to angle the incision (left). Slanting the cut toward the bud (3) or cutting too far above (2) or too near (4) the bud are all incorrect. Make the cut just above, and slanting away from, the shoot (1).

24

A common problem with hedges is lack of leaf cover at the base; sometimes they are not very thickly covered higher up, either. Part of the trouble is due to wrong training when the hedge was young, and part is due to poor soil and lack of food. In order to achieve a good thick cover low down, young hedge plants must be treated in autumn or early winter in one of three different ways. Some of the deciduous hedges and some of the evergreens should have their height reduced by a third, cutting to a good dormant bud, immediately after planting and any sideshoots cut back be about half. This is repeated in the second winter. Deciduous hedge plants such as blackthorn, hawthorn, tamarix and the mainly evergreen privet should be cut down very hard to within about 4-6in (10-15cm) of the soil. In the second winter, the new shoots subsequently produced should be reduced by half their length. The third method involves little work; the height of the plants is left alone and the sideshoots are only cut a little if they are straggling. This is repeated in the second winter. If these hedges are planted at the end of winter, they should not be cut then, but left until the next winter, which should be regarded as the first winter from the pruning viewpoint.

In the summer following the second winter, all hedges can be considered as established. The methods of clipping can then be divided into two groups. For the majority of hedges, leave the height alone, do no cut the leaders back, but cut the side growth hard to leave about a quarter of the new season's growth. When the hedge has reached the height required, trim thereafter to keep at that height and do the same with the sides when a suitable width has been reached. This annual clipping is required for the following: beech, cypress, cotoneaster and escallonia, *Euonymus japonicus,* hazel, holly, hornbeam, juniper, laurel, viburnum, pittosporum, pyracantha, spotted laurel, tamarix and yew. This should be done in summer; sometimes, in mild autumns, a second light trim is needed in mid-autumn. The laurels are best trimmed in early autumn only.

The second group, including blackthorn, hawthorn, *Lonicera nitida* and privet should have their top new growth cut back by about a quarter, until the height required is reached, and sideshoots should always be cut hard as with the first group. This trimming will be needed at least three times during the growing season, as all grow rapidly throughout the summer and sometimes into autumn. Combining this kind of trimming with spring feeding on light soils and dressing with rotted organic matter in autumn each year should ensure that the hedge provides a good cover all year if evergreen and for most of the year otherwise.

25

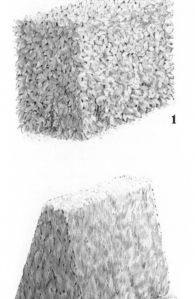

1

2

3

Above: Prunus lusitanica *(common laurel), with its glossy, dense foliage, is an example of a hedge that does not require a harsh cut. It is more suited to a light trim, carried out with a pair of small shears, to prevent excess damage to its distinctive leaves. The more formal habit suits coniferous-type shrubs, which look attractive when they are closely clipped (1). It is advisable to shape the hedges so that they are thinner at the top (2 and 3).*

Established hedges can be badly damaged at the top by the weight of snow, or by wind if the base is bare, and also if they have been clipped so that they are wider at the top than the bottom. The shape of a hedge in silhouette should be completely vertical or slightly tapered toward the top for greater strength and uniformity of appearance, which is so important with formal hedges. If snow settles on the top, the branches are likely to be pressed outwards.

Informal hedges are pruned when mature in the same way that shrubs are, since the object of any informal hedge is to obtain flowers. It should be left to grow virtually unchecked until flowering has finished, and then trimmed. It is worth bearing in mind that, to be effective, informal hedges should be at least 4ft (1.2m) wide.

Trees

There is little geneal maintenance of trees that needs to be done during the year, but there are some problems that occasionally occur and can kill the tree if not dealt with immediately.

Supporting in the first two or three years prevents wind-rock, in which the constant movement of the base of the trunk gradually produces a hollow in the soil around it. This collects water and leads to bark rotting and ultimately the death of the tree. Secure staking is essential and can be done with a single post, two similar ones with a cross bar or a single diagonal. For standards and half-standards, the support should extend about halfway up the trunk only. It should be removed in the third year, otherwise the trunk never thickens up as it should and the tree is less strong than it could be. Ties are important; too tight or left too long, they constrict the stem, cut into it and provide entry for disease. Sacking padding provides a home for pests and absorbs moisture, but there are kinds which avoid these problems.

Like shrubs, trees tend to be planted in places which are too small for them. If this has happened and a tree starts causing problems with shade or space, branches will have to be removed. If this is difficult it is better to obtain professional help, but if the branches are within easy reach and not too large they can be removed safely, by first making an undercut halfway through the branch near its junction with the trunk and a second on top some inches away from the first, until the branch snaps cleanly through. The remaining stump is sawn off so that there is a slight projection from the trunk. The wound will then callus over and heal much more quickly than if left flush with the trunk and a fungicidal paint can be applied.

When planting trees, remember that their roots can spread exensively underground, at least as much as the branches do above ground. House foundations and drains are the main hazards; small trees are unlikely to cause trouble, but trees such as weeping willows and poplars, particularly in clay soil, should be planted well away from the house and drainage system.

Some trees are prolific producers of new shoots from trunks and even roots; these are called suckers. Again, poplar is an example as are ornamental cherries, lilac and roses. In the lawn these suckers can be mown off, or they must be cut away at the point of origin. It is better if they can be pulled off as this will remove the eye completely, but it can lead to root damage or it may not be practicable. Application of a weedkiller will destroy suckers and is unlikely to harm the tree, but new ones will appear in their place needing treatment.

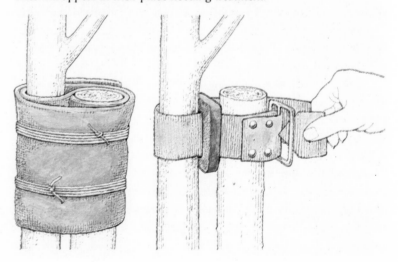

Removal of branches and top growth from trees must be done carefully (left). *Dead growth should always be cut away. Make sure that the cut is made level with the healthy trunk or branch (1 and 2). Damaged tips should be removed back to the healthy shoot (3). Supports should be tied to the tree or shrub so that they do not cut into the bark. Use padding* (right), *but be careful that insects do not hibernate beneath it, or use the special plastic tree-ties that can be loosened as the stem or trunk expands with growth* (far right).

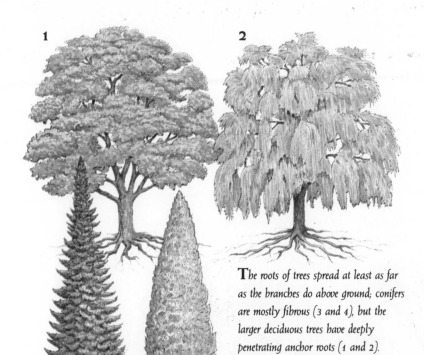

Laburnum flowers in early summer, and L. 'Vossii' makes one of the best small trees for the average yard (below). Its hanging clusters of deep yellow flowers can be as much as 12in (30cm) long, and it has no special growing needs. Rhus typhina (stag's-horn sumach) (left) is usually grown as a shrub, but can become a small tree, and has brilliantly coloured leaves in autumn.

The roots of trees spread at least as far as the branches do above ground; conifers are mostly fibrous (3 and 4), but the larger deciduous trees have deeply penetrating anchor roots (1 and 2). Shapes of trees can vary to fit into any kind of design. Dwarf conifers (below) can be used alone to excellent effect in borders.

Lawns

Where a new lawn is to be grown from seed, there are various hazards which endanger its survival, but which are easily avoided. Choose the right time of year; drought and heat or frost and waterlogging will prevent the lawn from establishing itself, and generally spring or early autumn are the best times to sow, when the weather is mild and likely to be moist rather than soaking wet. A badly prepared seed bed will result in thin seedling germination, bare patches, yellowing seedlings and slow growth. It must be evenly firm, of a friable nature and free of weeds and stones. An uneven surface will cause puddles after rain and seeds will be blown by wind or carried by rain into the hollows, which causes thick patches of seedlings to form, interspersed with bare patches on the bumps. Old seed and uneven sowing can produce the same effect and birds can also upset the regularity of the sowing. Even subsoil, brought to the surface in patches, can result in uneven or no germination.

Insufficient fallowing and inadequate advance weed control will produce a flock of seedling weeds along with the grass; besides a

Lawns are a popular and welcome addition to any yard if the area is large enough to handle one. They offer a feeling of space and provide an excellent foil to borders (right). A smooth, velvet-like turf, however, will not just present itself. It is the result of careful year-round management, which includes feeding, aerating, mowing, watering, top-dressing and raking. A lawn mower is one essential piece of equipment for any lawn. An electric mower (above) is a very effective machine and easy to handle anywhere. The lawn must be mown frequently, every five days during the growing season, and the surface should be kept perfectly level.

28

thorough preliminary cleaning, a special weedkilling solution can be sprayed onto the soil before sowing, which will kill the weed seedling, but not the grass. Damping-off, a fungal disease, attacks seedlings of all kinds and can cause a great deal of damage.

Laying a turf lawn is not advisable during a dry period. Dry soil and hot weather makes knitting of the turfs slow and difficult and once they have dried out the grass will be permanently damaged, if not actually dead. The wetter months are preferable, provided snow and frost are not forecast. As with seed, the soil surface must be level and firm and a spirit-level is useful for checking the lines of turfs as they are laid. To get a good close interlocking of the turfs, lay them in staggered rows, like the course in a brick wall, which will avoid four corners meeting and adding to to the problems of binding, and lay each turf slightly humped. As soon as each row is completed, gently knock the individual turfs flat. When you lay the next row knock the new row up against the previous one to further ensure successful knitting of the turfs. Finally, work a top-dressing mixture of sand, peat and loam into the cracks.

Both newly seeded and turfed lawns should be cut lightly when they have begun to grow, at about 1¾-2in (4-5cm) in height. To prevent the seedlings from being torn out of the soil by the mower, it is advisable to roll the new lawn lightly, but make sure the minimum possible rolling is done, to avoid damage to the soil structure.

Once the lawn is established, frequent mowing is necessary to ensure that the finer grasses predominate. Mowing needs to be done every five days in spring and early summer, then every seven until mid-autumn, and from then less often. If left for longer periods than these, the lawn will become more difficult to cut as the coarser grasses overcome the desirable fine ones. A sign of infrequent cutting or cutting when wet is ribbing, alternate ridges of short and long grass.

There are a number of problems that occur with mowing, which lead to weak grass and weed and moss encroachment. If the grass is not being cut as short as would be expected with the blade setting, and the grass tips are turning brown, then the mower blades need sharpening or resetting or the grass is being cut when it is wet. Some wiry grasses in particular show this tendency.

A trail of bare patches found after mowing along an otherwise grassy covering is probably due to an uneven lawn surface and not from mowing too closely. If this is not put right, weeds will soon cover the patches, but it is easily corrected by cutting an "H" shape in the turf, lifting and rolling back the flaps and removing the surplus soil. The cut turf, once back in place, will knit together rapidly.

Following the same routes every time the lawn is mowed will eventually produce the condition known as washboarding, in which the soil itself forms regular undulations running across the line of mowing. The same kind of effect occurs when a field is ploughed in the same

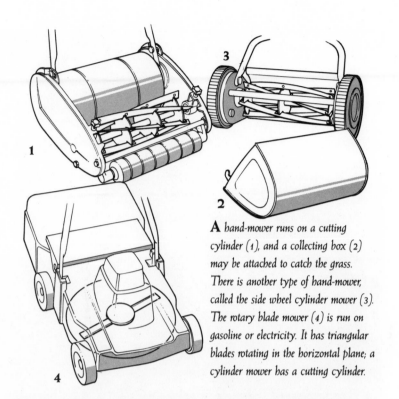

A hand-mower runs on a cutting cylinder (1), and a collecting box (2) may be attached to catch the grass. There is another type of hand-mower, called the side wheel cylinder mower (3). The rotary blade mower (4) is run on gasoline or electricity. It has triangular blades rotating in the horizontal plane; a cylinder mower has a cutting cylinder.

direction. It is a good idea to occasionally mow in a different direction in any case, as it improves the health of the grass.

Starting in spring, raking will get rid of the leaves, twigs, dead vegetation and worm casts that will have accumulated on the surface during winter. Feeding with a compound fertilizer should follow after the preliminary mowings, preferably applied to moist soil, when rain is due. If weeds are present, a weedkilling solution can be applied a week or two following feeding, or a combined fertilizer/weedkiller can be used if there is not much weed growth. Another spring job is aeration, to get air into the soil and enable surplus water to drain through. Frequent mowing, especially with cylinder mowers, compacts the soil surface to such an extent that it forms an almost impervious layer making it difficult for the grass's roots to function efficiently. A simple method is to push a garden fork into the soil 4in (10cm) deep, at intervals of a few inches all over the lawn. Autumn is another season when aerating is beneficial and in a drought, if penetration is possible, aeration will often revive the grass almost as well as watering would.

In autumn, spreading a top-dressing mixture of such ingredients as loam, peat and sand will keep the soil structure in good condition. Application is at the rate of about 2lb/sq yd (1kg/m²), put on evenly and worked into the turf at once with a broom or the back of a rake. Finally, raking off any leaves in early winter will avoid yellowing and weakening of the grass and the encouragement of worms. Autumn is also a good time for lawn repairs, such as re-seeding bare patches, removing small bumps and putting damaged edges to rights.

Techniques

chapter three

TECHNIQUES

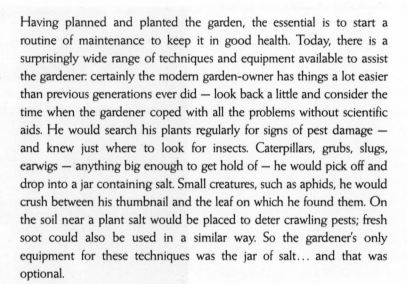

Having planned and planted the garden, the essential is to start a routine of maintenance to keep it in good health. Today, there is a surprisingly wide range of techniques and equipment available to assist the gardener: certainly the modern garden-owner has things a lot easier than previous generations ever did — look back a little and consider the time when the gardener coped with all the problems without scientific aids. He would search his plants regularly for signs of pest damage — and knew just where to look for insects. Caterpillars, grubs, slugs, earwigs — anything big enough to get hold of — he would pick off and drop into a jar containing salt. Small creatures, such as aphids, he would crush between his thumbnail and the leaf on which he found them. On the soil near a plant salt would be placed to deter crawling pests; fresh soot could also be used in a similar way. So the gardener's only equipment for these techniques was the jar of salt… and that was optional.

31

Once the basic structure of your garden has been created and the plants in place, maintenance is the key to keeping it healthy.

A basic set of the right tools and equipment is important for all garden chores. A digging fork and a sharp knife are vital and a budding knife is useful, especially if roses are increased by budding. A hand-fork, rake, hoe, pruning shears, string and a watering can are other requirements. For a lawn and hedge, a mower and hand-shears or a powered hedge-cutter will also be required. Hand-mowers are hard work for all except the smallest lawns and a mechanical mower will generally give a better finish. Hand-shears are convenient; buy a good pair which are well balanced, not too heavy, and whose handles are comfortable for your size of hand. They will be useful for cutting any awkward patches of grass and grass edges as well as hedges.

Rakes have a number of uses: raking up leaves, clearing rubbish and dead vegetation from lawns, raking weeds out of pools, breaking the soil down for seed beds, levelling gravel paths and drives and general tidying. A digging fork will do much basic cultivation and can double up as a carrier, like a pitch-fork; a hand-fork is useful for all weeding as well as planting small plants such as annuals, bedding plants and young perennials, although a long handled hoe will do the work more quickly when seedling weeds are the problem. A wheelbarrow is always necessary, and the standard, galvanised, metal kinds with a single rubber tire and two rear supports are still preferable. They are hard wearing,

long-lasting and balanced so that they can take a large amount of weight. It is also helpful to have some kind of easily transportable small carrier, such as a bucket, sack or box in which to carry tools or put weeds, plants and pots when working in the garden.

An essential addition to any garden is a wheelbarrow. The various types include the traditional model (1), the ball-wheeled (2) or the two-wheeled trailer (3). The traditional model is generally considered to be the most solid and practical. It is always important to make sure you have sturdy tools for heavy jobs, such as transporting, and also lifting.

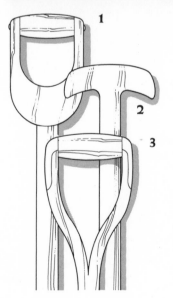

Above and left: Both spades and forks have three basic handle shapes: 'D' (1), 'T' (2) and 'YD' (3). They may also be made or covered in metal, plastic or wood. There is no specific advantage in any of the different materials, but it is always advisable to try out all combinations to find the one most suited to you and your type of garden. The shaft of the tool may also be made in different materials, and again, depending on the work required, choose either a sturdy or light material.

32

Two types of shears (1 and 2) and a pair of loppers (3) are a useful addition to any tool collection. A hand-fork (4) and trowel (5) are handy for intricate work, such as sowing or planting. However, a set of larger tools is also necessary. A sturdy garden fork (6) is an essential tool for any garden. It may be used, among other things, to break up soil, remove weeds and aerate lawns. An edge cutter (7) is a particularly useful implement for tidying up ragged lines around lawns and flowerbeds. A spade (8) is virtually synonymous with gardening, and is highly practical for digging and moving soil. The rake (9) will gather up debris and smooth over seed beds. Finally, two types of hoe, Dutch (10) and draw hoes (11), are both worth acquiring as they are excellent as weeding tools.

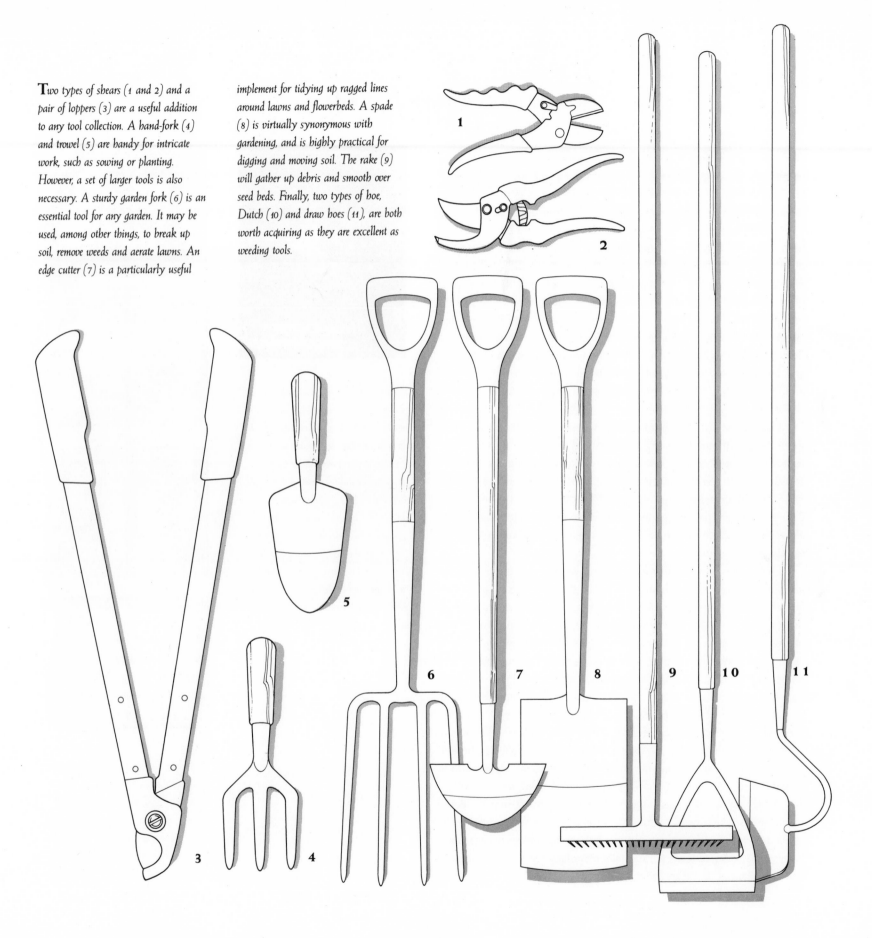

33

Digging and feeding

Once a yard is established, with its lawn, paving, borders and permanent plantings, digging consists of forking the top few inches of soil between the plants to aerate it, get rid of weeds and work in the remains of garden compost or to work in a fertilizer dressing.

Before planting individual shrubs, roses or trees, and before planting herbaceous borders, deeper cultivation is required. Single digging — digging to a depth which is equal to the length of the fork's prongs (tines), or the length of the spade blade — is sufficient for the smaller plants and where the soil is light. It is at this initial stage that it pays to mix in rotted organic matter at the same time. For deep-rooting and larger plants double digging is preferable. This means penetrating to a depth of two spits (spades) and then forking up the bottom of the hole and mixing bulky organics all through the soil to be returned. It is important to keep the topsoil, the first spadeful, separate and to return it to the top.

Digging helps to air the soil and allows water to soak through it and drain away without becoming stagnant and eventually toxic to plant roots. This, together with the addition of humus, revitalises the soil's constituents, producing an environment that enables roots to develop fully. Basic, preplanting digging should be completed a month or so before planting if possible; it should be done in spring for fallowing to allow weed seeds to germinate. Forking is needed in spring and autumn to tidy, break up and weed the soil.

Despite the large number of fertilizers available, it is not as essential for the gardener to use them as it is for the commercial grower or farmer, who is cropping intensively year after year, and needs to reap the biggest possible yield. For the gardener, annual mulching with rotted garden compost or a similar bulky organic in late spring or early autumn is generally all that is needed for medium to heavy soil. Sometimes such soils require a boost feed after wet winters or plants growing in them need bigger rations. Light soil, on the other hand, containing a lot of sand, stones, shingle, shale or grit, needs a second dressing of organic matter in late winter and regular additions of compound fertilizer, one in spring and a second halfway through summer. If a slow-acting organic compound is used, one application in spring will see the plants through the whole growing season.

Aside from dry fertilizers, there are concentrated liquid formulations which need diluting in water; these generally have to be applied frequently while plants are growing, once or even twice a week. Some of these liquid feeds are specially manufactured for application to leaves of plants — these are foliar feeds.

Beds need to be well prepared before planting can occur (above). This involves 'single digging' (right). Divide the area into two strips using garden string. Dig out a rectangular trench at the end of one of the strips — one spade deep and wide (1). Spread manure into the trench. Dig out the next trench (2), tossing the soil into the first trench (3). Do this up the first side and down the other (4), filling the last trench with the soil taken from the first. Double digging means that the trenches are two spades deep.

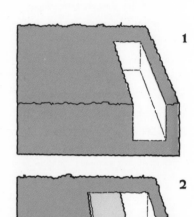

1

2

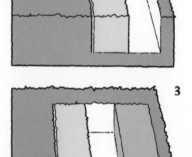

3

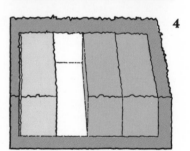

4

34

Planting appears to be a simple proposition, but it is probably responsible for as many sick plants and actual fatalities as all the other garden hazards put together. The most important point to remember is that a plant is a living organism, which breathes, eats and drinks. When it is out of the ground it should be regarded as being in a state of shock and, if it has been dug up rather than grown in a container, it will be seriously injured as well.

Roots are physiologically as well as literally a support system, and damage to them is unavoidable when digging up or transplanting. If possible, however, try to avoid breaking and disturbing the root system when lifting a plant. If tearing does occur, cleanly cut such roots off behind the break. It is also permissible to cut long roots back to a convenient length, since they are mainly present to ensure firm anchorage of the plant and not for supplying food and drink as the fine fibrous roots are.

Keep the roots moist until replanted, particularly the tiny ones; once they become dry, they will not function. It can happen very quickly, so it is a good idea to wrap the roots in plastic sheet as soon as the plant is dug up, and in hot weather to put the plant in the shade if you are not going to replant it immediately.

When planting, it is important to make the hole deep enough. Shallow planting means insecure anchorage and makes it more difficult for the plant to establish. It also bends the roots and often bunches and doubles them up, which effectively strangles them. Roots growing naturally are spread out evenly all through the soil, making the most use of nutrient and moisture content, so it is best to do the same when planting. If you are in doubt about the depth of planting, a good guideline is to arrange the plant so that the soil mark on the stem is level with the surface of the soil in its new site.

To give the roots as good a start as possible, use fine, crumbly, moist soil — potting compost is ideal, otherwise the original topsoil broken up — to fill in the hole and cover the roots. Do not use subsoil; if this depth is reached while digging, be careful to line the bottom of the hole with good soil as well. Very wet, sticky soil should be avoided, too, and if planting was necessary during dry weather, the soil should be well watered with a spray-like jet.

After planting, tread the soil down around the plant so that it is firmly secured, but without reducing the ground to a concrete-like consistency. Scratch the soil surface a little, so that it is not completely smooth and will allow rain to drain through and air to penetrate. This ensures the good health and proper functioning of the roots.

35

A *mulch is particularly beneficial to young trees and plants. It consists of either decayed manure, leaf mould, compost, peat, wet straw or sawdust. A layer of any of these should be placed in a circle around the base of the tree or plant. Make sure that the mulch is kept away from the trunk, otherwise mice will nest there, or the constant moisture will* rot *the bark. The mulch will conserve the moisture in the soil, supply additional nutrients and suppress weeds. A young shrub often requires this extra attention to encourage growth and young fruit trees which are just coming into fruit, are particularly grateful for the additional help.*

Watering

The most elementary and obvious aspect of plant survival is the supply of water. Without it plants wilt, and will die if they are starved for too long. Even if plants are revived with water after a drought there will still be problems, because the mineral nutrients required are absorbed in solution through the roots from the soil moisture. There is also a problem with many vegetables and fruit which do not get enough water in dry weather and, although such crop plants go on living, they could give much higher yields if they were regularly watered.

When the soil becomes baked and dry after weeks without rain and especially in hot, sunny weather, it cracks, and this movement of the soil causes mechanical damage to roots by tearing them. It also exposes them to light and results in even quicker drying out. Shoot growth ceases; leaves dangle limply, turn yellow and fall prematurely; buds drop off without opening.

Watering will be necessary at some time during the dry season; it may be required in cold springs when a harsh wind blows, and also sometimes in autumn, although at this time of the year heavy dews often supply enough moisture to tide the plants over. The method of application and the quantity of water supplied are both important. Turning a hose on with a single jet and leaving it to flood an area is wasteful of water and harmful to the plants. It makes puddles on the soil and pans the surface — makes it smooth and impenetrable, so that the water either stands on top or runs off to the nearest low point, without doing any good to the plants themselves. The plants will only really benefit if the water is applied as a spray, so that it is as much like a shower of rain as possible. There are nozzle attachments for hoses which will do this and many brands of sprinklers are available which can be turned on and left to provide the plants with a constant supply. Watering cans with fine or coarse holed spout attachments are good for individual plants and for seedlings. 'Dribble' hoses can be left on — the water seeps out through holes at intervals along the hose — and are especially good for crop plants in rows.

Application is best in the evening or early morning, as the plants take up plenty of water and store it ready for the heat of the day, but in emergencies all-day treatment cannot be avoided, although this does mean that some water evaporates and some is transpired almost as soon as it is absorbed. The amount that should be added is considerable; if enough water is not added at a time, roots are encouraged to develop close to the surface because the water does not penetrate deep down and they then dry out even more quickly. The lowest roots will not get any water at all, and on balance more harm than good is done. It is possible to work out how much water is required by keeping a check on the weekly rainfall: anything less than 1in (2.5cm) in the dry months or ³⁄₄in (1.8cm) at the beginning and end of the season will mean that watering is required to make up the difference. One inch of rain is equal to approximately $4\frac{1}{2}$ gal/sq yd (20 l/m²), and by working out how long it takes a hose to deliver $4\frac{1}{2}$ gal (20l) with a suitable degree of pressure, it can be calculated how long it will take to water a given area.

It is important to ensure that plants are well watered. A hose-pipe attachment is the most usual way of supplying extra water. An ordinary nozzle (1) is effective, but needs to be operated by hand. There is a simple sprinkler attachment (2) that sticks into the ground, but the rotating sprinkler (3) covers a larger area. The sophisticated, oscillating sprinkler has the widest range (4).

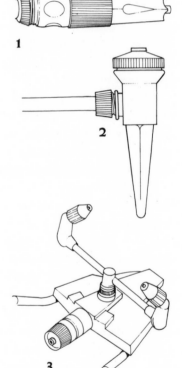

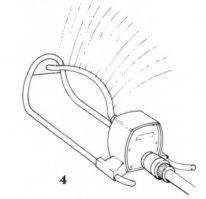

Removing dead growth

Plants die, branches break off, stems of roses and shrubs die back from the tips and flowers fade in the natural course of events. Left to themselves plants will rapidly become a clutter of dead and living growth. It is advisable to tour the garden every few weeks to remove anything that has died in the interim — dead growth will be brown, brittle and lifeless. This does not take long and is a powerful aid to plant survival. In autumn, leaves will be shed like confetti and dispersed by the wind, so it is worth removing them from the lawn and pool by raking, brushing or using mechanical leaf-sweepers. Leaf-mould is a very good source of humus and is what a heap of newly fallen leaves will become in time.

Continuously bad pruning will eventually result in a diseased shrub, with drooping and discoloured leaves.

Propagation

The most suitable time to propagate plants varies widely according to the type of plant and the method used. Spring is the most favoured time, since there is then a burst of vigour after the winter dormancy and a long growing season lies ahead during which the new plant can become well established before it has to face the rigours of its first winter.

But while many seeds and cuttings are started in early or mid-spring for these reasons, perennials and biennials tend to be sown in late spring, so that they are not too advanced by the onset of winter, but form sturdy, compact plants to pass safely through the severest weather.

Softwood, semi-hardwood and hardwood stem cuttings are taken at different times according to their development and to get the cuttings established in time to stand the winter or summer, as the case may be.

Root cuttings can be taken in late winter and are little trouble. Strawberries are rooted from runners in mid-summer, then planted out in late summer. Offsets of sedums and sempervivums can be taken at almost any time, though reasonable warmth helps them root.

Finally, bear in mind that the right time to propagate some plants is *never* — that is, if they are infected with some dreaded viral disease, for instance, in which case they should be destroyed. Other plants may be troubled by greenfly, red spider mites or mildew. You must then get them safely cleaned up before thinking of making more of them, or you will spread the trouble with the plant.

EQUIPMENT

You do not need to spend a great deal of money on tools and equipment to succeed at simple propagating. But such equipment as you do buy should be of good quality and right for the job.

Tools for taking and preparing cuttings should have really sharp stainless steel blades. Buy a budding knife, an efficient two-bladed pair of pruning shears with scissors action (as the anvil type tends to crush and injure soft stems, which can then rot) and possibly a scalpel for the cleanest cuts, from a reputable garden centre or nursery.

You will need a range of pots and seed trays for germinating seeds and rooting cuttings. The most useful pot sizes are 2½in (6cm), 3½in (9cm), 4½in (11cm) and 5in (13cm), plus some shallower 5½ (14cm) half-pots and standard-sized seed trays. How many of each you buy will depend on how much propagating you are undertaking and what types.

You will need a choice of soil-based and peat-based seed and potting mixtures, plus some sharp sand, perlite or vermiculite to add to their porosity, and peat to improve their texture and moisture retention. A mixture of peat and sand or perlite will be fine for rooting many cuttings.

To ensure efficient rooting of cuttings, you should get some rooting

38

Below: *Invest in best-quality cutting tools that stay sharp — pruning shears, pruning and budding knives, plus stout gloves to protect your hands.*

Above: *Basic tools for indoor propagating — plastic pots, watering can, sprayer, canes and maximum-minimum thermometer.*

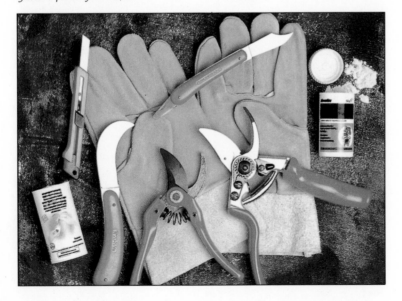

hormone powder or liquid. Even where it is not essential, it gives one added confidence.

To insert cuttings or seedlings into their growing medium without damaging them, make a small wooden dibber from a piece of dowel ⅜in (1cm) thick, sharpened to a blunt point with a knife. A wooden presser — a flat piece of wood fitted with handle — to prepare seed trays for sowing — can also be made from scrap wood.

Also homemade will be a measuring rod marked in feet and smaller divisions for setting out an out-door seedbed or planting out at fixed spacings. You will need a garden line, too, to get longer rows straight.

To keep seeds and cuttings moist while they develop, their containers will need to be covered with clear plastic film, supported on wire hoops or with a sheet of glass — or you may prefer to buy containers with purpose-made rigid clear plastic domes. An electric propagator with heating cables set in the base is a further sophistication which will give seeds and cuttings extra encouragement.

Some basic tools will be essential for outdoor cultivation. A border fork — lighter than a full sized digging fork — is most useful and less tiring to use. A steel rake is needed for levelling and fining the soil for a seedbed. Then you will need a hand-fork and garden trowel for planting.

For watering, you should buy a long-spouted can with a fine rose, suitable for greenhouse and outdoor use. Also a hand sprayer that gives a fine mist to moisten small seeds without washing them out of the soil. A similar sprayer should be kept for combating insect pests with chemicals. You may also need to consider investing in a garden hose and sprinkler to keep seedbeds watered in dry weather.

Equip yourself with a basic selection of pesticides and fungicides to deal with your plants' enemies, not forgetting slug bait to protect succulent seedlings from these voracious pests. Wire netting (or plastic netting) may be necessary to keep off pecking birds too.

Finally, a word of caution: keep all sharp tools, chemicals and plastic bags out of reach of children — preferably locked away when you are not using them.

BASIC METHODS

Garden plants are propagated in a variety of ways. Some respond to several different methods, others to only one. It is part of the gardener's skill to select the most suitable method for his plant and particular circumstances.

All the methods described here are comparatively simple, but they still need to be carried out carefully and accurately to ensure satisfying results. So, though you will probably be eager to turn straight to the methods themselves, do study all the other introductory sections, so that you can provide your cuttings and seedlings with the right conditions and aftercare and defend them from insect and fungal enemies.

Seeds

Raising seed is the first method to spring to mind, since it is nature's own. Many kinds of seeds will readily germinate at the right time of the year in the open ground, but others will need to be sown in pots or trays in a greenhouse or cold frame or on a light windowsill and gradually accustomed to outdoor conditions when they are large enough.

To get plants absolutely for free, you will want to save and sow seeds from your own plants. But be warned. While seeds from species — kinds that occur in nature — will produce progeny nearly identical to their parents, choice garden hybrids and special selections are more likely to give you inferior results as they revert to some earlier type in the plant's heredity. To succeed with such plants you will need to propagate them from a stem or root or division, which will faithfully reproduce their special characteristics, or go back to the seedsman for professionally raised seeds.

When you do save seeds from your own plants, make sure they are ripe, or nearly so. Collect them before the pods or capsules burst and the seeds are dispersed, if necessary tying bags over them to catch any seeds that fall. Seeds that are not fully ripe when autumn days turn damp, cold and misty will have to be taken under cover and ripened in the warm. Cut the whole seedhead, put if safely in an envelope, then spread on a plate in a cool greenhouse or on a sunny windowsill until ready. Sift or shake until the seeds can be packeted or put in airtight tins until sowing time comes round.

Some seeds, though ripe, will not germinate until their dormancy has been broken. Berberis and holly, for instance, must be stratified — that is, the seeds are spread between layers of sharp sand in a pan and left outdoors at the foot of a cold wall to be frosted. (Protect them from mice and other vermin with small mesh wire netting, or they could be eaten.) By spring they should be ready for sowing like other seeds.

To succeed with seed-sowing outdoors, choose a reasonably fertile patch of ground in good light and prepare it by forking it over, removing any weeds or other obstructions and break down any lumps. Tread it fairly firm, but not hard, then rake the surface down to a fine crumbly consistency. Water and leave to soak in if the soil is very dry.

Draw shallow drills (furrows) in the surface, about ½in (12mm) deep, then sow seeds thinly along the drill. Rake soil gently back to refill the drill and firm lightly in place with the head of the rake, so the seeds are in close contact with the soil. Mark ends of rows with canes and label with the name of the plant.

When the seedlings are large enough, lift them carefully with a hand-fork and set out separately at a suitable spacing in nursery rows to grow larger without overcrowding. Plant out in their permanent positions later in the season when large enough to fend for themselves.

The principles for seed-sowing indoors are the same, but the scale

Assemble suitable compost, clean pots or trays, seeds and labels to identify them before you start.

When sown, seeds should not be so close together that seedlings will be overcrowded when they germinate.

Loosely fill the container with compost, rap its base on the bench to settle and level it, then lightly firm surface to leave ¼in (6cm) below rim.

Tip some seeds into the palm of your hand, then sow thinly over compost surface — or sow direct from a corner of the packet.

Scatter a very shallow layer of compost over the seeds to cover them and keep them moist until they grow.

Water in gently with a fine-rose can or hand sprayer. Cover with a pane of glass or plastic. Ventilate daily. Keep warm.

39

is smaller and the conditions artificially controlled. Fill pots or trays with an open-textured mix specially formulated for seed-sowing, firm lightly in place, level surface and water and allow to drain. Again, sow the seeds thinly to avoid later overcrowding and cover with a shallow layer of the same compost. Cover the container with a sheet of glass or clear plastic and some paper to keep in moisture; shade it from bright light until seedlings appear, then promptly remove coverings, but make sure seedlings cannot get scorched.

As soon as the seedlings are large enough to handle, lift them carefully with a label, so their roots are not damaged and transplant them into trays of soil-mixture to give them more space. Handle them by their leaves, not by their vulnerable stems and set them gently at the right depth in small holes made in the soil with a wooden dibber. Push soil around them and firm lightly with your fingers. Water, ventilate, shade and feed as necessary so they grow into strong young plants ready for transplanting into pots or outdoors.

Cuttings

Stem cuttings provide a convenient means of propagating many kinds of plant, so the youngsters match their parents exactly. They fall into three categories according to the ripeness or woodiness of their stems. Each is taken at a different time of year and treated in its own way. *Softwood* cuttings are generally about 2in (5cm) long and taken in early summer and need close, warm (about 65°-70°F, 18°-21°C), humid greenhouse (or windowsill) conditions to root. They can be taken from young sideshoots of shrubs or as basal shoots arising from lupins, dahlias or delphiniums.

Semi-hardwood cuttings, of which bedding geranium (pelargonium) cuttings are typical, are 3-4in (7.5cm-10cm) long, firmer and rooted in pots but without specially warm or close conditions. *Hardwood* cuttings, 10-14in (25-35cm) long, generally of shrubs and woody plants, are taken in mid-autumn and inserted and overwintered in the open ground. Most root by the spring.

Whatever the type of cutting, select healthy shoots of typical growth with strong stems — neither flabby nor thin and weak. Trim across just beneath a leaf joint, where new roots most readily develop, remove all the lower leaves, so they are not buried where they will rot. Dip in hormone rooting compound, powder or liquid, then insert in a suitable rooting mixture. This is generally gritty with an open texture but low in plant foods. When the cuttings have rooted strongly they should then be moved into a more nourishing mixture which includes soil and probably fertilizers too.

Leaf bud cuttings are related kinds of cuttings in which a piece of stem bearing just one leaf bud is prepared and rooted in warmth. Leaf bud cuttings of camellias are taken in late summer and inserted upright in the rooting compost. Grapevines are propagated from single bud

cuttings ensuring that there is about an inch (2.5cm) of hardwood stem on either side of the bud. These are usually inserted horizontally in the surface of the soil mix after removing a sliver of wood from the lower side, and rooted at about 70°F (21°C).

Layering

This is a method of propagating that consists of rooting shoots while they are still attached to the parent plant and drawing nourishment from it. It occurs naturally on some shrubs, such as *Jasminum nudiflorum*, the winter jasmine, and *Forsythia suspensa*. If one of their drooping shoots

Above: *Hardwood cuttings are taken in autumn and rooted outdoors in slits in the ground with sharp sand in the base.*

Above: *Softwood cuttings are taken in spring and need close warm conditions to root.*

Above: *Half ripe cuttings, like those of bedding geraniums, are rooted in pots but need only moderate warmth and minimum attention.*

touches the soil, it is likely to develop roots, anchor itself there and start drawing nutriment from a fresh patch of ground. It is then simple for the gardener to sever the daughter plant from its parent, lift it carefully, so its roots are not damaged, and plant it (or pot it) where it is required to flower. Truly plants for free!

To imitate nature's behaviour, select a low-growing shoot that can be bent down to the soil, wound it where you want it to root by cutting it diagonally about half way through and prop the wound open with a sliver of wood. You could treat the wound with a hormone rooting preparation to make doubly sure of success. Peg down the shoot with a doubled-over wire pin, cover it with soil — or better still a sand/peat potting mixture that will encourage rooting — and stake the tip of the shoot upright so it will form a shapely plant when rooted and severed from its parent.

If layered in spring, a shoot should be rooted well enough to be cut from its parent in autumn and transplanted to a nursery bed to continue developing before it is eventually planted in its permanent position.

Tip layering is a related phenomenon, often seen on blackberry canes, for example. A long pendulous cane will form strong roots at its tip if it touches the soil and develop a new plant there. This could, of course, be severed and transplanted where required and will reproduce its parents' characteristics exactly.

Air layering

This is an ingenious development of layering in which the gardener brings the soil to the branch instead of bending it down to the soil. In this way we can layer many shrubs and trees that are not pliant enough to reach the ground.

Air layering a rhododendron.

A suitable shoot is cut upwards through the centre for 2-3in (5-7.5cm) and the wound held open with a matchstick while it is treated with rooting hormone, then filled and surrounded by moist sphagnum moss, when the matchstick is removed. The shoot and moss are then enclosed in a bandage of clear plastic film to keep in moisture while roots form. When the roots become visible, the shoot can then be severed from its parent plant and potted up. Keep it warm and close for a while until it becomes established, then gradually introduce it to normal conditions.

Runners, as formed by strawberry plants, are similar in principle to tip layers, since a plant forms at the end of each runner sent out by the plant. But it subsequently extends beyond the plant to form more young plants. When using this technique to propagate strawberries, a gardener will take only one plantlet — the first and strongest — from each runner. It is usual to root the plantlets straight into pots of potting compost so that, when severed from the parent, they can be planted out with the minimum of root disturbance and establish quickly.

Division

This is one of the most commonly used methods, particularly among clump-forming border plants, as it is so simple and effective. Just lift vigorous well-established clumps and divide them by pulling them apart with your hands, levering them apart with two hand-forks or border forks back to back, or resort to a knife. Select young healthy pieces with some good roots from the outside of the clump to provide new plants.

Division is normally undertaken in autumn or early spring. The hardest kinds like asters (Michaelmas daisies) can be divided in autumn or early winter, as their divisions are sure to survive the rigours of winter. But more tender kinds like pyrethrums are best left until early spring or even until just after they have flowered to avoid losses during winter following the shock of being torn apart.

It is inadvisable to divide plants in full leaf or flower, as the shock will result in at least temporary collapse. But if this is your only opportunity to secure stock of some desirable plant, you might risk it. Be prepared to lose the top growth for that season and to have to nurse the plant for some weeks until its roots have had a chance to re-establish. With care, you should have plants able to face the winter and give you a worthwhile display the next summer.

Offsets

Some plants, like *Sedum spathulifolium* and various sempervivums are typical offset formers, spreading clumps of leaf rosettes. Each of these rosettes may be removed with a short stem and a few roots and inserted in a gritty compost, where they will soon form independent plants. With little more attention than this, rosettes *without* roots can be encouraged to root and form new plants. Once you have one of these rosette-forming plants, you need never be without plenty of replacements.

Root cuttings

A number of border plants will obligingly make new plants from pieces of their thick fleshy roots. You may discover this by accident as I did by transplanting an acanthus and leaving some of its roots behind. It soon developed into an extra plant.

To propagate in this way, just scrape soil away from one side of a clump of the plant and cut away suitable lengths of root, about 1½in (2.8cm) long. Trim them straight across the top, slanting at the base, to make sure you get them the right way up, then insert into a gritty mixture suitable for cuttings, their tops level with the surface, to grow — usually without extra heat.

Phlox decussata is the typical example of a variant of this method. Take short lengths of its ⅛in (3mm) thick roots and lay them flat on the surface of a similar soil mixture, covering with a thin layer. These cuttings will also make new plants — and incidentally avoid transmitting any stem eelworm that may be in your phlox plants. Mint (culinary and ornamental) roots in the same way.

Lily scales and bulbils

Healthy lily bulbs, formed of loose fleshy scales, offer you an easy way of making more plants. Detach one or two scales from each bulb — do not take too many unless you are desperate to make a lot, or you will weaken the parent — and put them in a clear plastic bag of moist peat and sand mixture in a warm place. Each will develop a tiny plant at the base of the scale, and they can be set out in trays of soil-less or peat-based mix to grow on.

A few lilies, of which *Lilium tigrinum* and the popular variety 'Echantment' are most widely grown, form bulbils up their stems. These, about the size of sugar peas, can be detached when fully developed in midsummer and sown like seeds in trays to form more young lily plants — a real gift for the gardener!

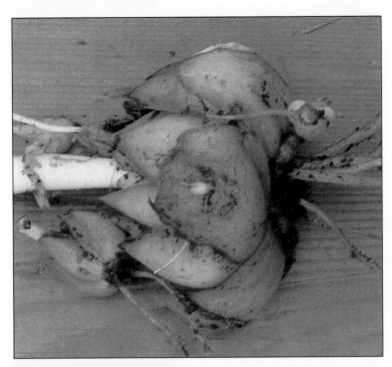

Above: *Bulb of* Lilium speciosum *showing plump scales used to form new young bulbs.*

Provide sharp drainage when propagating from root cuttings.

Lifted clump of Phlox decussata, showing thicker roots used as cuttings.

Lay 3in (8cm) lengths of root on surface of rooting compost, then lightly cover.

42

Pruning: Techniques and tools

Every effort should be made to help a plant recover from its pruning wound. Make sure the cut is as small and clean as possible, avoid unnecessary cuts and where possible make one cut instead of two.

THE RIGHT WAY TO PRUNE STEMS

It is important to sever the stem just above the growth bud. This applies to laterals on fruit and ornamental trees, for example, and branches on shrubs and rose bushes. A growth bud will usually be more pointed and slimmer than a flower bud although this rule does not apply to all plants. The reason for cutting back to a growth bud is that extension growth will subsequently take place; cutting back to a flower bud would yield just a flower and possibly fruit, after which growth would probably stop.

If you make the pruning cut too close to the bud, there is every chance that the bud will be damaged. If, on the other hand, the cut is too far away, a length of stem is left which is unlikely to heal properly, making it susceptible to disease; a cut sloping in the wrong direction and ragged and crushed stems — usually the result of blunt pruning shears — should be avoided for the same reason.

Cut above an outwards-facing bud, except on pendulous plants, where the buds should be upwards-facing. The cut must be positioned and angled to ensure that the bud is not damaged by the pruning tool and that the wound heals satisfactorily. Cut the stem at an angle, parallel to that at which the bud is growing, making the cut 1/8-1/4in (3-6mm) above the bud. The shorter distance is suitable for mild climates when the bud is less likely to dry out; in areas where there is a chance of very low air temperatures, the extra 1/8in (3mm) left above the bud will help to prevent dehydration. Avoid pruning in hard, frosty weather as this could badly affect the plant.

THE RIGHT WAY TO PRUNE LARGE BRANCHES

If lateral shoots are present on an unwanted branch, remove these first to reduce the weight. Then shorten the branch by stages, leaving a portion about 18in (45cm) long to be dealt with at the end. Make sure that the portions cut away do not damage lower branches as they drop to the ground; large pieces of wood should be lowered gently by rope, which must be in good condition to avoid accidents.

Above: *Buds that develop into blossom are usually fat and rounded, whereas growth buds tend to be smaller and pointed. The round bud on the left of the peach stem will produce blossom.*

Left: *Make the cut far enough away to avoid damaging the bud, but not so far as to leave a snag. The cut on the far right is correct; the others are not.*

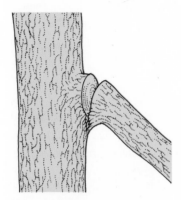

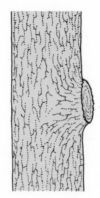

Above: *Avoid ripping the bark of a large branch by careless pruning. Otherwise an ugly wound will develop and the plant will be more susceptible to disease.*

REMOVING LARGE BRANCHES

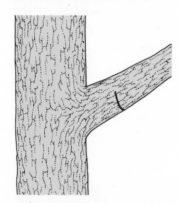

1 *After removing lateral shoots make the first cut 6in (15cm) away from the main trunk, underneath the branch and passing halfway through it.*

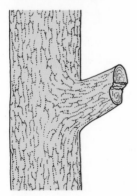

2 *Make the second cut 1in (2.5cm) out from the first and on the top side of the branch.*

3 *The final cut should be made close to the trunk, just outside the branch bark ridge. It should be angled away from the main trunk so as to form a mirror image of the angle of the ridge. Where a collar is present, the cut should be made just outside it, regardless of the angle.*

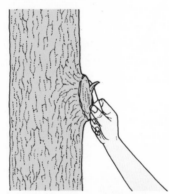

4 *Then smooth off the the ragged edges of the final cut with a sharp pruning knife.*

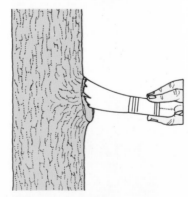

5 *If you wish, cover the pruned area with wound-healing paint (see text).*

Above: *Stubs are liable to rot when too much of the removed branch is left behind.*

Above: *The branch has been cut away too close for the wound to heal properly.*

Above: *The branches have been cut off at the right distance from the trunk to ensure quick and neat healing.*

44

Three cuts in all

Before tackling the remaining length of branch, attach a rope to it and secure the other end to a sturdy limb above. Using a saw, make the first cut about 6in (15cm) from the tree trunk on the lower side of the branch and take it about halfway through. Then cut through the branch by making a second cut, 1in (2.5cm) out from the previous cut. This staggered cut will prevent the bark tearing back into retained wood as the branch comes away.

The final cut should now be made just outside the branch bark ridge, angled away from the main stem to form a mirror image of the angle of the ridge. Where a branch collar is present the cut should be made just outside it, regardless of the angle otherwise the wound is liable to be too large. The final cut should never be flush with the main stem; this would inhibit the tree's natural healing of the wound. Stub cuts (when too much of the branch is left on the tree) should also be avoided for the same reason. Cutting large branches can be tricky. Always aim for a clean, smooth cut. Bark ripped by careless pruning will cause an ugly wound that will be prone to infection.

Smoothing and sealing the cut

In order to keep airborne disease spores from infecting pruning cuts, it is advisable to smooth the surface of saw cuts by using a sharp knife. This will also help to encourage the healing process and prevent rainwater from collecting on the surface of the wound and possibly causing rotting.

Wound-healing paint is available to brush on to pruning cuts and, according to one school of thought, will protect the cut from airborne disease spores. However, since there is likely to be a time lapse between pruning and the application of paint, disease spores may well have time to infect the wound and in that case would be sealed in. Critics of wound painting claim that it is doubtful whether painting has any real beneficial effect, other than to disguise large pruning cuts. It must be said however, that special wound-healing paint has been recommended by some advisers and used with success over the years, although its use has not always been substantiated by recent research work.

SELECTING THE RIGHT TOOL

There is a vast number of different kinds of pruning implements to choose from. Since they vary in quality and price, it is well worth hunting around for the best equipment in your price range; a well-made tool can last for many years and is a good investment.

Although smaller tools may cost less, it is false economy to purchase one that is not big or strong enough for the job in hand: lightweight tools make hard work of tough stems, and a strained, twisted blade causes damage to the plant as well as to the tool itself. Look closely at the general finish of the product, making sure the handle does

Above: *Wounds resulting from branch removal have healed nicely here.*

Above: *Smooth the surface of wounds using a sharp knife.*

not have rough edges and is therefore comfortable to hold with the bare hand — it is not always convenient to wear gloves. Another important factor is the quality of steel from which the tool is made: well-tempered, hard steel (with a bright finish) will keep a sharp edge longer than soft steel, which wears away faster.

How many different kinds of pruning tools you need will depend on the diversity of your plants and the size of your garden. If you need to use large tools only occasionally, it may be hard to justify their purchase. Local tool-rental firms often stock such items as chain saws, which can be hired for a comparatively small charge. However, there is

Use a long-arm pruner for the stems that are high up; some types have a curved saw blade attachment to cut off thick stems.

always the possibility that other gardeners may need to borrow a particular tool at the same time that you do, so if you are unlucky you might end up doing the work later than is ideal.

Pruning shears

There are basically two types of shears that you can use for stems up to approximately ³⁄₄in (2cm) in diameter. The anvil type consists of a single, straight blade that cuts against a more solid, broader strip of metal (anvil). To use anvil-type pruners, support the stem to be pruned squarely on the anvil, then bring the blade down through the stem. This type of secateur is available in various sizes, to be used on different thicknesses of stem. The blade is easily removed for servicing, and some models have a notch on the side for cutting wire.

The parrot type of pruning shear has two curved cutting blades, resembling a parrot's bill in shape, with a scissor action. The design has been modified considerably since it was first produced because the blades sometimes tended not to cut tough wood cleanly. That is unlikely to happen with modern blades, provided you use the tool correctly and do not twist it when you are cutting the stem. This type of secateur is particularly useful for soft stems and for cutting close to a narrow crotch. As with the anvil type, a notch is often provided for cutting wire, and a design with swivel handle grips is also available, which means that if you twist the secateurs the blades do not shift.

Long-handled pruners

If you need to prune stems more than ³⁄₄in (2cm) in diameter, it is best to use long-handled pruners, which have strong cutting blades and handles up to 2¹⁄₂ft (75cm) long to give added leverage. They will cut stems up to 1¹⁄₄in (3.5cm) in diameter and are useful for removing growth from the centre of a plant that may be difficult to reach with hand pruners. One type has been designed with self-adjusting jaws, and another with a ratchet mechanism; both make cutting stems of various thicknesses and densities much easier.

Pole pruners

Pole pruners are useful for reaching high branches. They have a single, usually wooden handle 7-20ft (2-7m) long. The head forms a hooked blade that looks like a inverted J. This is passed over the stem to be cut and then worked by a long length of rope or high-tensile galvanised steel wire. Although you can use pole pruners to cut stems up to 1in (2.5cm) thick, be careful not to prune too large a branch. If the wire becomes strained, it may straighten out at the handle or even break. There is also the possibility that the blade may jam in the stem you are trying to cut. Some models have levers or pulleys that enhance the leverage and allow you to remove large branches more easily.

Hand shears

These long-bladed implements are used for clipping hedges and other dense growth, such as mature heather. They should be used for comparatively soft wood and thin stems — but a notch is usually provided to accommodate obstinate, thicker stems. The blades should be kept sharp by grinding so that they cut cleanly; otherwise too much strain may be placed on them so that they warp and become less effective.

Curved saws

When access to a plant is restricted, a curved saw often provides the solution. The saw is sturdy, yet comfortable and light to handle. Although the pointed end of the blade is narrow enough to enter a confined space, it can still tackle comparatively large branches. There are short-handled and long-handled versions, the latter allowing you to remove high branches while standing on the ground. This long-armed instrument, known as a pole saw, needs to be used with great care, since high branches can fall with alarming speed after they have been cut.

Two-edged saws

These saws have a cutting edge on both sides of the blade: one has fine teeth, the other coarse teeth for large branches. This type of saw needs to be handled carefully to avoid scarring adjacent branches.

Folding saws

These saws, which can be used only for branches of small diameter, have a blade that folds back into the handle. This is especially useful when you are pruning on a ladder, since when you have finished using the saw it can be slipped into a pocket.

Chain saws

Chain saws, which are available in various sizes and are powered either by liquid fuel or by electricity, will remove stout branches or fell an entire tree. They are used mainly by professionals, such as foresters and tree surgeons, trained in their use. If you decide to use one, you should take great care in operating it and avoid working from any precarious position, such as on a ladder. Chain tension is very important and should be checked periodically with the special tool provided with the machine.

Mechanical hedge trimmers

Mechanical hedge trimmers are particularly useful for clipping large hedges, saving you time and aching arms. They are also versatile enough to trim shrubs and ground cover. A long blade with sharp teeth moves backwards and forwards alongside a fixed blade; different models have wide or narrow spaces between the teeth, and it is important to choose the correct one for the particular job to be done. The smaller models cope well with stems up to ¼in (6mm) thick; heavier work requires a larger machine. Look for Teflon-coated blades; these make the trimming even easier and faster.

Most hedge trimmers are powered by electricity, through an extension cable or from a battery; but petrol-powered models are also available. It is absolutely essential that an extension cable be kept out of

Above: *Long-handled pruners are ideal for awkward areas.*

47

Above: *The long-handled pole pruner enables high branches to be cut while standing on the ground, but look out for falling wood.*

When access is restricted, the curved saw provides the answer to many an awkward situation. (Above) The first, second and third cuts.

the way of the blades at all times, whether they are moving or not, since cutting through it could be lethal. It is best to pass the cable over your shoulder so that it is always behind you, not dragging in front of your body. The cable should, of course, be in good condition and earthed. Wear rubber-soled footwear when using a hedge trimmer and use it only on a dry day. Never use the trimmer if you have to stand in a wet spot. Although petrol-powered trimmers tend to be heavier, they have the advantage of being safer and can be used in wet weather.

TOOL MAINTENANCE

Since even the best of tools will suffer through neglect, good maintenance is essential. A wipe with an oily rag after use usually removes any stains from the blade and, at the same time, gets rid of most disease spores that may have collected on the trimmer. Persistent stains can be removed by steel wool or emery paper.

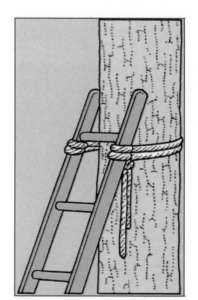

LADDERS

You may sometimes need ladders or steps to reach high branches. Aluminium ladders are rot-proof and easier to carry than the wooden kind; the rungs on both are inclined to work loose in time and should be inspected occasionally and tightened if necessary. Hinges are also prone to wear unless they are oiled. One final tip: if you intend to prune a tree from a ladder, secure this to the tree with rope. In this way any falling branches that rebound from the ground cannot dislodge the ladder.

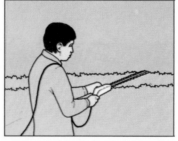

Above: *Make sure that the cable of the electric hedge trimmer passes over your shoulder, out of the way of the cutting blades.*

Pruning shrubs

Every shrub goes through an annual cycle of growth, leaf development, budding, flowering and in some cases fruiting. Each stage occurs at more or less the same time each year and is influenced by such factors as day length, temperature, soil moisture and, of course, pruning. It is therefore very important to take each plant's life cycle into account when planning how and when to prune it.

While not all shrubs require pruning every year, most are improved by occasional pruning. For example, *Cornus alba* benefits from having older wood cut away, which encourages bright red young stems to appear.

Old shrubs can often be rejuvenated by careful pruning so that they become attractive and productive once more. Very old, congested shrubs can be dealt with most conveniently in two stages: remove dead and weak growth one year, as the first stage of renovation, and carry out the normal pruning recommended for the shrub the following year, as the second stage.

WHEN TO PRUNE

The initial training of young shrubs should be aimed at establishing a good framework. On young evergreens select three or four strong shoots and remove their tips, cutting back to an outward-facing bud; remove all other stems entirely, cutting them back to soil level. Prune subsequent growth in late spring the following year by thinning out overcrowded shoots. This encourages an open-centered plant through which air can circulate.

On young deciduous shrubs, select up to five vigorous stems and shorten any lateral shoots to approximately half their length, again cutting back to an outwards-facing bud. Remove the remaining stems completely. Cut back subsequent growth by half during the following

*C*ut the flowered shoots of Erica *back by no more than one-half when the flowers have faded.*

*S*hrubs that flower on the previous year's growth should be pruned back hard to new growth right after flowering, in the spring or summer.

winter and thin out any overcrowded growth at the centre.

Established shrubs need to be pruned at different times and by different methods, according to whether they are grown principally for their flowers (and/or fruit) or their foliage or stems, and whether, on flowering shrubs, flowers are produced on old or new growth.

Flowering shrubs

Shrubs producing flowers on the previous year's growth usually flower during spring and early summer. They include Forsythia, *Kerria japonica*, *Philadelphus*, *Pieris* and Weigela. Shrubs like these should have their flowering shoots pruned immediately after flowering so that the plants put all their energy into producing new extension growth rather than developing old wood and seed heads.

Certain shrubs, such as hibiscus and some species of berberis produce flowers on the current season's growth. Plants in this group often respond best to hard pruning of the previous year's shoots in late winter or early spring, before new growth appears. Some shrubs of this type, such as *Buddleia davidii*, can be strong growers and, unless pruned in late autumn or early winter, may suffer damage from strong winds.

Shrubs grown for foliage or stems

Most shrubs grown for their foliage require only occasional pruning to keep them within bounds. The best time to do this is before new growth starts in spring, since any winter-damaged stems can be removed at the same time.

However, shrubs with brightly coloured or interestingly shaped leaves can have these features enhanced by pruning back hard in late winter or early spring. This encourages strong, vigorous growth and large leaves.

Shrubs with variegated or otherwise attractive leaves occasionally produce a single shoot with plain green leaves which tends to be more vigorous than the normal growth. You should deal with such mutations as soon as you notice them, by cutting off the shoots where they arise — otherwise, the entire plant will eventually revert to plain green.

Some shrubs are grown mainly for their brightly coloured bark. One of the finest, *Cornus alba*, can be made more striking by cutting its stems back to just above ground level each spring. Others should be pruned less severely. In all cases the new growth produced the following summer is vigorous and matures well to withstand the coldest of winters.

Above: *Brown leaf tips on* Prunus laurocerasus *are winter-damaged. Prune off in spring.*

Cut out mutations such as this on Weigela florida variegata *as soon as they appear, otherwise you may end up with a different plant!*

Above: *Shrubs that flower on this year's growth should have last year's wood cut back to two or three buds from the main stem in late winter or early spring, before new growth appears.*

Pruning wall plants

The true climbers fall into three categories: plants with their own natural support, such as aerial roots which act as suction pads on a wall or fence; plants that twine their stems, tendril or other parts around a support; and plants with hooked thorns. Other plants, though not true climbers, tend to grow in such a way as to cover structures and are also included in this section.

When acquiring a bare-rooted plant, cut off any damaged roots, remove any weak or damaged shoots, and shorten the remainder by half.

TRUE AND SOFT STEM CLIMBERS

During their first year true climbers and plants with soft stems require very little pruning; they should be allowed every opportunity to establish themselves. In subsequent years follow the instructions given in the plants list that follows. One important general point to remember is that you should remove shoots growing outwards, away from the support; do not prune those growing inwards because they are needed to provide and reinforce support for the plant.

WOODY STEM CLIMBERS

For plants that develop woody stems, formative pruning during the early years is needed to establish a good framework. In the case of woody deciduous climbers, it will ensure that during the dormant period, when only the framework can be seen, the plant will still be attractive.

PRUNING NON-SELF-SUPPORTING CLIMBERS

1 *Carefully remove the plant from its support and lay it on the ground.*

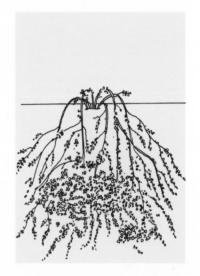

2 *Prune away the dead growth and very old growth with hard bark.*

3 *When this is done rearrange the plant over its support and tie it if necessary.*

Left: *Abelia floribunda can be used in the garden as a climber, but should be treated like a shrub when pruning.*

Pruning hedges

Many yards benefit from a hedge for one reason or another: it provides privacy, a boundary, shelter from wind, and a screen to hide unwanted views. Hedges are often used to divide features in a large garden, and smaller gardens can be made to look bigger by a well-placed hedge.

PRUNING NEW HEDGES

Except for conifers, hedge plants generally benefit from light trimming during the first spring and after planting: reduce the leading shoots to a uniform height and cut side shoots back to form a straight line. During the following year or two, prune the plants lightly in this way right through the growing season. However, slow-growing plants that are well furnished with side branches need only misplaced shoots removed, while, at the other extreme, fast-growing plants need to be cut back hard to encourage growth from dormant buds near ground level.

On evergreens it is important to complete all pruning by the end of the active growth period, so that stems will have the opportunity to ripen before winter. Otherwise, frost may well damage the soft tissue. With deciduous plants, an alternative method is to cut stems made the previous growing season back by half during winter.

PRUNING ESTABLISHED HEDGES

Once a hedge has reached the desired height, trim it once a year, after the flowers have faded (but bear in mind that with pruning at this time fruit will be forfeited) or, in the case of a non-flowering hedge, in midsummer.

Make sure to prune a hedge so that its base is wider than its top. This will enable the lower leaves to receive a fair share of light. In addition, less damage is likely from the weight of snow collecting on the top of a narrower-topped hedge.

Pruning shears are the most convenient tool to use for young plants and informal hedges that are allowed to grow more naturally. They are also the best for broad-leaved plants, since the leaves will not be damaged in the way that they would be by using shears. Mechanical trimmers and shears are ideal for small-leaved formal hedges (those clipped into very well-defined shapes). They should be used flat against the face of the hedge. To ensure that you cut the top of a hedge level, insert a pole into the ground at each end and stretch a line tautly between them as a guideline.

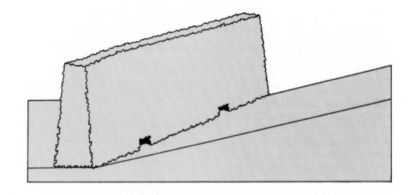

Above: *To protect plants growing higher on a slope from frost in cold regions, cut 6in (15cm) gaps at 6ft (2m) intervals in the base of the hedge growing lower down the slope.*

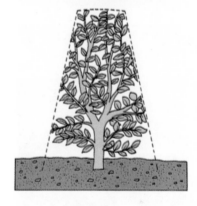

Above *and* left: *During their first summer after planting, hedges, with the exception of conifers, will require light trimming by cutting the leading shoots to a uniform height. Secure a taut line between two poles to get this. The side shoots should be cut back to straight lines. Note that the hedge should eventually be wider at the base.*

Roses are the most popular of garden plants. Enthusiasts fill every available space with them, but the average gardener will probably be content with a bed of hybrid teas, floribundas, one or two species of roses or shrub roses in a mixed border and perhaps a rambler or climber trained up a wall, over an archway or horizontally along a trellis or fence. Miniature roses are attractive and can be grown successfully in containers.

PRUNING NEWLY PLANTED ROSES

On all newly planted roses, cut back any dead stems to healthy wood, just above a bud. Remove the weaker of any crossing stems, again cutting back to just above a bud. Entirely remove any spindly stems. After this standard pruning, any further initial pruning and subsequent maintenance pruning should be carried out as follows according to the type of rose.

Hybrid teas, floribundas, grandifloras, polyanthus

In spring, just before growth starts, cuts maiden roses back hard to buds approximately 4½in (11cm) from the ground. However, if the rose was

PRUNING NEWLY PLANTED ROSES

Newly planted roses are all pruned much the same way, no matter what the type.

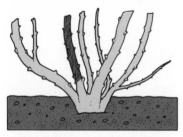

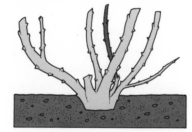

1 *Cut all dead stems back to healthy wood.*

2 *Look for crossing stems and cut back the weaker ones to just above a bud.*

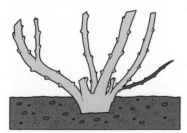

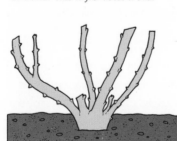

3 *Remove all spindly stems.*

Larger *blooms result from disbudding.*

53

planted in autumn and has very long shoots, these should receive a preliminary pruning after planting by cutting them back by half to avoid wind damage.

Maintenance pruning should also be carried out in spring, before new growth appears. Remove winter damage at the same time. The standard spring pruning procedure is first to remove any winter-damaged stems and any dead or diseased wood; next, thin out the centre of the bush to allow air and sunlight to penetrate and to facilitate spraying; then cut back any weak growth to one or two buds from the main stem. The extent to which the rest of the plant will need pruning depends on various factors. For example, strong-growing plants require less pruning than weaker ones. However, as a general rule cutting wood made the previous year back by half should provide a good garden display and sufficient flowers for cutting. If you want numerous early flowers it is best to prune more lightly; conversely, late flowering, with fewer, larger blooms and more vigorous growth results from more severe pruning. So you should regulate your pruning according to what you want and what the plant needs.

On weak-growing roses with thin stems, the previous season's growth should be cut back hard, by two-thirds, to produce stronger stems more likely to resist weather damage and to provide better cut blooms.

A second pruning in late autumn is beneficial: remove any damaged stems and cut back long shoots to avoid damage from winter winds and cold.

Climbers and ramblers

Maiden climbers do not require any initial pruning, other than the

Above: *Light pruning encourages earlier flowering.*

Above: *Hard pruning produces sturdy growth and later flowering.*

Above: *Rose shoots damaged by late frost should be cut back to a healthy lateral.*

PRUNING HYBRID TEA ROSES

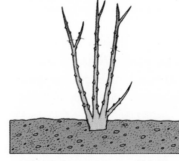
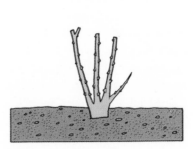

1 *After planting prune away all dead wood and weak and spindly growth.*

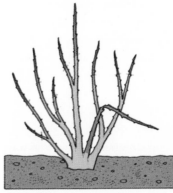
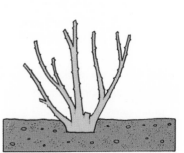

2 *The following spring and every spring thereafter cut back last year's growth by half. Weak-growing bushes can be pruned more severely to encourage growth.*

standard procedure described. Established plants are best pruned during late autumn by cutting back the old flowered shoots to within 3in (7.5cm) of the main stem.

After planting ramblers, cut them back to a bud approximately 1ft (30cm) above ground level — if this has not already been done at the nursery. Prune established plants during autumn. You may need to thin out vigorous growers each year by removing old stems to ground level or back to a strong lateral. The only other pruning necessary is to cut back lateral shoots which have flowered to about 3in (7.5cm) from the main stem.

Tie-down roses

Tie-down roses can be trained horizontally on frames or wires. With this method, flowering stems develop more uniformly than on an upright plant, since the sap tends to spread through the stems evenly instead of rising to the buds at the tips.

After planting, cut back to three or four buds from the union (where the top growth arises from the rootstock). This will encourage vigorous growth the following year. In winter this growth should be tipped back

54

to firm growth and then tied to the framework with garden string. Subsequent pruning consists of cutting old shoots that have flowered back to two buds and removing old congested stems, either completely or back to a strong-growing lateral.

Shrub roses and species roses

Shrub roses and species roses do not require any but standard pruning immediately after planting. Thereafter, shrub roses need little maintenance pruning other than removing dead or weak growth and thinning out when necessary. For species roses the only pruning necessary is to cut invasive growth back to a strong-growing lateral shoot; anything more drastic can ruin the appearance of the plant.

PRUNING TIE-DOWN ROSES

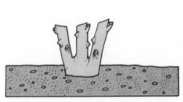

1 *Prune back to three or four buds that emerge from the union at ground level immediately after planting.*

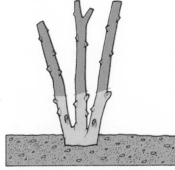

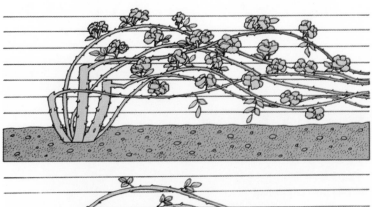

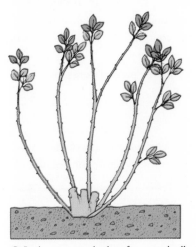
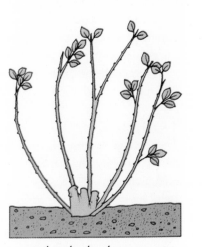

2 *In the winter, cut back to firm growth all vigorous growth produced in the previous year.*

55

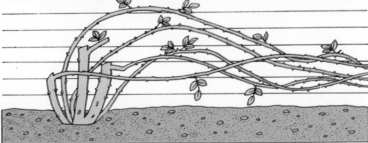

Above: *Established climbers are best pruned in late autumn by cutting back the old flowered shoots to within 3in (7.5cm) of the main stem.*

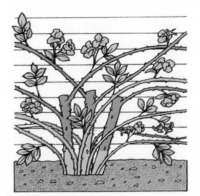
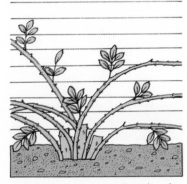

Established ramblers are pruned during autumn when vigorous growers are thinned out by removing very old stems to ground level or back to a strong lateral, where one exists.

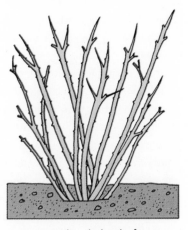
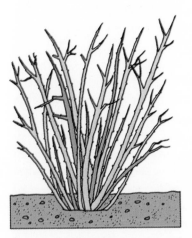

Above: *The only pruning necessary with species roses is to reduce the length of any invasive growth to a strong lateral.*

Generally, deciduous trees are best pruned just before the sap rises in spring (provided severe frost is not expected); otherwise they may bleed. (Certain trees, such as *Betula* and *Acer* are inclined to lose a considerable amount of sap when cut at other times of the year.) It has been suggested, however, that wounds heal more quickly when the tree is in full leaf, because gumming of the sap-conducting tissue and callus formation over the wound is brought about more quickly. It is also claimed that air-borne disease spores likely to attack an open wound are less numerous during hot, dry weather. Pruning before sap rises, during the dormant season, induces vigour in the plant, though it should also be taken into account that it may well reduce that year's flowering and fruiting. If these are more important to you than the tree's vigour, you can delay pruning until the summer.

Non-coniferous, evergreen trees should be pruned during early and mid-spring, as and when necessary.

TRAINING

There is a great sense of satisfaction in training a young tree that, given the opportunity and depending on species, may grow for decades or even hundreds of years.

Lateral growth

On both grafted and nongrafted trees, laterals will develop. If you keep them, the main stem will thicken at the expense of height; if you remove them, the main stem will remain thin but grow taller than it would otherwise have done. The best approach is a compromise. Remove all lateral growth from the bottom third of the main stem during the dormant season. On the middle third, reduce laterals to three buds. Leave the upper third unpruned, unless a double leader develops, in which case cut the weaker shoot out.

Standard trees

Pruning during the following two years depends on the type of tree. A standard — a tree with a trunk clear of laterals up to approximately 6½ft (2m) — is the best choice for a small garden. Allow an intended standard to grow up to about 7ft (2.25m); then cut growth back to firm wood just before the sap rises in spring. Any secondary growth from the lowest third of the trunk should be cut away. At the end of the two years, when the plant has become well established, all laterals from the middle third of the main stem should be removed, allowing a good crown to develop.

Once a standard tree is mature, little pruning should be necessary except to remove dead or crossing branches and any laterals that develop lower than the desired crown. Strong water shoots arising from

TO REMOVE OR NOT TO REMOVE LATERALS ON A TREE

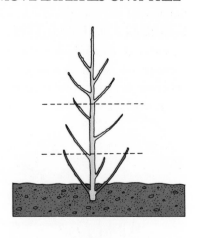

1 *When the lateral growth is kept on a young tree, the tree increases its girth faster than when it is removed.*

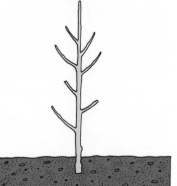

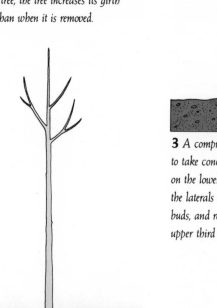

3 *A compromise is often the best course to take concerning laterals: remove laterals on the lower third of the trunk, shorten the laterals on the middle portion to three buds, and retain the lateral growth on the upper third of the trunk.*

2 *When laterals are pruned away the trunk stays thinner but grows taller faster.*

56

previously cut areas should be removed completely. Any branches extending too far can be cut back to a suitable sublateral (growth arising from a lateral). Old wood is best removed each winter to stimulate young replacement shoots.

Larger trees

Where space is available to grow a large specimen, the bare portion of trunk can be extended to 8½ft (2.5m) or more. Taller trunks can be especially effective on trees such as *Nyssa sylvatica* that tend to have lower branches which curve down to the ground as they mature. On all grafted trees shoots arising as suckers should be removed at an early stage.

Unless a weeping tree has already undergone formative pruning, cut the leader and lateral shoots back to two or three buds each winter until the tree reaches the desired height. With trees that do not produce a vertical leader naturally, it will be necessary to tie the leading shoot to the supporting stake.

When training a tree into a shape such as a column or pyramid, do not remove laterals from low down on the main stem, unless they are overcrowded, damaged or crossing.

SHAPING A WEEPING TREE

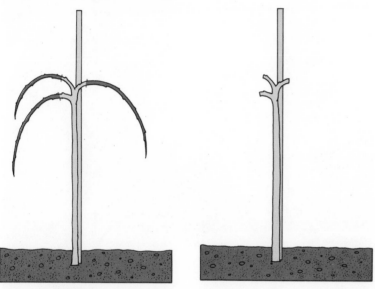

1 *Cut the leader and the lateral shoots back to two or three buds every winter until the tree has reached a suitable height.*

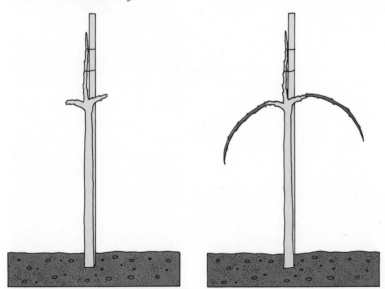

2 *If there is no obvious leader, drive a stake next to the tree and tie the longest middle shoot to it. Continue to prune back the shoots until the tree has reached the desired height.*

GENERAL MAINTENANCE PRUNING

Wood should be removed from a mature tree with care and consideration for its shape. For example, it is often better to take out an unwanted branch completely, rather than cut it back, otherwise the shortened branch may well produce a lateral that will simply replace the original branch.

If a tree is lop-sided, cut the lateral shoots on the weak side back hard to within two or three buds and prune the strong side only lightly. Vertical shoots competing with the leader should be shortened or removed. On a tree that produces a large amount of short-stemmed, congested growth, especially towards the centre of the plant, thin out this growth to allow air to circulate and light to penetrate.

Once formative pruning has been completed, deciduous and non-coniferous evergreen trees require comparatively little in the way of maintenance to keep them looking attractive.

RESHAPING A LOPSIDED TREE

1 *First, hard prune the lateral shoots on the side that is weakest by cutting them back to two or three buds. Lightly prune the strong side.*
2 *As the tree grows, prune any vertical shoots that compete with the leader.*

58

Troubleshooting

chapter four

TROUBLESHOOTING

Vivid colour and vigorous, lush growth distinguish the healthy garden. Some gardens, however, despite all efforts, just do not flourish. Plants look dusty, tired and colourless; growth is slow and stunted. This type of garden, where cultivation has been attempted but has failed to produce satisfactory results, is often difficult to remedy, as opposed to those cases where the main problem is outright neglect. Locating the underlying cause is the main difficulty. Any number of hazards — from weeds, pests, diseases to nutrient deficiencies and weather damage — can affect a garden's health. While it is possible to treat each of these in a specific way once diagnosed, much can be done to prevent garden ailments in the first place by maintaining a good standard of hygiene so that adverse growing conditions are avoided.

Keeping the garden free from debris does not necessitate destroying the natural habitat of local wildlife. It is possible to retain a nature reserve, long-lasting and self-generating, where natural controls supplement the gardener's vigilance, while at the same time satisfying your basic requirements for beauty and relaxation. Weeds are a major problem. They should be uprooted and placed on the compost pile, not left lying around in containers to encourage plant marauders. Dying or dead growth should be dug out as soon as seen and burnt. Compost piles should be enclosed in some way, even if only by wire netting, and lawn sweepings placed on the pile or allowed to rot separately into leaf-mould. Every six weeks during the spring and summer cut back new rose, shrub or climbing growth as well as branches of trees that overhang paths or impinge on smaller plants. In the case of a bad insect infestation, cut off and destroy the whole shoot.

These basic measures will ensure an overall level of hygiene and go far to promote health and vigour in the garden. More specific problems, however, demand specialised attention.

59

Rose leaves suffering from caterpillar damage.

Weeds and weedkillers

What is a weed? A practical definition is 'a plant growing where it is not wanted'. In this context garden plants as well as wild plants are included. But, from the gardener's point of view, a weed is a wild plant — a member of the native flora — which is growing among, and competing with, cultivated garden plants. Weeds compete with our garden plants for food, water and light, and they can seriously reduce growth and cropping if not controlled.

There are two groups of weeds — annuals and perennials. Members of the first group are short-lived plants, completing their life cycle from seed germination to seed production within one year. Once they have set seeds they die.

Examples are chickweed, groundsel, shepherd's purse, and bittercress. Generally they are easily controlled: by hand weeding, hoeing while the seedlings are tiny, mulching with organic matter or black mulching polythene, or by applying a weedkiller like paraquat and diquat. They can even be prevented from germinating, by applying to weed-free soil among garden plants what is known as a 'soil-acting' weedkiller, such as simazine. This will keep the soil free from annual weeds for many months, provided the film of chemical on the soil surface is not broken by cultivating.

Perennial weeds are not so easy to eradicate, although with modern weedkillers this is not the problem it used to be. Perennial weeds live for a number of years and can become permanently established if not controlled. Examples are ground elder, bindweed, couch grass, mare's tail, docks, dandelions, creeping thistle, buttercups, bracken and brambles or wild blackberries.

It is these more difficult weeds that we are considering here. The main reason they are more difficult to eradicate than annual weeds is that many of them are deep rooting, like docks and dandelions. Mare's tail is the extreme example, for it sends roots several feet into the soil. Some weeds, like ground elder, bindweed and couch grass, spread by means of rhizomes or underground stems.

If the roots or rhizomes of perennial weeds are left in the ground during digging they will send up new growth from them. Even little pieces of root or rhizome left in the soil are capable of producing new plants.

Many perennial weeds in the past have proved somewhat resistant to weedkillers, but formulas are changing, and with the range of weedkillers introduced in recent years even the most resistant perennial weeds can now be effectively controlled.

Convolvulus arvense
(Field bindweed)
Type: *Perennial; spreads by rhizomes; creeping stems*
Control: *MCPA + dicamba, glyphosate*

Equisetum arvense
(Mare's tail, horsetail)
Type: *Perennial; very deep rooting*
Control: *Difficult, glyphosate*

Veronica chamaedrys
(Germander speedwell)
Type: *Perennial; lawn weed; forms dense mats*
Control: *MCPA + dicamba + ionoxyl, ionoxyl + mecoprop*

Achillea millefolium *(Yarrow)*
Type: *Perennial; lawn weed; spreading mats*
Control: *2,4-D + mecoprop or fenoprop*

Taraxacum officinale *(Dandelion)*
Type: *Perennial; deep tap root*
Control: *In lawns 2,4-D + mecoprop or fenoprop; elsewhere glyphosate*

Rumex obtusifolius *(Broad dock)*
Type: *Perennial; deep tap root*
Control: *Glyphosate, dichlorbenil*

Sagina procumbens *(Pearlwort)*
Type: *Perennial; lawn weed; moss-like mats*
Control: *Ioxynil + mecoprop*

Aegopodium podagraria
(Ground elder)
Type: *Perennial; spreads by rhizomes; common in shade*
Control: *Glyphosate, dichlobenil*

Tussilago farfara *(Coltsfoot)*
Type: *Perennial; very deep rooted; often on clay soil*
Control: *Can be difficult, glyphosate, dichlobenil*

Pteridium aquilinum *(Bracken)*
Type: *Perennial; strong spreading rootstock; mainly on acid soils*
Control: *Difficult, 2,4-D + 2, 4, 5-T*

Polygonum aviculare *(Knotgrass)*
Type: *Annual; mat former*
Control: *Paraquat, simazine, propachlor*

Cardamine hirsuta
(Hairy bittercress)
Type: *Annual; rapidly spreads by seeds*
Control: *Paraquat, simazine, propachlor*

Ranunculus repens
(Creeping buttercup)
Type: *Perennial; spreads by runners; moist places*
Control: *Glyphosate, dichlobenil*

Bryonia dioica *(White bryony)*
Type: *Perennial; climber; often in hedges*
Control: *Glyphosate, dichlobenil*

Hedera helix *(Ivy)*
Type: *Perennial; climbing or trailing; problem in hedges*
Control: *2,4-D – 2, 4,5,-T*

60

DIGGING THEM OUT

The time-honoured practice of digging out perennial weeds still holds good; but it is time-consuming, and, as mentioned earlier, every piece of root or rhizome must be removed. It is of course sensible to remove any perennial weeds while digging.

Roots and rhizomes must not be put on the compost heap, or they will continue growing; it is better to dispose of them by burning or, if facilities exist, dumping them in a local landfill.

USING WEEDKILLERS

The most effective method of controlling perennial weeds is to use one of the more modern weedkillers. If the garden, or part of a garden, is badly infected, then the first priority should be to completely eradicate weeds before planting or cropping. This may mean leaving the ground fallow for a complete growing season while weed control is being undertaken.

Weedkillers are best used when weeds are in full growth. Weedkiller containing the chemical glyphosate will kill most perennial weeds. If couch grass is the problem, then use a weedkiller containing alloxydim sodium.

For tough woody perennials like brambles and bracken, use a brushwood killer, containing the chemicals 2,4-D and 2,4,5-T.

If perennial weeds are growing among established plants, such as shrubs, fruit trees and bushes, and perennial-border plants, you can still use glyphosate and alloxydim sodium.

Obviously you have to be especially careful when using weedkillers among established plants, but they are safe if used as directed by the makers. If there are only a few perennial weeds among plants then carry out 'spot treatment' — that is, treatment of individual weeds with a weedkiller. The old method was to apply the weedkiller with an old paint brush, but today there are available proprietary 'spot weeders', usually containing glyphosate. Basically they consist of a cannister of weedkiller which feeds an applicator, usually a sponge-rubber pad. The tool has a long handle, and you simply dab each weed to cover it with the chemical — very easy and safe, with no risk of splashing nearby plants with weedkiller.

A 'spot weeder' is of course extremely useful for controlling weeds in difficult places, such as on a rock garden where weeds may be growing between rocks and are impossible to dig out. It can also be used for weeds growing at the base of hedges.

WEEDS IN PATHS

Perennial weeds can grow almost anywhere, and it is not unusual for them to grow through cracks in paving or concrete, or through gravel paths and drives. There are proprietary weedkillers available especially for use on paths or drives. Most contain several chemicals to control annual as well as perennial weeds, such as paraquat, diquat, simazine, and aminotriazole.

Before using any weedkiller, read the manufacturer's instructions on use thoroughly and follow them to the letter.

61

Plantago lanceolata
(Ribwort plantain)
Type: *Perennial; lawn weed*
Control: *2,4-D + mecoprop or fenoprop*

Rorippa sylvestris
(Creeping yellow cress)
Type: *Perennial; creeping stems, very deep rooting*
Control: *Very difficult, glyphosate*

Poa annua *(Annual meadowgrass)*
Type: *Annual; lawns and cultivated ground; seeds freely*
Control: *In lawns regular mowing; elsewhere paraquat, simazine, propachlor*

Urtica dioica *(Stinging nettle)*
Type: *Perennial; generally found on rich soil*
Control: *MCPA + dicamba, dichlobenil, glyphosate*

Plantago major *(Great plantain)*
Type: *Perennial; lawn weed; deep tap root*
Control: *2,4-D + mecoprop or fenoprop*

Rumex acetosa *(Common sorrel)*
Type: *Perennial; lawns and cultivated ground*
Control: *In lawns 2,4-D + mecoprop or fenoprop; elsewhere glyphosate*

Oxalis corniculata
Type: *Perennial; spreads by bulbous rhizomes*
Control: *Difficult, glyphosate, dichlobenil*

Bellis perennis *(Daisy)*
Type: *Perennial; lawn weed; seeds freely*
Control: *2,4-D + mecoprop or fenoprop*

Cirsium arvense *(Creeping thistle)*
Type: *Perennial; spreads by creeping stems*
Control: *MCPA + dicamba, glyphosate*

Agropyron repens *(Couch grass)*
Type: *Perennial; vigorous rhizomes*
Control: *Alloxydim sodium, dalapon*

Rubus fruticosus *(Bramble)*
Type: *Perennial; clambering stems, often found in hedges*
Control: *2,4-D + 2, 4, 5-T*

Trifolium repens *(White clover)*
Type: *Perennial; lawn weed, mat-forming*
Control: *Can be difficult, 2,4-D + mecoprop*

Garden pests

Any creature that enters the garden and does something to impair the beauty or development of a plant is called a pest. When pest damage becomes unacceptable, we need to control it by reducing the pest's numbers, but there is no excuse at all, however, for attempting annihilation or an overkill. Certainly there is no need to endanger the whole insect population, friend and foe alike.

Never spray open blooms, where friendly insects may be at work, and never let spray drift out of sight or over a hedge where it might reach a neighbour or an innocent animal.

Whenever your plants appear to need help, see if the following check-list of pests and the means of getting rid of them is of any help to you. Having chosen a chemical remedy, handle it with the maximum possible care.

ANTS

Ants are more of a nuisance than a pest, but they encourage aphids and transport them to clean plants — in fact they are less likely to operate where there are no aphids. Aphid control (see below) is thus a help to ant control.

Ants love dry soil like that usually found in rock gardens (where tunnelling can cause havoc by looseneing stones), but their additional fondness for sweet things can lead to their undoing. Mix equal quantities of borax powder and fine granulated sugar, and place half-teaspoonfuls of the mixture where they are working. Workers then carry quantities of the poison back to their nests to be shared out, and all eat fatal doses. There are also several proprietary ant-killers available, most of them based on sodium tetraborate.

APHIDS (blackfly and greenfly)

Aphids infest a vast range of plants, causing damage by sucking the sap, mainly from young shoots. They breed rapidly, especially in warm conditions, and repeated sprays may be needed to keep them under control. Derris, fenitrothion, malathion, or systemic insecticides can all be used in sprays.

APHID, woolly

Colonies of this pest cover themselves with white, waxy 'wool' which it is difficult to penetrate with spray. Protected thus fairly securely they do severe damage to the bark of the tree or shrub they are infesting — such as hawthorn, cotoneaster and pyracantha. The wound they make is then prone to attack by canker spores.

The waxed colonies can be removed with a small brush dipped in denatured alcohol or by a forceful jet of aphicide spray — derris or fenitrothion are useful aphicides. Tree wounds caused by the pest should be treated with a canker paint.

CAPSID BUG

Chrysanthemums, dahlias and several other flowers commonly have holes in their leaves made by this pest. Spray with fenitrothion or pirimiphos-methyl.

CATERPILLAR

The countless types of caterpillars attack a large range of plants. Picking off the pests by hand is still one of the most useful controls, but for a chemical control use derris, pyrethrum, pirimiphos-methyl, or HCH.

CHAFER GRUB

This fat, curved grub of the chafer beetle feeds on the roots of many flower plants for a large part of the year. Its attack on the roots of chrysanthemums and dahlias is sometimes fatal. It is a long-term nuisance, taking two years to mature. The adult beetle eats holes in leaves, but such damage is rarely serious. The grub is the real menace — and can be controlled by raking bromophos into the soil.

EARTHWORM

Although the earthworm does a lot of good to the soil, and is to be appreciated in most parts of the garden, its presence in a lawn is distinctly unwanted. Its casts do considerable damage: whenever dry enough to be crumbled, however, they should be knocked down.

In circumstances in which worms become even more of a nuisance, they can be cleared through the use of chlordane worm-killer applied according to the maker's directions.

EARWIG

Blooms of dahlia, chrysanthemum and many other plants are commonly damaged severely by this pest. To trap them, hang small plant pots half filled with hay upside down on canes. The pest feeds at night, and after feeding is attracted to the hay in the pot as a place to rest. On checking the pots each morning, it should be possible to reduce the numbers in quick time. To protect plants without trapping, there are several effective insecticides available, including fenitrothion, HCH and trichlorphon.

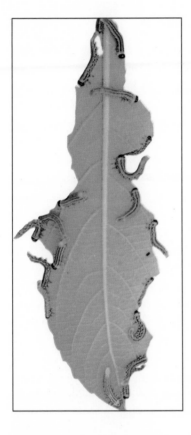

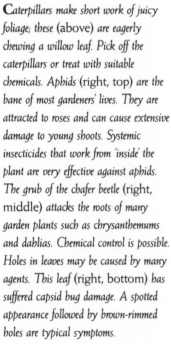

Caterpillars make short work of juicy foliage; these (above) are eagerly chewing a willow leaf. Pick off the caterpillars or treat with suitable chemicals. Aphids (right, top) are the bane of most gardeners' lives. They are attracted to roses and can cause extensive damage to young shoots. Systemic insecticides that work from 'inside' the plant are very effective against aphids. The grub of the chafer beetle (right, middle) attacks the roots of many garden plants such as chrysanthemums and dahlias. Chemical control is possible. Holes in leaves may be caused by many agents. This leaf (right, bottom) has suffered capsid bug damage. A spotted appearance followed by brown-rimmed holes are typical symptoms.

FLEA BEETLE

The name follows from the curious fact that this little beetle jumps like a flea, attacking *Alyssum* and wallflower, among others, and making a multitude of holes in their leaves. Spray or dust with derris or HCH.

FROGHOPPER OR SPITTLEBUG

The effect of this creature is known as cuckoo spit, because of the mass of froth in which each froghopper hides. The froghopper is a tiny pinkish insect about $\frac{1}{8}$in (3mm) long. Lavender, rosemary and carnations are particularly likely to be attacked. The damage done is small and can be reduced by just knocking off the froth with a jet of water. For chemical control, spray forcefully with HCH, fenitrothion or malathion.

GALLFLY

These tiny mites feed on the stems of trees and shrubs, and the internal irritation causes the tree to produce lumps — galls — which enclose the mite and protect it. Because of this wooden barrier it is difficult to achieve chemical control. The damage done is not severe, but can spoil the tree's appearance.

LEAFCUTTER BEE

Neat, semicircular pieces are cut from the leaves of roses, laburnum and other plants by the female bee in order to make her nest. Damage is rarely significant although it occasionally occurs on a large scale. If it becomes unacceptable, watch till the bee reveals her nest, probably in decayed wood or old brickwork, and attack there with HCH.

LEAFHOPPER

Almost any plant is liable to attack by this insect, which jumps (hops) if disturbed when feeding on the undersides of leaves. Attacked leaves take on a pale, mottled look; if the attack is severe, the entire plant becomes unsightly. There are also suspicions that the insect transmits virus diseases. Control with fenitrothion or malathion.

LEAF MINER

Pale, irregular, twisting lines on a leaf give away the fact that this insect grub is tunnelling under the skin. There are several species of leaf miner and various plants are attacked, but chrysanthemums are particularly vulnerable; damage to them can sometimes be fatal. In turn, however, leaf miners are vulnerable to repeated sprays with HCH, especially if started immediately the first signs of attack are seen.

Alternatively, examine the tunnelling carefully; where it ends is where the miner has stopped to rest. Cut open the leaf at that spot and the little pest can be removed forthwith.

63

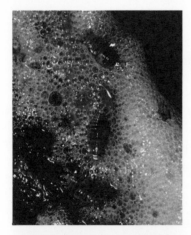

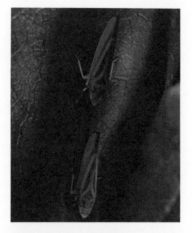

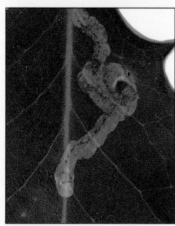

*Cuckoo spit (above, top) is an apt
description of the froth that appears on
some plants. In the froth lie the
froghoppers that produce it as a sort of
'smoke screen'. The froth and the
froghoppers can be washed off with water.
The symmetrical patterns produced by
the leaf cutter bee (above) are easily
identifiable. It is the female bee
taking home leaf pieces for her nest that
causes all the trouble. Ideally, destroy the
nest. These really quite attractive insects
(right, top) are leafhoppers. Besides
causing leaves to pale they may also
transmit plant viruses. The leafminer
plots a telltale trail (right, middle) as
the grub journeys through the tissues of a
leaf. Leatherjackets (right, bottom)
are the tough-skinned larvae of the cranefly.*

64

LEATHERJACKET

The tough skin of this crane-fly larva gives it the name — and also
indicates why control is difficult. It feeds on plant roots and can cause
substantial bare patches when operating under lawns. It can also cause
the deaths of young plants. Where the soil surface is kept loose, birds
can reduce the infestation. For chemical control when deemed essential,
use methiocarb and rake it in thoroughly. On lawns, spread a plastic
sheet at night in damp weather; the pests then come to the surface
under the sheet ready to be disposed of the next morning.

MOLE

The chief food of the mole is the earthworm, and so chlordane worm-
killer on lawns can be an effective control. Beneath shrubs and plants its
tunnelling may be fatal, but getting rid of the tunneller is difficult
because it travels long distances. Putting a smoke dispenser in the tunnel
under its latest mole-hill is not likely to be immediately effective,
therefore. Trapping, however, calls for skill and experience; and smoke-
generating mole-killers should be persevered with.

NARCISSUS FLY

Damage is done more by the maggot than the fly, although of course
the fly starts it all by laying its egg close to the bulb. A heavy dusting of
HCH around the bulb may deter the fly.

The maggot works unseen inside the bulb and damage is not
noticed until the plant collapses, or the bulb is dug up and found to be
soft or rotting. Harvested bulbs should be examined with care, as should
all new bulbs from store. Soft ones should be destroyed.

RED SPIDER MITE

If normally green-leaved trees and shrubs develop a bronze leaf colour,
examine the leaves through a magnifying glass and you are likely to see
tiny mites and a little fine silky webbing.

This is the red spider mite. Worst attacks generally occur in early
summer and early autumn. Spray thoroughly with dimethoate,
fenitrothion, or pirimiphos-methyl.

RHODODENDRON BUG

As it feeds on the undersides of the leaves, this bug causes the surfaces
of the leaves to become mottled, the edges to curl downward, and the
underneaths to turn rusty brown. First attacks come in early summer;
spraying should be carried out immediately, with malathion or HCH,
and should be repeated two or three times at three-weekly intervals.

ROSE SLUGWORM

Leaves attacked by this pest take on a strange look: the green tissue on the surfaces disappears, leaving only a transparent inner skin. Derris or permethrin, administered immediately, controls it.

SAWFLIES

There are several species of sawfly which infest various plants, inserting their eggs into plant tissues. The eggs hatch into caterpillars which then feed on the leaves. The leaf-rolling sawfly causes leaves to curl and distort. Pick off infested leaves where possible, and spray the remainder with permethrin or primiphos-methyl.

SLUGS AND SNAILS

Both these creatures attack almost any plant in the garden and do considerable damage if not kept in check. However, the two best-known molluscicides — metaldehyde and methiocarb — give reasonable control.

Stones, bricks, boxes, pieces of timber, almost any loose item left lying on the ground can be used by them as a hiding place and should be cleared away. Rockeries too must be checked regularly or the stones may become nesting places.

SWIFT MOTH

The caterpillar of this moth lives in the soil and attacks the roots of various herbaceous plants, bulbs, corms, and tubers, doing serious damage if not controlled. Sprinkle bromophos wherever the pest is suspected of being active; stir or rake it into the soil.

THRIPS

Also known as thunder flies, these small insects damage petals, leaving pale spots. Gladioli seem particularly prone to attack. Spray with permethrin or derris.

WEEVILS

There are several species of weevil, all of which feed on plants at night, spending the day in the soil or in plant debris. Attention to cleanliness and the incineration of such debris is thus a sound precaution. Where plants have been eaten, HCH dust stirred into the soil close to plants is a further precaution, for weevil larvae feed on roots.

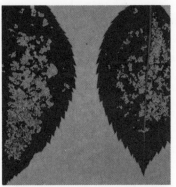

The distinctive skeletal appearance of these leaves (left, middle) *has been caused by the rose slugworm. The larvae of sawflies* (above) *are caterpillars that feed on succulent leaves. As mature insects they cause many problems for gardeners; the activities of the leaf-rolling sawfly are all too evident on this rose* (left). *Slugs are notorious garden pests, particularly in moist shady corners. Holes in leaves* (top) *and slime trails are telltale signs of their presence. Fortunately, excellent deterrents are now available and being improved all the time.*

65

WHITEFLY

The outdoor species of whitefly is not a major pest and can be controlled by fenitrothion if attacks are severe. The greenhouse whitefly, however, can be a menace, feeding on the undersides of leaves. Spray with permethrin and repeat every three days for three weeks. That makes seven sprays in all, and the three-day interval between each must be adhered to strictly. The reason so many sprays are needed to clear out the infestation is that three stages of the pest are present: eggs, nymphs, and flies (the flies are like mini-moths). There may be survivors at one stage or another after each spray up to the seventh.

WIREWORM

This is the larva of the click beetle. It eats the roots of various flowering subjects, and damage can be severe. It is often present in great numbers near where grassland has been recently dug up for cultivation. Bromophos or HCH should be worked into the soil near affected plants.

WOODLOUSE

Some people suspect this creature of nibbling roots, but it is more generally believed to feed only on decayed wood. About the size of a ladybug, it has a hard grey shell and rolls itself into a ball when scared. Where it is considered a menace, it can be controlled by HCH dust.

66

Weevils come in all shapes and sizes. Both adults and larva cause problems in the garden. The adults, such as the hazel weevil (above) feed at night on the leaves. The evidence of their passing is clearly seen on these rhododendron leaves (left and below). The U-shaped notches cut into the leaf edges are characteristic of the ½in (12mm) vine weevils. Most leaf weevils attack at the height of summer. Control consists of clearing away plant debris where they congregate and incineration of affected leaves. The weevil larvae live in the soil and attack roots, particularly those of ferns and rockery plants.

ANTHRACNOSE OF WILLOW

A mild form of canker is the first symptom among weeping willows in a wet start to summer. Attacking young foliage as it opens, it is often fatal however.

A liquid copper fungicide applied early enough, and repeated frequently enough, might keep it off.

ARMILLARIA

Armillaria is a fungus which attacks large numbers of trees and shrubs. Honey-coloured toadstools appear on the surface under the infected tree or bush, from which follows the alternative name honey fungus. Leaves turn dark brown and die. Black growths like bootlaces appear on the plant's roots, giving rise to an alternative name for it, bootlace fungus.

There is no cure, and the fungus spreads quickly. The only treatment is to dig out and burn every scrap of root, and treat the ground with formaldehyde.

ASTER WILT

This form of verticillium wilt is a minute fungus which attacks only asters. All infected plants have to be destroyed.

BACTERIAL CANKER

Poplar, ornamental *Prunus*, and some willows are attacked by this bacterial infection. Typical canker wounds characterise it: a small area bare of bark surrounded by rough, swollen bark. It is best to remove infected branches completely and then treat all the cut ends with canker paint promptly to avoid further damage.

BASAL ROT

Affecting daffodils and lilies, the rot starts at the base of the bulb and soon spreads. Infected bulbs must be discarded. Protect fresh stocks by dipping in benomyl.

BLACKLEG

A frequent cause of failure among cuttings of pelargonium, this condition begins on the cut end and may go unnoticed for a while. It can be avoided where fresh sterilised compost is used, and with clean tools and equipment. If caught in time, the cutting can be trimmed back to clean tissues and rooted in fresh compost which should remove the problem of blackleg altogether.

The toadstools produced by honey fungus appear at the base of an affected tree or shrub in the autumn. Just beneath the bark a network of fungal filaments spreads throughout the tree as evidence of the infection.

BLACK SPOT

This serious disease of roses was unknown in industrial towns and cities in the days when every chimney belched out smoke and fumes. It is generally accepted that sulphur in those fumes served as an effective fungicide against black spot.

As its name indicates, the disease produces black spots. These appear on the leaves, but the fungus also attacks the shoots. It is a killer, and there is no known cure.

Frequent preventive sprays in infected areas are necessary. There are several new fungicides which help to control the spread of the disease, including some with systemic action. One sophisticated new spray combines several substances in a cocktail to take care of most rose troubles; it contains triforine, dinocap and sulphur (as fungicides), with permethrin (as insecticide) and a foliar feed.

BOTRYTIS (also known as GREY MOULD)

Found on many subjects in periods of heavy humidity, the mould's main victims are chrysanthemums, dahlias and peonies. Both leaves and flowers are attacked. Infected leaves and blooms should be removed and the plants sprayed thoroughly with benomyl.

BUD DROP

Buds of various plants may drop unopened for no discernible reason. In fact, it seems commonly to be due to climatic and physical conditions at the time the buds were forming. Perhaps the plants were too dry, or the temperature was fluctuating too severely (too hot by day and too cold by night). No chemical control corrects it. A good mulch of moisture holding material around the plants, plus watering in dry spells, may help the plants to recover.

CANKER

This is a general term to describe infections in open wounds on trees and shrubs. Both bacteria and fungi may be involved. Heavily infected branches should be cut back to clean wood, that is, to the point where the cambium and the bark are seen to be white. Any browning indicates that the canker is still there. Infected wood should be put into the incinerator, and wounds should be treated with a canker paint.

CHLOROSIS

A large range of plants suffer chlorosis at times; it makes their green leaves turn pale or yellow, or even white, due to a mineral deficiency which in turn is caused by an upset in the acid-alkali balance, 'locking up' a soil constituent.

Plants which prefer a somewhat acid soil (rhododendrons, for instance) rapidly become chlorotic in a limy soil. When chlorosis

The familiar black spot of roses (above) is also caused by a fungal infection. Chemical sprays can prevent or contain the infection but not cure it outright. Botrytis is clearly present on this pelargonium leaf (below). Rife in humid conditions, this fungus causes leaves, stems and flowers to develop brown patches with a fluffy grey mould.

Where bark has become damaged, canker (above) may set in. Caused by fungi and bacteria, this infection may kill branches that it encircles.

occurs, the soil should be tested; subsequent plantings should be selected with care. In mild cases, sequestrenes (sequestered iron, for example) applied to the soil may be enough to enable plants to recover.

CLEMATIS WILT
This fungal trouble afflicts young specimens of the larger-flowered clematis, such as the 'Jackmaniis'. If the plant is set so that 2in (5cm) of the base of the stem is below soil level, and if wilted shoots are removed promptly, the young plant usually recovers and fresh shoots spring from the base. Apart from cutting wilted shoots back to clean wood, it is helpful to spray plants with benomyl or a copper fungicide.

CORAL SPOT
Clusters of small, red, raised spots on dead wood are the signs by which to recognise this fungus. But its spores are airborne and they can infect living trees through wounds or cuts. It is important to clear up any dead wood promptly, and to trim off dying branches of all trees before fungus growths appear.

DAMPING OFF
The strange name applies to a disease caused by parasitic fungi which afflicts small seedlings, especially if crowded or too damp. It can be avoided by using sterilised seed compost and by sowing thinly. A mild attack caught in time can be arrested by watering with a mixture called cheshunt compound, made by mixing finely-ground ammonium carbonate (11 parts) and copper sulphate (2 parts). Dissolve one ounce in two gallons of water (three grams to one litre of water) and water the seedlings with it.

DIE-BACK
Die-back is a gradual death from the tip, or cut end, of a shoot back to its junction with a main branch or trunk. It may be due to a faulty or badly-placed pruning cut or to damage. The remedy is to cut back to clean wood and to treat the cut with a canker paint.

FAIRY RINGS
The lawn toadstool *Marasmius oreades* quickly produces a circular patch of darker green than the rest of the lawn which then spreads in ever-widening circles, finally being made up of two dark green rings with a straw-coloured nearly-bare ring in between them. Marasmius is extremely virulent; no matter how much effort is made to remove infected grass and soil, if a tiny spot is left infected it will rapidly take over again. Many people just keep trying to reduce the effect by watering the treble ring with iron sulphate. The dosage rate is half an ounce to a gallon of water to each square yard (15 grams to 5 litres to 1 sq metre).

FIREBLIGHT
Cotoneaster and hawthorn are prone to this bacterial disease which, in some countries, is a notifiable one. The wisest treatment is to grub out and burn — although with skilled care, and severe cutting back, experts are sometimes able to save the plant.

FUSARIUM PATCH
Also known as snow mould, this fungal disease afflicts lawns. It is encouraged by giving too much nitrogen in autumn lawn treatments, thereby producing soft growth too near the onset of winter. The trouble begins as a small area of yellowing grass which then becomes hay-coloured and lifeless. Treat with mercurised lawn sand at four ounces to the square yard (125 grams to the square metre).

FUSARIUM WILT
This fungal condition can generally be avoided by clean cultivation. All the same, it also occurs particularly where a susceptible species such as Dianthus is grown for too long on one patch of soil. Affected plants are stunted in growth, with a yellowing of the leves which then wilt as if lacking moisture. Infected plants should be destroyed and, because the fungus is soil-borne, the soil should be sterilised.

GREY MOULD see BOTRYTIS

HONEY FUNGUS see ARMILLARIA

MAGNESIUM DEFICIENCY
The deficiency shows itself as a bronzing in the spaces between the veins of green leaves. Sometimes an excess of potash 'locks up' the magnesium. To correct the deficiency, magnesium sulphate can be sprinkled lightly on the soil and raked in, or can be dissolved at $3^1/_2$ ounces to a gallon (20 grams to a litre) of water and poured over the plant. Some of the liquid is absorbed through the leaves, the rest works through the roots.

MANGANESE DEFICIENCY
This deficiency usually goes hand in hand with iron deficiency, which causes a chlorosis and shows as a yellowing of leaves. Sequestrenes, applied in accordance with the makers' directions, correct the deficiency.

MILDEW (downy)
Among plants affected by downy mildew are poppy and sweet pea. Leaves turn yellow on the upper side as a greyish mould forms on the underside. Spray thoroughly with mancozeb.

69

MILDEW (powdery)

The powdery condition is more serious than downy mildew and attacks a wide range of plants, coating leaves and stems with its white powder. Nipping off infected tips of shoots can help control it, but it is wise to spray with benomyl or other suitable fungicide.

RHODODENDRON BUD BLAST

Flower buds attacked by this fungus turn brown, with black bristles of fungal spores, but do not drop off. Indeed, they become tough to remove. Cut them off and burn them. No fungicide appears effective, but since the disease is sometimes carried by leafhoppers, a spray with derris or other aphicide in late summer is a wise precaution.

RINGSPOT

Carnations seem most affected by this fungus which produces dark rings of spores on their leaves. Infected leaves should be picked off and burned promptly, and the rest of the plants sprayed thoroughly with a copper fungicide like mancozeb.

Leaf spot is the general name for a host of fungal infections that plague a wide range of plants; ringspot on carnations is one such infection. The very dark spots on these leaves of Acer (above, left) are also caused by a kind of leaf spot. The presence of viruses in plants is often difficult to diagnose; many of their symptoms resemble those caused by other disease organisms. The spotted and discoloured appearance of this dahlia leaf (above, right) points to an incurable viral infection. The dusty white symptoms of powdery mildew (right) are much easier to identify but not much easier to cure. Spray regularly with a fungicide to ward off the infection.

70

Rust fungus (left) is distinctive for the bright orange powdery residue it produces on the affected plant. Sprays will help to prevent it but destruction of infected parts is the only cure. The tangled knots of dense branches seen in certain trees may be caused by a fungus. These so-called witches' brooms (right) should be cut out if they can be reached. Be sure to paint cut branches against canker.

RUST

Raised spots of reddish brown are seen on many shrubs and trees, caused by fungi and are termed rust. If infected leaves are removed and burned promptly, there should be no need to take any further action. Where attacks are serious, spray with benomyl.

TULIP FIRE

Symptoms of tulip fire are small fungal growths which appear on bulbs; if these are seen, the bulbs should be discarded immediately. On such bulbs that are planted, scorched areas develop on the leaves and spots on the petals. Dig up and burn infected bulbs, and spray the remaining plants with mancozeb or thiram.

VARIEGATION LOSS

In plants whose leaves are normally variegated — with yellow or cream streaks or margins — a shoot with plain green leaves may be produced if there is insufficient light. The remedy is to cut the affected shoot clean out and to ensure that the plant gets maximum light thereafter.

VIRUSES

Virus diseases cause plants to become distorted, or stunted in growth; the infections are carried in microscopic particles which are spread by insects but enter only through wounds. Diagnosis is tricky; there is no cure, and the remedy is prevention. Avoid damaging plants, and keep insects — particularly aphids — well clear.

WITCHES' BROOMS

The name given to abnormal growths which appear on some trees, particularly conifers and birch. The growths take the form of a dense bunch of small shoots coming from one spot.

It is doubtful whether they do serious harm, even though they are caused by a fungus. However, it is easy, and perhaps wiser, to cut them off right up to the trunk and treat the wound with a canker paint.

71

An A-Z of plants for your garden

chapter five

AN A-Z OF PLANTS FOR YOUR GARDEN

Whichever plant you choose to grow in your garden, it is important to provide the right conditions and care. The needs of different plants vary, and so do the pests and diseases to which they are susceptible. Plant by plant, this alphabetical section provides all the information necessary for successful gardening, from special growing requirements to individual problems and solutions.

73

Choosing the plants for your garden can be a time-consuming and yet most stimulating pastime.

Ageratum houstonianum (Ageratum, Floss flower)

Clusters of tiny fluffy, powderpuff-like flowers of primarily blue but sometimes pink or white cover 6-12in (15-30cm) mounded plants that have heart-shaped leaves

Seeds can be sown outdoors after all danger of frost has passed, but better results are obtained by starting seeds indoors six to eight weeks earlier. Do not cover seeds as they need light to germinate which takes five to 10 days. Space plants 6-8in (15-20cm) apart in sun or light shade. Ageratum prefers rich, moist, well-drained soil and grows best under moderate heat and humidity. Ageratum flowers fall cleanly as they fade. Leggy plants can be sheared back.

Alternanthera ficoidea (Alternanthera, Copperleaf)

Alternanthera is grown for its ornamental foliage which is green, red with orange, yellow, yellow with red, rose, purple and copper, or blood red. It is a neat, trim plant only 6in (15cm) high. The plant is generally sheared, preventing the inconspicuous flowers from blooming.

Alternanthera is grown from divisions or cuttings as it cannot be propagated from seed. It is best to take root cuttings in the late summer and overwinter them in a greenhouse or a hot bed, setting them into the garden in spring after danger of frost has passed. Set plants 8-10in (20-25cm) apart in a warm, sunny location and an average garden soil. Keep plants clipped, especially if they are being used in a pattern.

Althaea rosea (Hollyhock)

Most hollyhocks are stately 4-6ft (1.2-1.8m) plants, but there are dwarf varieties that grow only 24in (0.6m) high. Both have stiff spikes of paper-like flowers on top of maplelike leaves. Flowers may be single or double in a wide range of colours except blue. Some hollyhocks are perennials or biennials but can be grown as annuals.

Start seeds indoors six to eight weeks before the last frost, not covering the seeds which need light during the 10 to 14 day germination. Set plants 18-24in (46-60cm) apart in full sun or very light shade. Soil should be rich, moist and well drained. Tall hollyhocks need staking. Cut flowers as they fade; hollyhock self-sows easily but plants will be inferior. It is susceptible to rust.

Anchusa capensis (Summer Forget-me-Not, Bugloss)

Summer forget-me-not has clusters of tiny ultramarine flowers on showy, spreading plants that grow 9-18in (23-46cm) tall. Foliage is coarse, lance-shaped and hairy.

Above: *Ageratum houstonianum* 'Madison'.

Alternanthera ficoidea 'Brilliant' (top); *Althea rosea* (above).

Sow seeds directly into the ground after all danger of frost has passed, or start plants indoors six to eight weeks earlier. Germination takes 14 to 21 days. Plant summer forget-me-not in full sun, 10-12in (25-30cm) apart. Soil should be light, infertile, dry and well drained. Cut back after flowering to encourage a second bloom.

Arctotis stoechadifolia (African Daisy)

Modern hybrids of the African daisy have yellow, white, pink, bronze, red, purple, brown and orange flowers and grow only 10-12in (25-30cm) tall. Flowers bloom all summer but close at night.

Seeds can be sown outdoors in early spring as soon as the soil can be worked, but for best results, start them indoors six to eight weeks before the last frost, when the seedlings should be set outside. Germination takes 21 to 35 days.

Set plants 12in (30cm) apart in full sun and in a light, dry, infertile, sandy soil. African daisies grow best where nights are cool. Remove faded blooms regularly to prolong flowering and improve appearance.

Begonia x semperflorens-cultorum
(Wax Begonia, Fibrous Begonia)
Wax begonia has neat mounds of round foliage and single or double flowers. The tiny blooms of white, pink, rose, or red appear continuously over waxy green, bronze, brown or variegated foliage on a plant that grows 6-12in (15-30cm) high.

Start seeds indoors 12 to 16 weeks before the last spring frost. The seeds are fine and dusty and need light during the 15- to 20-day germination period. Set plants 6-8in (15-20cm) apart in partial shade; hybrid wax begonias can be set in full sun if temperatures do not exceed 90°F (32°C). In hot areas, select bronze-leaved wax begonias over the green-leaved forms for their greater heat resistance. Soil should be very rich, fertile, well-drained, and of average moisture.

Brachycome iberidifolia (Swan River Daisy)
Masses of fragrant, 1½in (4cm) daisylike flowers in blue, red, rose, white or violet with dark centres smother 9-18in (23-46cm) mounded plants in summer. Under the flowers, the almost invisible foliage is featherlike.

Start seeds indoors four to six weeks before the last frost. Germination takes 10 to 18 days. Set plants 6in (15cm) apart in full sun and rich, moist soil. Swan River daisy is not a long-blooming plant, so successive plantings should be made three weeks apart to ensure continual bloom. Swan River daisy refers cool temperatures.

Browallia speciosa 'major' (Browallia)
Stems grow 8-18in (20-45cm) long and carry a multitude of purple, blue or white starlike to bell-shaped, velvety, 2in (5cm) flowers.

Sow seeds indoors six to eight weeks before frost danger has passed. Do not cover seeds as they need light during the 14- to 21-day germination period. Transplant plants into the garden two weeks before danger of frost has passed. Plant browallia 6-10in (15-25cm) apart in part shade in a rich, moist, cool, well-drained soil.

Catharanthus roseus (Madagascar Periwinkle, Vinca)
Periwinkle has leathery, green leaves and waxy, five-petalled flowers of white, pink or rose on 3-10in (7.5-25cm) spreading or upright plants. Use it in planters, in beds and borders, or as a ground cover, especially where adverse growing conditions exist, as it tolerates heat, drought and air pollution.

Start seeds indoors 12 weeks before the last frost and cover the seeds which need darkness for the 15- to 20-day germination. Plant periwinkle in full sun or part shade in any well-drained garden soil. Spreading varieties are planted 24in (60cm) apart; upright varieties 6in (15cm) apart.

Cleome basslerana (Spider Flower)
Named for the shape of its petals, spider flower has 6-7in (15-18cm) flowers with long stamens and strongly fragrant florets of white, rose, pink or lavender. Compound leaves have five to seven leaflets and two spines at the base of each leaf. Conspicuous seed pods are long and slim. At the back of the border or in a large bed, the waving 3-6ft (1-2m) stems of spider flower are most attractive.

Sow seeds outdoors after all danger of frost has passed, or start seed indoors four to six weeks earlier. Germination takes 10 to 14 days. Plant spider flower 2-3ft (0.6m-1m) apart in average to infertile soil, in a warm spot that receives full sun. It will withstand high heat, and is very drought resistant.

Coreopsis Tinctoria (Calliopsis)
Calliopsis has daisylike, 1¼in (3cm) flowers that can be bright red, yellow, pink or purple, some solid coloured, some banded. Slender and wiry stems are 8-36in (20-90cm) tall.

Seeds can be sown outdoors in midspring, but earlier flowering will result by starting seeds indoors six to eight weeks before outdoor planting. Seeds germinate in 5 to 10 days and need light to germinate. Transplant carefully, as calliopsis resents having its roots disturbed; space plants 8-12in (20-30cm) apart. Calliopsis likes full sun and light, dry, infertile sandy soil with excellent drainage. Keep flowers clipped as they fade to keep plants neat and producing more flowers.

Brachycome iberidifolia (top left);
Catharanthus roseus (left); *Cleome basslerana* (above).

Cosmos (Cosmos)

Cosmos fills the garden with clusters of bushy plants with slender stems, and single or double daisylike flowers that have wide and serrated petals. There are two cosmos species. *C. bipinnatus* is known as the Sensation type and is 3-4ft (1-1.3m) tall with lacy foliage. Flowers are 3-6in (7.5-15cm) across and lavender, pink or white. 'Sensation Mixed' and 'Day-dream' are good varieties. *C. sulphureus* is called the Klondyke type. Its foliage is denser and broader, plants are generally shorter, and flowers are yellow, red, gold or orange.

Seeds may be sown outdoors after all danger of frost has passed, or started indoors five to seven weeks before the last frost. Germination takes 5 to 10 days. Plant cosmos 9-24in (23-60cm) apart, depending on their ultimate size, in full sun and in a warm spot. Soil should be dry and infertile. To keep plants neat, cut off faded flowers. Tall types may need staking.

Dianthus (Pinks, Carnation, Sweet William)

The dianthus genus is a large one, with members known as pinks, Sweet William and carnation. Flowers are red, white, pink, rose or lilac and most have petals with lacy edgings that look as if they were cut with pinking shears. All have a delicious fragrance, reminiscent of cloves or other spices.

D. barbatus, Sweet William, grows 12in (30cm) high and has blooms that appear in dense, round clusters. *D. chinensis*, China pink, grows 6-18in (15-45cm) tall, with single- or double-frilled, flat-topped flowers. Foliage is grasslike and grey-green.

Dianthus seeds should be started indoors six to eight weeks before the last frost; germination takes 5 to 10 days. Space plants 6-12in (15-30cm) apart in full sun and light, rich, alkaline, well-drained soil. Cut back plants after they bloom to encourage further flowering. Dianthus prefer cool to moderate climate and high humidity. Some dianthus, particularly the newer hybrids may be perennial in areas where winters do not go below 0°F (−18°C.)

Gaillardia pulchella (Gaillardia, Blanket Flower)

Flowers of gaillardia are double, ball shaped, 2½in (6cm) across and in a brilliant colour range of red, bronze, butterscotch and maroon, with fringed petals tipped in yellow. Neat plants grow 10-24in (25-60cm) tall.

Seeds may be sown outdoors after all danger of frost has passed or started indoors four to six weeks earlier. Germination takes 15 to 20 days. Plant them a distance apart equal to their ultimate height. Soil should be light, sandy, infertile and well drained. Gaillardia prefers full sun and is heat and drought tolerant. Remove flowers as they fade. In humid, cool areas, watch for signs of fungus disease.

Gomphrena (Globe Amaranth)

Globe amaranth has round, mounded, papery, cloverlike flowers. Plants grow 30in (75cm) tall and have long cutting stems. *G. globosa* has blooms that come in a range of colours from purple through lavender, rose, pink, orange, yellow and white. *G. Haageana* has red bracts and yellow flowers.

Start seeds indoors six to eight weeks before the last frost. Germination takes 15 to 20 days. Cover seeds well as they need darkness to germinate. Speedier germination can be achieved by soaking the seeds in water before sowing. Seeds can be sown outside after all danger of frost has passed, but the plants will bloom later in the summer. Set plants 10-15in (25-38cm) apart in full sun. Globe amaranth tolerates drought and heat. Soil should be sandy, light, fertile and well drained. To dry flowers, cut blooms before they are fully open and hang them upside down in an airy, cool, dry spot.

Helianthus annuus (Sunflower)

Plants with large, coarse, hairy, somewhat sticky leaves are topped with large, single, daisylike yellow flowers with centres of dark red, purple or brown, or double flowers of gold. There are dwarf forms of sunflower that grow to only 15in (38cm), but the traditional, well-known plant reaches 4-6ft (1.3-2m) or more.

Sow seeds outdoors after all danger of spring frost has passed. Seeds can be started indoors and will germinate in 10 to 14 days, but sunflower grows so fast that this is not necessary. Plant 2-4ft (0.6-1.3m) apart in full sun and a light, dry, infertile, well-drained soil. Stake to support tall plants. Sunflowers grow best where summers are hot.

Dianthus barbatus (top left); Gaillardia pulchella (left); Gomphrena globosa (above).

Helianthus annus (above);
Hunnemannia fumariifolia (right).
Impatiens balsamina (bottom left).
Kochia scoparia forma *trichophylla*
(bottom right).

Hibiscus moscheutos (Hibiscus, Rose Mallow)

Shrubby plants of varying heights from 18in-6ft (45cm-2m) are filled during summer with large, usually single, five-petalled, pink, white or red flowers with a prominent tubular structure protruding from the centre of the flower. The stems are downy and the leaves are hairy.

Seeds may be sown outdoors after all danger of frost has passed, or sown indoors six to eight weeks earlier. Seeds have a hard coating. Either clip the seeds with a knife or scissors, or soak them in water until they sink, when they are ready to be planted. Germination takes 15 to 30 days. Plant dwarf hibiscus a distance apart equal to its ultimate height. Tall hibiscus should be planted a distance apart equal to about two-thirds of its ultimate height. Hibiscus like full sun or light shade and rich, well-drained, moist soil. It tolerates high temperatures in summer as long as it is kept well watered.

Hunnemannia fumariifolia (Mexican Tulip Poppy)

This annual looks like a cross between a tulip and a poppy. Flowers are yellow, 3in (7.5cm) across, and ruffle-edged. Downy, smooth, finely divided, fernlike blue-green leaves cover the 2ft (0.6m) plant.

Sow seeds outdoors after all danger of frost has passed, or start seeds indoors four to six weeks earlier. Germination takes 15 to 20 days. Mexican tulip poppy dislikes transplanting, so grow it in individual peat pots to lessen transplanting shock. Plants should be set 9-12in (23-30cm) apart in a warm location and full sun. Soil should be light, dry, infertile, well drained and slightly alkaline.

Impatiens balsamina (Balsam)

Balsam blooms are waxy, borne close to the stem, and can be single but are usually double. They look like roses or camellias in shades of white, pink, red, purple, lavender, salmon or yellow, and are sometimes solid coloured, sometimes spotted. Plants grow 10-36in (25-90cm) tall and are clothed with pointed, toothed leaves.

Seeds may be sown outdoors after all danger of frost has passed or, for earlier bloom, start seeds indoors six to eight weeks earlier. Germination takes 8 to 14 days. Plant balsam 6-15in (15-38cm) apart in full sun or part shade in a rich, fertile, moist, well-drained soil. Balsam is heat tolerant.

Kochia scoparia forma trichophylla (Summer Cypress, Burning Bush)

For most of the summer, kochia adds little to the garden, but in early autumn, it starts to turn bright cherry red and becomes a real attraction. Looking like a conifer, the plant is dense, globe shaped, 3ft (1m) tall, and has narrow, feathery foliage. The greenish flowers are insignificant and all but invisible.

Seeds can either be sown outdoors after all danger of frost has passed, or started inside four to six weeks earlier. Do not cover seeds which need light during the 10- to 15-day germination period. Space plants 18—24in (45-60cm) apart in full sun and dry soil with excellent drainage. Plants grow best in hot weather. To keep them in symmetrical shape, they can easily be sheared. Seeds drop easily and quickly sprout, which can be somewhat of a nuisance.

77

Lavatera Trimestris (Mallow)

Pink, red or white 4in (10cm) blooms are cuplike, resembling hollyhocks, and form in the upper leaf axils. Leaves are dark green and maplelike, and often turn bronze in cool weather. Plants have hairy stems and grow 2-3ft (0.6-1m) tall.

Lavatera seeds can be started indoors in early spring, but they are hard to transplant. Therefore, it is better to sow seeds in place outdoors in midspring. In mild areas, seeds can be planted outdoors in autumn to germinate and grow the following spring. Germination takes 15 to 20 days. Plant lavatera in full sun, 15-24in (38-60cm) apart, in dry, well-drained soil. Keep faded flowers picked to prolong blooming. Lavatera performs best where nights are cool.

Lobelia erinus (Lobelia)

Grown primarily for its outstanding multitude of small blue to purple flowers, lobelia also has varieties with white or pink blooms. Plants grow 4in (10cm) tall and spread to cover an area 10in (15cm) across.

Start seeds indoors 10 to 12 weeks before the last frost. Do not cover the seeds and provide them with a warm (75°F, 24°C) environment during germination, which takes 15 to 20 days. Plant lobelia 8-10in (20-25cm) apart in full sun or part shade in rich, moist, well-drained soil. Lobelia does best where summers are cool. Flowers fall cleanly as they fade. Leggy plants can be cut back to encourage compactness and heavier bloom.

Lobularia maritima (Sweet Alyssum)

Domed clusters of tiny, sweetly scented flowers of white, rose, lavender or purple cover plants that grow 3-4in (7.5-10cm) tall and 12in (30cm) across. Foliage is linear and needle like.

Seeds may be sown outdoors several weeks before the last expected frost, or started indoors four to six weeks earlier. Do not cover seeds as light is necessary for germination, which takes 8 to 15 days. Seeds are very prone to damping off. Set plants 10-12in (25-30cm) apart, in full sun or partial shade and average, well-drained soil. Sweet alyssum prefers to be kept moist but will tolerate drought. Although it prefers cool nights, it will grow successfully, if not as floriferously, in hot areas. Flowers fall cleanly as they fade, and plants can be cut back if they become leggy to encourage compactness and further bloom.

Mimulus × hybridus (Monkey Flower)

The monkey flower's blooms are tubular and two lipped, and look like a cross between a petunia and a snapdragon. Blooms are yellow, gold or red, often flecked with a contrasting colour and reminiscent of a monkey's face. Plants grow 6-10in (15-25cm) high.

Seeds should be started indoors six to eight weeks before the outdoor planting date. Do not cover seeds which need 13 hours of light per day to germinate, which takes 7 to 14 days. Plant outdoors in early to midspring as soon as the soil can be worked, 6in (15cm) apart in rich, moist, well-drained soil. Mimulus does best in part shade or shade, although it will grow in full sun if temperatures are cool and humidity is high.

Nemesia Strumosa (Pouch Nemesia)

Racemes of tubular, cuplike flowers that have pouches at their bases bloom in white, yellow, bronze, blue, scarlet, orange, gold, pink, cream and lavender, in solids and bicolours. The leaves are attractive and finely toothed. The 8-18in (20-45cm) plants are useful in rock gardens, edgings, borders and containers.

Sow seeds outdoors after all danger of frost has passed, or, for better results, start seeds indoors four to six weeks earlier. Seeds must be completely covered as they need darkness to germinate, which takes 7 to 14 days. Plant 6in (15cm) apart in full sun or light shade and rich, moist, well-drained soil. Pinch back when planting into the garden to induce bushiness. Nemesia grows best where summers are cool and the humidity is low.

Mimulus x *hybridus.*

Lavatera trimestris (left); *Nemesia strumosa* (above left); *Nierembergia hippomanica* (above).

Nierembergia hippomanica (Cupflower)

Cup-shaped, blue violet blooms cover 6-12in (15-30cm) mounded plants that have hairy, fernlike leaves.

Start seeds indoors 10 to 12 weeks before the last spring frost. Germination takes 15 to 20 days. Plant 6-9in (15-23cm) apart in full sun to light shade in light, moist, well-drained soil.

Papaver (Poppy)

Poppies have single or double, crêpe-paper-like flowers with large black centres. Stems are branching and wiry over deeply cut leaves. *P. nudicale*, Iceland poppy, has flowers of white, pink, yellow, orange or red on 1ft 0.3m) stems. *P. Rhoeas*, corn poppy or Shirley poppy, grows to 3ft (1m) and has flowers of red, purple or white.

Seeds can be sown outdoors in either late autumn or early spring. Seeds may also be started indoors, but cool (55°F, 13°C) temperatures are required and the plants are difficult to transplant. Cover seeds completely as they need darkness to germinate, which takes 10 to 15 days. Sow Shirley poppy seeds successively every two weeks during spring and early summer for continual blooming. Set plants 9-12in (23-30cm) apart for full sun and rich, dry soil with excellent drainage.

Perilla frutescens (Beefsteak Plant)

Toothed, deep reddish purple leaves have a metallic bronzy sheen. Although the 18-36in (45-90cm) plant bears pale lavender, pink or white flowers in late summer, it is primarily grown for its foliage.

Sow seeds outdoors after all danger of frost has passed, or start them inside four to six weeks earlier. Do not cover seeds as light is necessary during the 15- to 20-day germination. Transplant carefully as beefsteak plant does not like having its roots disturbed. Plant 12-15in (30-38cm) apart in full sun or light shade in average to dry, fertile soil with good drainage. Pinch when 6in (15cm) tall to induce bushiness. If allowed to bloom, it self-sows readily.

Phlox drummondii (Phlox)

Annual Phlox is a compact, mounded plant growing 6-18in (15-45cm) tall. The flowers are round or star-shaped and flower in clusters. Colours include white, pink, blue, red, salmon and lavender.

Seeds may be sown outdoors in spring as soon as the ground can be worked or started indoors in individual pots 10 weeks earlier. A cool room is critical for germination, which takes 10 to 15 days. Cover the seeds as they need darkness to germinate. Annual phlox is very prone to damping off. Plant in full sun, 6in (15cm) apart, in rich, light, fertile, moist, well-drained soil. Keep faded flowers removed; shearing the plants back will encourage compactness and further bloom. Phlox is fairly heat-tolerant although some decline in flowering may be seen in midsummer.

Nemophila menziesii (Baby blue eyes)

Baby blue eyes has decorative, heavily cut leaves and bell-shaped, highly fragrant flowers that are usually blue with white centres. Trailing stems spread to fill a space 12in (30cm) across and 6in (15cm) high.

Sow seeds outdoors in early spring as soon as the soil can be worked. In warm areas, seeds can be sown in autumn for colour the following spring. Seeds can also be started inside six weeks before the outdoor planting date, provided a 55°F (13°C) temperature can be maintained during germination, which takes 7 to 12 days. Set plants 8-12in (20-30cm) apart in full sun or, preferably, light shade. Soil should be light, sandy and well drained. Baby blue eyes self-sows readily, so it acts almost as a perennial in cool areas, where it grows best. It also benefits from being sheltered from the wind.

Primula x polyantha (above);
Salpiglossis sinuata (right); Sanvitalia
procumbens (below).

Primula (Primrose)

Primroses are a large group of 12in (30cm) plants with large, oblong or heart-shaped textured leaves and bright flowers in many colours, some with interesting contrasts and markings.

Sow seeds outdoors in the late autumn or early spring, or start plants indoors up to six months before outdoor planting. Germination takes 21 to 40 days. Do not cover the fine seeds which need light to germinate. Space plants 8-10in (20-25cm) apart in part shade and rich, moist, fertile, cool, slightly acid, well-drained soil.

Rudbeckia hirta (Gloriosa Daisy)

Related to Black-eyed Susans, gloriosa daisies grow 8-36in (20-90cm) tall and have single or double flowers of gold, yellow, bronze, orange, brown or mahogany, often zoned or banded, with brown, yellow, green or black cone-shaped centres.

Start seeds indoors six to eight weeks before the last frost. Germination takes 5 to 10 days. Space plants 12-24in (30-60cm) apart in full sun or light shade in average garden soil. Gloriosa daisies are heat- and drought-tolerant. Cut flowers as they fade. They are susceptible to mildew.

Salpiglossis sinuata (Painted Tongue)

Painted Tongue has tubular, velvety, heavily veined or textured trumpet-shaped flowers of purple, red, yellow, blue and rose. Plants grow 24-36in (60-90cm) tall; foliage and stems are slightly hairy.

Seeds can be sown outdoors in midspring, several weeks before the last expected frost, or started indoors eight weeks earlier. Seeds are very fine and should not be covered. Since they also need darkness to germinate, cover the seed flats with black plastic until germination occurs in 15 to 20 days. Plant painted tongue in full sun, 8-12in (20-30cm) apart in rich, light, moist, alkaline soil with excellent drainage. Mulch to keep the soil cool. Painted tongue does best where summers are cool. Tall varieties may need to be staked.

Sanvitalia procumbens (Creeping Zinnia)

Small, oval, dark green leaves set off sprightly, single or double, daisylike blooms of yellow or orange with purple centres. Plants grow 4-8in (10-20cm) tall and spread 10-16in (25-40cm) wide.

Seeds may be sown outdoors after all danger of frost has passed or started indoors in individual pots four to six weeks earlier. Seeds need light to germinate, which takes 10 to 15 days. Set plants 5-6in (12.5-15cm) apart in full sun and in light, open, well-drained soil. They tolerate drought. Flowers fall cleanly as they fade.

Verbena x *hybrida.*

Senecio cineraria and *S. vira-vira* (Dusty Miller)
Dusty Miller is a common name given to a number of plants that have silver and/or grey, velvety, lobed or deeply cut foliage and no significant flowers. They are grown exclusively for the leaves and are used as buffers between strong colours, as borders, or as edgings in gardens often enjoyed at night, when the grey foliage seems almost luminescent. Plants grow 8-24in (20-60cm) high.

Start seeds indoors 8 to 10 weeks before the last frost. Germination takes 10 to 14 days. Space plants 12in (30cm) apart in full sun or light shade. Soil should be light, sandy, dry and well drained. If plants start to get leggy, they can be sheared back.

Thunbergia alata (Black-Eyed Susan Vine)
Vines grow 6ft (2m) high and have dense, dark green, arrowhead-shaped leaves. Flowers are bell-shaped and tubular, and white, yellow or orange. Flowers bloom both in clear colours, and with black eyes.

Sow seeds outdoors after all danger of frost has passed, or start them indoors six to eight weeks earlier. Germination takes 15 to 20 days. Plant in full sun or very light shade in light, rich, moist, well-drained soil. Space plants 6in (15cm) apart and provide a support if you wish them to climb. Pick faded flowers as they form to keep the plants trim and productive. Black-eyed Susan vine grows best with a long, moderate temperature growing season.

Tithonia rotundifolia (Mexican Sunflower)
Mexican sunflower, except for a dwarf variety, grows 4-6ft (1.3-2m) tall and has large, daisylike flowers of orange-red or yellow. The leaves are large, grey and velvety.

Start seeds indoors six to eight weeks before the last frost, or outdoors after frost danger has passed. Germination takes 5 to 10 days. Do not cover seeds as light appears to be beneficial for germination. Plants should be spaced 2-3ft (0.6-1m) apart in full sun and dry garden soil with good drainage. Mexican sunflower is very heat- and drought-resistant.

Torenia fournieri (Wishbone Flower)
Bushy plants grow 8-12in (20-30cm) tall and are covered with small flowers that have light violet upper lips and dark purple lower lips. In the throat of the flower is a pair of stamens that looks like a wishbone.

Start seeds indoors 10 to 12 weeks before the last frost; germination takes 15 to 20 days. Wishbone flower prefers part or full shade, and rich, moist, well-drained soil. Set plants 6-8in (15-20cm) apart.

Verbena x hybrida (Verbena)
Verbena creates a stunning show of colour in red, white, violet, purple, blue, cream, rose or pink. Flowers bloom in clusters on spreading or upright 8-24in (20-60cm) plants.

Start seeds indoors 10-12 weeks before the last frost. Cover the seed flat with black plastic until germination occurs, which takes 20 to 25 days. Germination of verbena is usually low, so sow extra heavily. Refrigeration of seeds for seven days prior to sowing may help. Verbena is particularly prone to damping off, and to powdery mildew when grown in heavy soil in humid condition. Plant spreading types 12-15in (30-38cm) apart, and upright types 8-10in (20-25cm) apart. Select a spot in full sun with light, fertile, well-drained soil. Verbena is tolerant of heat, drought and poor soil, but is slow to become established.

Zinnia elegans (Zinnia)
Zinnias grow from dwarf, 6in (15cm) plants to tall varieties almost 4ft (1.3m) high. Flowers range from tiny buttons to huge, cactus-shaped blooms in every colour of the rainbow except true blue.

Seeds can be sown outdoors after all danger of frost has passed or started indoors four weeks earlier. Germination takes five to seven days. Zinnias should be planted a distance apart equal to one-half of their ultimate height. Do not crowd them as they need good air circulation to inhibit mildew, which can be a major problem; see Diseases, earlier. Zinnias like full sun and a rich, fertile, well-drained soil. They are tolerant of heat and drought.

81

Adenophora (Ladybells)

Ladybells have delicate, ¾in (18mm), blue or purple bell-like flowers from mid to late summer on long-lived plants growing 2-3ft (60-90cm) tall.

They grow in sun or light shade with a humus-rich, moist, well-drained soil. They do not transplant readily. Group several plants together about 12 in (30cm) apart for greatest effect. Hardy to −40°F (−40°C). Propagate from seed and cuttings.

Amsonia (Blue Stars)

This low maintenance perennial has loose, rounded clusters of pale blue, ½in (12mm), star-shaped flowers on stiff 2-3ft (60-90cm) stems that provide a gentle contrast to other stronger-coloured flowers in spring and early summer.

The narrow, glossy, willow-like leaves remain attractive all season long before turning yellow in the autumn.

They grow in average moist or dry soil in full sun or light shade. Adding humus to the soil and mulching will encourage best growth, but don't overfertilize or growth will be too open. Plants form clumps 18-24in (45-60cm) wide and should be planted singly or in small groups 18in (45cm) apart towards the middle of a border. Hardy to −40°F (−40°C). Divide in spring.

Anchusa (Bugloss, Alkanet)

Resembling forget-me-nots, bugloss is favoured for the airy sprays of intensely coloured, dark blue flowers in bloom over a long period in summer.

They prefer deep, humus-rich, well-drained soil with full sun or very light shade. Cutting back after flowering encourages a second blooming. The coarse, hairy foliage may flop unless staked. Plants do not live very long but self-sow readily. Division is needed every two to three years. Plant singly or in groups of three near the back of a border, spacing plants 18in (45cm) apart. Hardy to −40°F (−40°C). Propagate by division or root cuttings in spring or autumn. Can be affected by leafhoppers and mosaic.

Arabis (Rock Cress)

Although rock cresses are usually grown in the rock garden, two species are also of particular merit as an edging or accent plant along walls, banks, or other landscape features. Creeping 8in (20cm) mounds of soft grey-green leaves mark *Arabis caucasica,* while *A. procurrens* forms a compact

mat of tiny, glossy evergreen leaves.

They must have loose, well-drained, limy soil of only average fertility and full sun. Cut back the flowers after blooming. Set plants 8-12in (20-30cm) apart. Hardy to −40°F (−40°C). Divide in spring or seed to propagate. Will rot in hot, humid summers and suffer from gall midge; club root; white blister; downy mildew.

Aruncus (Goat's Beard)

Deserving to be more widely grown, goat's beard (*Aruncus dioicus,* also known as *A. sylvester)* is a handsome, large, shrubby plant. Plants grow 3ft (90cm) or more across and 5ft (1.5m) or taller with magnificent creamy white, feathery clusters of tiny flowers in early summer. The leaves are segmented and stems branch readily.

Long-lived, they grow best in partial shade and tolerate a wide range of soil conditions, but prefer a humus-rich, moist soil. Plants will tolerate full sun if soil is kept consistently moist. Plants seldom need staking, neither are they invasive. Set plants 24-30in (60-75cm) apart. Cut the stems off to several inches (cm) tall in the autumn. Hardy to −30°F (−34°C). Although sometimes difficult and seldom needed, divide in spring or autumn, if desired.

Goat's beard is seldom bothered by pests and diseases except by sawflies or occasionally caterpillars in spring.

Adenophora *confusa* (left); *Arabis caucasica* (above).

82

Baptisia australis (left); Chrysogonum virginianum (above).

Asarum (Wild Ginger)

Forming a dense mat of shiny, heart-shaped leaves 6in (15cm) tall, European wild ginger (*A. europaeum*) is an excellent ground cover for fully to partially shaded areas. In areas with milder winters, the glossy foliage remains evergreen. In spring, purple-brown, bell-shaped flowers 1in (2.5cm) or less across bloom at ground level.

Besides shade, they must have moist, well-drained, humus-rich soil to grow well. Set plants 8-12in (20-30cm) apart and 1in (2-5cm) deep. Hardy to −20°F (−28°C). Divide in spring to propagate. Seldom bothered by pests and diseases except where slugs and snails are a problem.

Aubrietia (Purple Rock Cress)

A splendid staple of the spring garden, purple rock cress (*Aubrietia deltoidea*) forms 6in (15cm) tall mats of downy, grey-green leaves that spread to 12in (30cm) or more across, the ½in (12mm) or larger flowers may be purple, rose, red or lavender, depending on the cultivar.

It thrives in full sun but tolerates partial shade and needs sandy, well-drained soil containing lime and a cool, moist climate for best growth. In areas with hot summers, plants are short-lived. Shear the plants back after flowering, except ones in walls, which should just be deadheaded. Space 6-8in (15-20cm) apart. Hardy to −20°F (−28°C). Divide in autumn or take cuttings in autumn and overwinter in a greenhouse. Can suffer from white blister or mildew.

Baptisia (False Indigo)   *Backyard.*

A lush, elegant, shrubby plant, false indigo (*B. australis*) has sturdy, upright, 3-4ft (90cm-1.2m) branching stems with blue-green leaves and pea-like, 1in (2.5cm), deep blue flowers.

Long-lived and never invasive, it is difficult to transplant so choose its location well. Tolerant of dry soil because of its taproot, it grows in full sun to partial shade in average to humus-rich, well-drained soil. Space plants 2ft (60cm) apart. Hardy to −40°F (−40°C). Sow seed outdoors as soon as ripened or in the spring.

Brunnera (Siberian Bugloss)

Rough, heart-shaped leaves and blue forget-me-not-like flowers in spring make this a useful, low-maintenance, long-lived specimen plant.

Although tolerant of full sun and a wide range of soils, it does best in humus-rich, moist but well-drained soil in partial shade. Remove faded flowering stems, or leave if self-seeding is desired. Space plants 12in (30cm) apart. Hardy to −40°F (−40°C). Propagation is seldom necessary, but division is possible in spring or autumn.

Centranthus (Red Valerian)

Red Valerian (*Centranthus ruber*, sometimes listed as *Kentranthus ruber* or *Valeriana ruber*) grows readily, especially in cool-summer areas, and blooms for much of the summer. The large, showy heads of small red, pink or white fragrant flowers bloom again if the spent stems are cut back.

The bushy plants grow to 3ft (90cm) tall with blue- or grey-green leaves. Although not long-lived, red valerian is easily propagated and plants self-sow readily, except for the white-flowered type.

It grows in average, well-drained soil in full sun to partial shade. In poor soil, plants will be shorter than their usual 3ft (90cm); in poorly drained soil they will probably not survive the winter. Set plants 12-18in (30-45cm) apart. Hardy to −20°F (−28°C).

Chrysogonum (Golden Star, Green-and-Gold)

Golden Star (*C. virginianum*) grows 4-6in (10-15cm) tall with small, pointed leaves and delicate, star-shaped 1½in (4cm) golden yellow flowers. In mild climates, the leaves are evergreen. Leaves vary from smooth to hairy and dark green to grey-green.

Growing best in light to full shade, the plants bloom all summer, especially in cooler climates or if the soil remains evenly moist but well-drained. Spreading by seed or rooting stems, golden star makes a good ground cover, edging, or accent in a shaded wild flower or rock garden; it does not become invasive. Set plants 12in (30cm) apart in humus-rich, moist but well-drained soil. Hardy to −20°F (−28°C). Divide in spring or autumn.

Coreopsis (Tickseed)

The sunshine-yellow, daisy-like flowers of tickseed brighten borders and meadow gardens for much of the summer, especially if faded flowers are

83

Erigeron (above); *Galium odoratum*
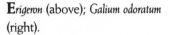
(right).

clipped off, or if plants are cut back by one-third after the first flush of bloom. Very easily grown, the flowers are very long-lasting when cut.

The species needs full sun, but both threadleaf and eared tickseed can tolerate light shade. Soil need only be average, but must be well-drained. Set plants 12in (30cm) apart. Hardy to −30°F (−34°C). Divide in spring every three or four years except for *C. grandiflora*, which is usually started from seed each year. All types can be started from seed. Can suffer from froghoppers and slugs.

Dictamnus (Burning Bush)

A very long-lived, low-maintenance perennial, burning bush (*D. alba*, also called *D. fraxinella*) grows to a shrubby 2-3ft (60-90cm) tall with glossy, dark green leaves that remain attractive until frost. Produced in numerous long spikes in early summer, the 1-2in (2.5-5cm) white blooms are good for cutting.

It has deep roots, so does not transplant well and needs several years to become established, at which time it tolerates drought. Grow in full sun or very light shade with humus-rich, moist but well-drained soil. Set plants 3ft (90cm) apart. Hardy to −40°F (−40°C). Seed sown outdoors in the autumn sprout the following spring; seeds saved until the spring will germinate more readily if boiling water is poured over them. It may be three or four years before new plants bloom.

Digitalis (Foxglove)

Foxglove's tall spires of velvety, dotted bells rising from low clumps of leaves provide a dramatic statement in the early summer garden. Common foxglove (*Digitalis purpurea*) is a biennial growing 4ft (1.2m) or

taller with 2in (5cm) flowers in white or shades of pink or purple; plants readily self-sow. The Merton hybrid foxgloves *(D. × mertonensis)* are perennials with pink, rose, or red flowers on spikes growing to 3ft (90cm) tall.

They grow best in a humus-rich, moist but well-drained soil and full sun or partial shade. Remove faded flower stems if self-sowing is not desired; this may also encourage re-blooming. Set plants 12-18in (30-45cm) apart. Hardy to −30°F (−34°C). A winter mulch of evergreen branches is helpful where there is little snow cover. Divide in spring after blooming. Seed sown outdoors in late summer for flowers the following year. Crown and root rot may develop if the ground is over-wet in winter.

Erigeron (Fleabane)

Resembling asters, with 2in (5cm) delicate, daisy-like flowers in shades of blue, pink, or white with yellow centres, fleabanes bloom during early and mid-summer.

They do best in sandy, well-drained soil, and full sun in regions with cool summers but will withstand hotter temperatures with light shade. Set plants 12-18in (30-45cm) apart. Deadhead regularly to prolong blooming. Hardy to −10°F (−23°C). Divide or make basal cuttings in early spring.

Euphorbia (Spurge)

Although there are over 1600 different spurges, only a few are of horticultural interest. Spurges are characterised by showy bracts, with very tiny flowers in the centre. They have a milky sap, which can be a skin irritant.

Long-lived, these spurges grow best in full sun in dry, sandy soil. Light shade is beneficial in hot areas. Plants readily self-sow. Set plants 12-18in (30-45cm) apart. Hardy to −20°F (−28°C). They do not transplant well, but if necessary, divide in early spring. Can suffer from grey mould.

Gaillardia (Blanket Flower)

Blanket flowers readily produce brightly coloured, daisy-like, 3-4in (7.5-10cm) blooms for much of the summer. The flowers are various combinations of yellow, gold and red, often with purple centres.

They tend to be short-lived in fertile, moist soils, but last longer with full sun in average to poor, very well-drained soil, especially in winter. Deadhead and trim back plants in late summer for more bloom in the autumn. If plants do not bloom, divide them in early spring. Set plants 6-18in (15-45cm) apart. Hardy to −40°F (−40°C). Divide in early spring; make basal cuttings in late summer or root cuttings in autumn and overwinter in a coldframe. Downy mildew can effect the plant.

84

Galium (Sweet Woodruff)

A low-maintenance ground cover for shaded areas, sweet woodruff (*Galium odoratum*, also known as *Asperula odorata*) is used fresh as an herb. Small, star-shaped fragrant white flowers are scattered across the tops of the 6-8in (15-20cm) mounds of thin, whorled leaves in spring and early summer.

It prefers partial shade in moist but well-drained, humus-rich soil. Plant 12in (30cm) apart. Hardy to −30°F (−34°C). Divide in spring or autumn, as desired, although seldom required.

Gypsophila (Baby's Breath)

The billowing clouds of tiny white or pink flowers of baby's breath provide a fine-textured addition to the flower garden as well as to both fresh and dried bouquets. The thin, wiry, branching stems have a few narrow, grey-green leaves.

It grows in full sun with average, well-drained, alkaline soil. Plant 1-2ft (30-60cm) apart, in early spring. Many named varieties are grafted; set the graft union 1-2in (2.5-5cm) below the soil. Hardy to −30°F (−34°C), applying a loose mulch in winter after the ground is frozen. The best kinds are purchased as grafted plants. Ordinary forms are grown from seeds or cuttings.

Heliopsis (False Sunflower)

Vigorous, bold plants with dark green foliage, false sunflowers have abundant clusters of golden, daisy-like flowers 2-4in (5-10cm) across, with slightly darker centres, blooming from summer through autumn.

Although drought-tolerant, they grow best in full sun with average to humus-rich, moist but well-drained soil. Deadhead regularly to prolong blooming. Set plants 2ft (60cm) apart. Hardy to −30°F (−34°C). Divide in early spring every three or four years. Seed in spring or summer.

Hesperis (Sweet Rocket, Damask Violet)

Sweet rocket (*Hesperis matronalis*) is a lovely, cottage garden plant, resembling phlox, with wonderfully fragrant elongated clusters of lavender, purple, mauve or white ½in (12mm) flowers from late spring to midsummer.

It thrives best in full sun or partial shade with moist but well-drained alkaline soil. Set plants 18in (45cm) apart. Deadhead regularly to prolong blooming. Hardy to −40°F (−40°C).

Hibiscus (Rose Mallow, Hibiscus)

Exotic and bold, rose mallow (*Hibiscus moscheutos*) makes a dramatic statement in the garden with the 6-12in (15-30cm) saucer-shaped flowers on 3-6ft (90cm-1.8m) plants with broad leaves. Blooming from midsummer to autumn, the flowers may be white or shades of pink or red.

They grow best in full sun with humus-rich, moist soil. Light shade and drier soil are tolerated once plants are established. Long-lived and resenting disturbance, they are also slow to sprout in the spring. Set plants 3ft (90cm) apart. Hardy to −20°F (−28°C), but in areas with a low of 0°F (−18°C) or less, a winter mulch is desirable.

Although seldom necessary, divide in spring, setting the leaf buds 4in (10cm) deep.

Aphids and mealy bugs can affect the plant and bud drop may develop if soil too dry or night temperature too low.

Iberis (Candytuft)

One of the best spring-blooming plants, the 2in (5cm) clusters of white blooms of candytuft (*Iberis sempervirens*) are set off by the dense, fine-textured, dark evergreen leaves on creeping woody plants 6-10in (15-25cm) tall and 2ft (60cm) wide.

It grows best in full sun with a humus-rich, neutral to alkaline, moist but well-drained soil. Prune stems back halfway after flowering to keep the plant bushy. Once well-established, leave undisturbed and it will be long-lived. Set plants 15in (38cm) apart. Hardy to −30°F (−34°C). Take cuttings in early summer or divide in early summer after flowering. Flea beetles can be a problem.

Lavandula (Lavender)

An old-fashioned garden favourite, lavender is beloved for the scent of its flowers and leaves as well as for its effectiveness as a specimen plant. Needle-like, grey-green leaves and lavender, purple, pink, or white flowers provide a fine-textured, softly blending plant for the garden. Flowers are produced from early to late summer, and they can be used in fresh arrangements or dried for use in pot pourri and sachets. Lavender (*L. augustifolia*) grows 1-3ft (30-90cm) tall.

It needs full sun and sandy, alkaline, well-drained soil that is not too fertile. Prune back old wood in the spring. Set plants 12in (30cm) apart. Hardy to −20°F (−28°C). A winter mulch in climates of 0°F (−18°C) or colder if necessary. Take cuttings in early summer. Froghoppers and leaf spot can be a problem.

Lobelia (Cardinal Flower, Great Blue Lobelia)

With the right growing conditions, both species (*L. cardinalis, L. siphilitica*) can offer intensely coloured spikes of asymmetrical flowers from summer to autumn above low-growing clumps of leaves.

Both species grow best in light shade but tolerate full sun if the soil is always moist. A wet or moist, humus-rich soil is preferable. Staking may be needed. Although not always long-lived, they readily self-sow

85

with the right growing conditions. Mulching keeps soil moist, improves hardiness, and encourages seedlings to grow. Set plants 12-18in (30-45cm) apart. Propagate through seed, remove and replant offsets in early autumn. Rhizoctonia, stem rot and virus disease affects cardinal flowers.

Lupinus (Lupin)

Lupins (*Lupinus* × 'Russell Hybrids') have showy 2-3ft (60-90cm) spikes of 1in (2.5cm) pea-like flowers in shades of white, yellow, pink, red, blue or purple, either solid or bicolored, in early summer. The bushy plants have hand-shaped grey or bright green leaves. Lupins grow best in areas with cool, moist summers and they usually live about four years and do not readily transplant once established.

They do well with either full sun or light shade and need humus-rich, moist but well-drained soil. Set plants 18-24in (45-60cm) apart. Deadhead regularly to promote second flowering. Mulch to conserve moisture and provide winter protection. Hardy to −40°F (−40°C). Propagate through seed, which must be nicked with a file to germinate readily or take stem cuttings, with a portion of the root attached, in spring. Crown and root rot; honey fungus; powdery mildew; mosaic and other virus disease can affect lupins.

Lythrum (Purple Loosestrife)

Varying widely in height and flower colour, purple loosestrife is a very adaptable, low-maintenance, bushy plant that blooms from early summer until autumn. Foliage is small and willow-like, providing fine texture in the garden, and the spikes of ¾in (18mm) flowers are produced abundantly.

Although they naturally grow in wet meadows and beside streams, they also do well in moist, well-drained soil and even withstand dry conditions. Full sun is best, but light shade is tolerated. Set plants 18in (45cm) apart. Hardy to −40°F (−40°C). Divide in spring or autumn, or take root cuttings in early summer.

Macleaya (Plume Poppy)

Best used as a specimen plant near a building or hedge, plume poppy (*Macleaya cordata*, also listed as *Bocconia cordata*) is bold and dramatic with its rounded, scalloped blue-green leaves with silvery undersides on 6-10ft (1.8-3m) stems. Fluffy, 12in (30cm) plumes of ½in (12mm) petal-less flowers bloom during summer, and the seed pods are attractive until frost.

It grows best in light shade in hotter regions, but full sun is tolerated in cooler areas. Plant in average moist to well-drained soil, spacing 3-4ft (90cm-1.2m) apart. Hardy to −30°F (−34°C). Divide in spring.

Nepeta (Catmint)

Related to Catnip, two very similar types of catmint are lovely in the garden because their delicate texture and colour blend so readily with other flowers and plants. The sprawling mounds are useful as an edging, in a rock garden, in raised beds or walls, or at the front of beds and borders. Small, heart-shaped, hairy grey leaves densely cover the 12-18in (30-45cm) plants. Spikes of ¼in (6mm) softly coloured blue or white flowers in spring and early summer may rebloom if plants are cut back by half after the first blooming.

They grow best in full sun in sandy, well-drained soil. Plants have more compact, attractive growth in poor soil and are tolerant of drought and hot summers. Set plants 12-18in (30-45cm) apart. Hardy to −40°F (−40°C). Catmint may be divided in spring and it can be affected by powdery mildew.

Physostegia (Obedient Plant)

Easy to grow, obedient plant (*Physostegia virginiana*, also listed as *Dracocephalum virginianum*) grows in bushy clumps 2-4ft (60cm-1.2m) tall with stiff, wand-like spikes of pink, magenta, rose, lilac, or white tubular 1in (2.5cm) flowers.

It grows best in full sun with average, moist, slightly acid soil. Drier soil is tolerated, especially in light shade, but plants will be shorter. Set plants 18-24in (45-60cm) apart. Hardy to −40°F (−40°C). Divide in spring every other year.

Platycodon (Balloon Flower)

Forming 18-30in (45-75cm) tall, stiffly bushy plants, balloon flower (*Platycodon grandiflorum*) derives its common name from the shape of the bud, which opens into a 2in (5cm), cup-like, star-shaped blue flower.

This easily grown, adaptable plant does not start to sprout until late in the spring, so the location must be marked well. Blue- and white-flowered cultivars thrive in full sun, but pink flowers fade unless in light shade. Provide average to sandy, well-drained soil; poor drainage in winter is fatal. The plants may take several years to become established, and if moved, must be dug deeply to get all of the long roots, which spread slowly. Division is seldom necessary and the plants are long-lived. Plants also self-sow, but not rampantly. Staking is necessary with taller cultivars. Deadhead regularly to prolong blooming. Set plants 12-18in (30-45cm) apart, with the crown just below the soil surface; a group of three plants in the middle of a bed or border is most effective. Although hardy to −40°F (−40°C), some loose winter protection is often necessary for plants to survive. Cut off outer sections of crown in spring when shoots are 1in (2.5cm) tall to propagate.

86

Physostegia virginiana (left); Smilacina racemosa (above).

Polygonatum (Solomon's Seal)

The different forms of Solomon's seal are all similar in appearance, with arching, unbranched stems of pointed, oval leaves and drooping, tubular, white or cream flowers in late spring and early summer.

The rhizomatous roots spread slowly forming handsome colonies. Long-lived, it is seldom invasive and division is rarely needed. It thrives in humus-rich, moist but well-drained soil; dry soil is however tolerated. Set plants 18-24in (45-60cm) apart. Hardy to −30°F (−34°C). Divide in spring or autumn.

Salvia (Salvia)

The Genus *Salvia* is a very large one, with annual, biennial and perennial forms, including the popular annual scarlet salvia as well as the culinary herb sage. The longest-lived perennial sage, easiest to grow and best for low-maintenance gardens, is violet sage *(Salvia X superba, also listed as S. nemorosa)*, which has an abundance of 6-12in (15-30cm) stalks of dark purple, ½in (12mm) flowers.

It does best with full sun and average, well-drained soil, and is tolerant of drought. Poorly drained soil in winter is usually fatal. Set plants 12-18in (30-45cm) apart. Deadhead regularly to prolong blooming. Although hardy to −20°F (−28°C), a loose winter mulch is beneficial. Divide in spring or autumn. Red spider mites can affect the plant as can physiological disorder in young plants caused by too low temperatures.

Scabiosa (Scabious, Pincushion Flower)

Above clumps of finely cut, grey-green foliage, scabious *(Scabiosa caucasica)* sends up stalks of blue, lavender-blue or white, 2-3in (5-7.5cm), richly textured flowers throughout the summer that are excellent for cutting. It grows 12-18in (30-45cm) tall.

It is easily grown in full sun with sandy to average, neutral to alkaline, well-drained soil. It does not do well under very hot conditions, unless grown in light shade. Set plants 12in (30cm) apart. Hardy to −40°F (−40°C). Deadhead regularly to prolong blooming. Divide in spring, if necessary. Slugs, snails and mildew can affect the plant.

Smilacina (False Solomon's Seal)

False Solomon's seal *(Smilacina racemosa)* has 18-36in (45-60cm) arching stems of pointed oval leaves resembling Solomon's seal. The flowers, produced in late spring, are 4-6in (10-15cm) feathery clusters of tiny creamy-white blooms, that, in late summer, become clusters of bright red berries.

It grows best in slightly acid, humus-rich, moist but well-drained soil. Space 12-18in (30-45cm) apart. Hardy to −30°F (−34°C). Divide in spring, which is seldom necessary except for increase.

Stokesia (Stokes' Aster)

Stokes' Aster *(Stokesia laevis)* forms stiff, branching plants with long, narrow leaves that are evergreen in warmer climates. Flowers are lacy, fringed, blue or white, and 4in (10cm) across on 12-24in (30-60cm) stems.

Long-lived, it grows well in full sun with average, well-drained soil. Poor drainage in winter is usually fatal. Set plants 12-18in (30-45cm) apart. Deadhead regularly to prolong blooming. Hardy to −20°F (−28°C), with a loose winter mulch beneficial in colder areas to prevent roots heaving out of the ground. Divide in spring every four years.

Thermopsis (Carolina Thermopsis)

Resembling lupin, Carolina Thermopsis *(Thermopsis villosa, also listed as T. caroliniana)* has 8-12in (20-30cm) long spikes of ½in (12mm) yellow, pea-like flowers on stout stalks 3-5ft (90cm-1.5m) tall in early to midsummer. Plants slowly spread to form clumps 3ft (90cm) across.

It grows easily in poor to average, well-drained soil in full sun, although light shade is tolerated. Staking may be necessary with older plants or in windy sites. Set plants 2-3ft (60-90cm) apart. Hardy to −40°F (−40°C). Division is seldom necessary and difficult because of the deep roots. Take cuttings in late spring.

Viola (Violet, Pansy, Heartsease)

Diminutive violets and pansies have been grown and loved for centuries. Of the hundreds of species and many cultivars, some are weeds and others rare plants for the collector's garden. A few species can be singled out for use in front of beds and borders, in wild flower gardens, as a ground cover, or as an edging along paths. The flowers can be used in tiny bouquets.

Most types grow well in light shade, except as noted. Average to humus-rich, moist but well-drained soil is preferred. Set plants 12in (30cm) apart. Divide in spring and beware mosaic, leaf spot and rust.

87

Tulips

EARLY TULIPS
Singles
Many of the oldest tulips in cultivation fall into this class. 'Keizerskroon' is carmine scarlet deeply edged golden yellow, and 'Prince Carnival' is yellow flamed red. 'Keizerskroon' is one of the very oldest tulips in the classified list, being in cultivation since 1750. Other very old early tulips are 'Yellow Prince' (1785) and 'Silver Standard' (1637). Many more of these varieties, such as the forcing tulip 'Brilliant Star', were introduced in the latter half of the nineteenth century. Most of the single early tulips are between 10 and 15 inches (25-40cm) high. A number of them are stated to be scented, but that seems to be an exaggeration.

Doubles
Double tulips were first mentioned in histories in 1665, but it was nearly two centuries later before any significant information became available about the early doubles. The dominant feature of this class of tulip is 'Murillo' and its many sports, of which there are 101. The sports of 'Murillo' are in all shades of pink, red, yellow and orange and even the deep violet purple of 'David Tenniers'. They all grow about 10in (25cm) high and bloom outdoors in mid-April. Some of the more popular of these sports include 'Peach Blossom' (bright pink), 'Orange Nassau', 'Goya' (salmon scarlet and yellow). 'William Kordes' (cadmium orange) 'Williamsoord' (carmine and white) and 'Mr van der Hoef' (yellow).

MID-SEASON TULIPS
Darwin hybrids
The original Darwin hybrid tulips were the result of crosses between Darwin tulips and *Tulipa fosteriana*. They now include the result of crosses between other tulips and botanical tulips, which have a similar habit and in which the wild plant is not evident. Many of the early Darwin hybrids were raised by DW Lefeber and introduced during the Second World War. 'Holland's Glory', 'Lefeber's Favourite', 'Dardenelles' and 'Red Matador' appeared in 1942.

The first non-red Darwin hybrid was 'Oranjezon', usually called 'Orange Sun' and the first non-red introduced as a Darwin hybrid was 'Gudoshnik' (1952). 'Orange Goblet' and 'Big Chief' arrived in 1959, and 1960 brought 'Vivex'. Since those days, mutations of the original plants have given mostly golden sports, but there have been other striped and edged sports of many of the original reds.

There are some excellent Darwin hybrids in which pink is the predominant colour. 'Dawnglow' is a pale apricot flushed carmine with a hint of orange on the interior. Being a sport of 'Red Matador', raised

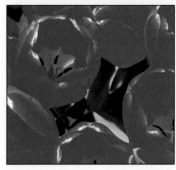

'*Keizerskroon*' (left); '*Orange Nassau*' (below); '*Oxford*' (bottom left).

from fosteriana crossed with Mendel, it needs to be planted reasonably early to give a good show.

Triumph Tulips
The Triumph tulips are an excellent race. They are mostly extremely robust and reasonably vigorous and they give an excellent show, mostly towards the end of April.

In the years following the First World War, Triumph tulips were introduced in considerable numbers. They are a cross between a single early and a May-flowering tulip. They are robust although perhaps slightly less vigorous than the Darwin hybrids, but they have a much greater range of colour. It is perhaps in the violet purple range of colours that these tulips are so valuable. The most popular is probably 'Attila', a light purple violet.

There are several good whites in this section, possibly the best is 'Carrara', formerly a cottage tulip. 'Kansas', 'Hibernia' and 'Pax' are also good. There are also a number of good pinks, an old favourite is

88

'Peerless Pink', a pure satin pink. Another old variety, 'Pink Glow', is a satin rose.

Many of the reds and yellows appear to have been superseded by the Darwin hybrids of a similar colour, but there are still some that are well worth growing. 'Alberio' is cherry red with a creamy edge and is the sport parent of so many of the parrot tulips. 'Robinea' is a good cardinal red and the brownish red 'Cassini', though fairly old, is still extremely vigorous.

There are several good orange tulips in this section: 'Adorno' (salmon orange), 'High Society' (orange red edged pure orange), 'His Highness' (clear bronze tinged orange throughout) and 'Mary Housley' (apricot orange).

LATE TULIPS

Singles

This is a very large list, comprising the popular Darwin tulips together with most of the cottage tulips and both the Dutch and English breeder tulips. Against these additions to the list, the lily-flowering and later the fringed and viridiflora tulips have been taken out of the list.

Usually the first to bloom is 'Mirella', a beautiful tulip of unusual shading. It has a long oval head with buff rose petals and a broad flame of raspberry red rising from the base. Inside, it is silver rose shading through carmine to a black blue base. The first early Darwin to appear is the ever popular 'Demeter', a rich plum purple variety. 'The Bishop' is an excellent violet purple, 'Dorie Overall' is dark petunia violet edged mauve and 'Cum Laude' is dark campanula violet.

'La Tulipe Noire' is a deep purple black, and its fame has derived as much from the novel by Alexandre Dumas as from its own quality. 'Queen of the Night' is a deep velvet maroon and 'Black Diamond' is a dark reddish brown on the exterior and a dark dahlia purple inside. Both of these varieties look black at a distance. Two cultivars are classified as absolutely black: 'Black Beauty' and 'Black Pearl'.

Doubles

Double late tulips are often called peony-flowering tulips. The history is somewhat murky but it is known that most of the early varieties had very weak necks and the flower heads tended to hang because of their weight.

'Blue Flag (Bleu Celeste)' was raised in 1750. It is a light violet and may still be obtainable, but almost all the other cultivars now on sale have been raised since 1932. 'Lilac Perfection' is an excellent lilac and one of the best in this section.

Some of the most popular members of this section are bicolours. 'Coxa' is carmine vermillion edged white. It has a sport, 'Orange Triumph' which is orange red flushed brown with a narrow yellow edge. Also very popular is 'Nizza', which is yellow with red stripes.

89

Lilies

This is not a complete list, but it covers some of the species that are readily available. Other species are only likely to be grown by more advanced growers.

In this list the perianth segments, ie the similar-looking petals and sepals, are all referred to as petals.

L. Bolanderi
A species from the western United States with funnel-shaped flowers of a deep red merging into a yellow throat. The inner part of the petals are also spotted with purple. These flowers appear in midsummer on stems that reach up to 3ft (90cm). It is not a stem-rooting lily and has delayed hypogeal germination. Unfortunately it is not long-lived and needs to be regularly resown to keep it going. Plant in a sunny position, preferably in a humus-rich soil; however, this lily can be grown on alkaline conditions.

L. Cernuum
This is a delicate little, Turk's-cap lily from northeastern Asia that only grows to 2ft (60cm) or so. The scented flowers are a deep rich pink, marked with purple spots. They appear from early to midsummer. The species produces stem roots and seed which has immediate epigeal germination. The bulb is not very long-lived, and so the plant needs propagating regularly to ensure its survival. It grows well in rock gardens and is tolerant of lime.

L. Davidii
This Chinese lily comes from the west of the country. It produces up to 20 Turk's-cap flowers, each orange-red in colour with deep purple spots. It is easily grown from seed (immediate epigeal germination) and hybridises readily, giving many hybrids and strains in cultivation; indeed, the true wild plant is rarely seen. It flowers from mid- to late summer. *L. davidii* is a stem-rooting plant that will grow up to 5ft (1.5m) or more in some of its varieties such as *macranthum*. It will just about tolerate limy soils as long as humus has been added.

L. Humboldtii
This is a Californian lily which carries sometimes quite large numbers of Turk's-cap flowers in midsummer. A bright orange, speckled with maroon spots, they have the added advantage of being fragrant. These are carried on stems that can reach up to 8ft (2.5m) high. The bulbs are sub-rhizomatous and lack stem roots. It has a variety, *L. h.* var. *occelatum,*

which does have these stem roots, as well as having spots that are ringed in crimson, reaching right to the tips of the petals. Both produce seed that has delayed hypogeal germination. Plant out in a very well-drained soil in either sun or light shade.

L. Iridollae
A Turk's-cap species from the south-east United States. The flowers are yellow with brown spots and appear from mid- to late summer on stems that can reach up to 6½ft (2m) in height. The bulbs are stoloniferous and there are stem roots present. Germination is immediate hypogeal. It grows in a moist soil in full sun or light shade.

L. Mackliniae
This species was not introduced into culitvation until just after the Second World War. It is a beautiful species with nodding bell-shaped flowers that are a pinkish purple on the inside and darker on the outer surfaces of the petals. Flowering takes place during early to midsummer. It is a stem-rooting species that grow up to 3ft (90cm) tall. Germination is immediate epigal. It is a bit tender and might need protection, but otherwise it is easy to grow as long as it has a neutral or acid soil and light shade.

L. Michiganense
This is a species from the eastern United States. The flowers are Turk's-cap in shape and vary in colour from orange to red, spotted in a deeper red or purple. These are borne from early to midsummer on stems that reach up to 5ft (1.50m) high. The bulb is stoloniferous and there are no stem roots present. The seed has delayed hypogeal germination. Plant out in a moisture-retentive soil in full sun.

L. Occidentale
This is a lily from the western United States that bears nodding Turk's-cap flowers coloured crimson shading to orange in the throat, with purple spots. They are carried on stems that grow up to 6ft (1.80m) in height and appear around midsummer. Germination is delayed hypogeal. Plant out in a moisture-retentive soil in sun or part shade.

L. Rubellum
This is a lily of great charm from Japan. The flowers are funnel-shaped and of a delicate shell pink, which is set off well by the shiny green leaves. The flowers appear in early summer and are sweetly scented. *L.*

rubellum is not a very tall plant reaching up to only 2ft (60cm) or a little more. It is stem-rooting and germination is delayed hypogeal. It prefers a moist, lime-free soil in a partially shaded position.

L. Wigginsii
This Turk's-cap lily from the western side of the United States is a rich yellow dotted with purple spots. It flowers about midsummer and grows to 4ft (1.20m) tall. It is a rhizomatous bulb with occasional stem roots. The seed has delayed hypogeal germination. Grow in an acid, moisture-retentive soil.

Cardiocrinum Cordatum
Formerly known as *Lilium cordatum*, this is another similar species, this time coming mainly from Japan. It is shorter than *C. giganteum*, growing up to 6ft (1.80m) tall, but in most other respects, including flower colour, is similar to it. It is monocarpic and needs replacing each year.

91

Above left: L. cernuum

Above right: L. occidentale

Above: L. rubellum

Left: L. wigginssii

Climbers

Bougainvillea (Bougainvillea)

These are extremely colourful climbers with which many people from northern areas have fallen in love. The sun is the key to these plants; they are decidely tender and can only be grown in frost-free areas. However, more people now own conservatories and these make an excellent place in which to over-winter bougainvilleas, as long as the temperature does not drop below 46°F (8°C). The temperature should be raised a few degrees in the spring to bring the plants into growth.

Bougainvilleas are happy in any fertile soil and though they like the full sun they will take a little shade. They can be trained into a variety of shapes, including arches or standards, or even hedges, if your greenhouse needs a room divider.

Propagation is from heeled summer cuttings. Bougainvilleas can grow very big if left to their own devices, and pruning is undertaken in early spring, when lateral spurs are cut back almost to the main stems.

Clematis (Clematis)

This is one of the finest groups of plants ever to be introduced. The flowers vary from insignificant wisps to large, full-blown cartwheels. The colours cover a large part of the spectrum between blue and red.

Most clematis are rampant climbers and will easily climb up to 3m (10ft) or often even more, but some of the New Zealand green-flowered species that have recently been introduced into cultivation reach only 30cm (1ft) or less and are very dainty, with attractive seed heads.

Clematis are happy with most soils. It is often said that they need limy soils to do their best but you should take little notice of this; there are many fine specimens that have never seen a hint of lime. Many are plants of the sun and look best in full sunlight provided their roots are kept cool and out of the sun.

Propagation seems a bit of a mystery to some people, but most clematis come readily from cuttings taken in midsummer.

Jasminum (Jasmine)

Jasmine is one of those groups of plants that gardeners always love to have around. They are not necessarily spectacular — comfortable might be a better word — but they do tend to do the right thing at the right time. Winter jasmine has flowers in winter, when there is not much else about; common jasmine and some of the others produce a delicious scent on warm evenings. Jasmines are either shrubs with arching stems or climbers, and the latter, if trained, will grow up to considerable heights. The flowers take the form of yellow or white stars on the end of short tubes. The shrubby versions look like broom, with green stems and small trifoliate, almost non-existent, leaves. The climbers have larger, more positive leaves. Several are hardy, taking temperatures down to 7°F (−14°C), but others are much more tender and need protection, as much to protect the flower buds as the plant inself. A good flow of air is important, but they all grow well against walls.

They will tolerate most soil conditions and seem to thrive in sun, though they can survive in light shade once they have become established.

Propagation is from half-ripe cuttings or from layers, and in practice the plants will often self-layer. Pruning should be under-taken after flowering, when most of the flowering stems should be removed, plus any dead or old wood that was forgotten the previous year. So often, jasmine looks like a tangle of dead wood with a few flowering stems.

Lonicera (Honeysuckle)

Many gardeners are often surprised when they discover the number and variety of honeysuckles. The one that really comes as a surprise is *Lonicera nitida*, which is very commonly used as a hedging plant (it has very small oval leaves and is sometimes mistakenly called privet). This does flower, but very insignificantly, so we will leave it and move on to the more floriferous varieties, of which there are basically two types; those that climb and those that are bushes.

Above: Bougainvillea x buttiana *Apple Blossom*

Right: Jasminum officinale

There are no difficulties over soil conditions, for honeysuckles will grow almost anywhere. Sun or light shade makes little difference, except that most undoubtedly flower better in full sun, though some actually prefer light shade.

Propagation is from seed or half-ripe cuttings. Pruning is needed to keep everything tidy: dead wood should be cut out and some of the old wood should be removed from shrubby species every year.

Solanum (Solanum)

This is a very large genus that includes potatoes, tomatoes and deadly nightshade. It is an extremely diverse group of plants, including two very good flowering climbers that ought to have a space found for them. They are both a bit on the delicate side, but if grown against a wall they should survive most winters: they might be cut back but will quickly regenerate without apparent loss of flowering ability. They both have typical potato-like flowers, in one species these are white and in the other, blue. The flowering is profuse and prolonged, continuing from spring to late fall. If supported, these delightful and rewarding climbers will grow to more than 6m (20ft).

They seem to thrive on any soil as long as it is free draining. Both species like full sun.

Both can be grown up a wall or over a trellis and are a spectacle in their own right with a long flowering period. Propagation is from summer cuttings. The only pruning is to keep the plants tidy and to remove any frosted wood.

Wisteria (Wisteria)

These are indeed handsome plants. A sizeable wisteria in full bloom, with hundreds of large blue tassels hanging beneath the airy feathery leaves, sends the pulse racing. Unfortunately you cannot rush out and buy a fully grown tree to wrap around your house; it takes time and patience. The flowers are typical of the pea family, Leguminosae, to which wisteria belongs. They erupt in spring in long chains; these are similar to laburnum, except that here the flowers are a soft blue. The different forms include whites as well as several minor variations on the lilac-blue theme. The foliage is like ash leaves, with several small leaflets along a central stem (this is called a pinnate leaf). The trunks become old and gnarled as they age and add to the character of the plant. All wisterias are fairly hardy, though you should seek advice when choosing a species for a cool zone. And a sunny wall is beneficial; this is for better flowering, rather than for protection from winter cold.

They are not too fussy about the kind of soil in which they grow as long as it is reasonably well drained. Do not over-feed.

Propagation is by layering in spring or taking late-summer cuttings. Grafting can also be used for some of the special forms.

Above: Lonicera x tellmanniana

Above: Solunum crispum
Glasnevin

Below: Wisteria floribunda
Multijuga

93

Roses

SPECIES ROSE

Species roses are those that occur naturally in the wild. They are found throughout the northern hemisphere from east to west, but not south of the equator. Species roses hybridise freely in the wild. There are at least 200 wild roses known today. Most species have single flowers with five petals. They self-pollinate, and form hips which produce seeds that will grown true to parent plant.

On the whole, species roses bloom once, early in the season. This bloom is quite spectacular as the plant produces a large quantity of flowers. Following the flowers are the brightly coloured hips which are attractive to us and to birds.

Species roses are fairly easy to grow, requiring little care. They are vigorous, but some are more cold tolerant than others. Some species can grow very large, up to 2.7m (9ft) tall by 2.7m (9ft) wide. Others sprawl, making them suitable as ground coverers, while some are good hedge material. They include: *Rosa banksiae, R. multiflora, R. pomifera, R. rugosa* and *R. spinosissima.*

OLD GARDEN ROSES

It is a matter of much debate, what roses should be considered to be old garden roses. Whether the China and tea roses should be in a separate classification from the European varieties and from the varieties that arose from their subsequent hybridisation is a matter for the scholars. The subclasses of old garden roses include Gallica, damask, alba, moss, centifolia, Portland, China, tea, Bourbon, Noisette, and hybrid perpetual.

The American Rose Society decreed that time should judge which roses are considered old garden varieties. Any roses in a class that was established before 1867 are thus deemed old garden roses, even if the particular variety was not introduced until after that date. Why 1867? That was the year that La France, one of the first hybrid tea roses, was introduced, thus ushering in the era of modern roses (hybrid teas, floribundas and grandifloras).

Right: *'Commandant Beaurepaire'*

Far right: *'William Lobb'*

HIGHLY RECOMMENDED OLD GARDEN ROSES

RED
Rosa gallica officinalis (G)
'Crimson Globe' (M)
'Nuits de Young' (M)
'Souv. d'Alphonse Lavallée (HP)

YELLOW
R. banksiae lutea (Sp)
R. hugonis (Sp)

WHITE
'Coquette des Alpes' (B)
'Dupontii' (Misc OGR)
'Leda' (D)
'Mabel Morrison' (HP)
'Mme Hardy' (D)
'Nastarana' (N)
R. banksiae banksiae (Sp)

PINK
'Celsiana' (D)
R. centifolia cristata (C)
'Marie Louise' (D)
'Paul's Early Blush' (HP)
'Rose de Meaux' (Ch)
'Souv. de la Malmaison' (B)

MAUVE
'Celina' (M)
'Charles de Mills' (G)
R. rugosa rubra (Sp)
'Tuscany' (G)

BLEND
'Commandant Beaurepaire (B)
'Louis Philippe' (Ch)
'Mutabilis' (Ch)
R. foetida bicolor (Sp)
'William Lobb' (M)

KEY: B—Bourbon, C—Centifolia, Ch—China, D—Damask, G—Gallica, HP—Hybrid Perpetual, M—Moss, Misc OGR—Miscellaneous Old Garden Rose, N—Noisette, Sp—Species

94

MODERN SHRUB ROSES

The term 'shrub rose' is perhaps a misnomer, as it does not denote the size, shape, or habit of a rose in this context, but rather a group for classification purposes. The hybrid roses that are in a class that was in existence before 1867 are considered old garden roses; those classified later are modern roses. There are several subclasses of shrub roses: hybrid eglantines, hybrid musks, hybrid rugosas, hybrid spinosissimas (some are old garden roses), and shrub roses. The last class is a catch-all for those roses that do not fall into any of the other four subclasses.

The characteristic that is common to all the shrub roses is their toughness. Some are species that grow true from seed, while others are man-made cultivated varieties. They vary in height from 60cm (2ft) to 3m (10ft). Flowers range through white, pink, red, orange, yellow and purple. The older varieties are not recurrent, but some newer introductions bloom continuously throughout the growing season.

Above: Rosa gallica officinalis
Apothecary's rose, Red rose of Lancaster

Left: *Cécile Brunner*

Below: *Golden Wings*

95

HIGHLY RECOMMENDED SHRUB ROSES

RED
'Dortmund' (K)
'F J Grootendorst' (HRg)
'Hansa' (HRg)
'Summer Wind' (S)
'Will Scarlet' (HMsk)

YELLOW
Fruhlingsgold' (HSpn)
'Golden Wings' (S)

WHITE
'Blanc Double de Coubert' (HRg)
'Nevada' (HMoy)
'Weisse au Sparrieshoop' (S)

PINK
'Canterbury' (S)
'Cécile Brunner' (Pol)
'Cerise Bouquet' (S)
'China Doll' (Pol)
'Flamingo' (HRg)
'Raubritter' (HMac)
'The Fairy' (Pol)
'Wanderin' Wind' (S)

BLEND
'Alchymist' (S)
'Applejack' (S)
'Cornelia' (HMsk)
'Dr Eckener' (HRg)
'Dornroschen' (S)
'Paulii Rosea'

KEY: Hmac—Hybrid Macrantha, HMoy—Hybrid Moyessii, HMsk—Hybrid Musk, HRg—Hybrid Rugosa, HSpn—Hybrid Spinosissima, K—Kordesii, Pol—Polyantha, S—Shrub

HYBRID TEA ROSES

Hybrid teas are the largest group of modern roses and are still the most widely grown of all roses. Think of a rose and the image that comes to mind usually has the characteristics of the hybrid teas; long pointed buds opening to elegant, high-centred, fragrant flowers of diverse colours on long straight stems.

Hybrid teas grow from 60-180cm (2-6ft) tall. With their long stems, most are good cut flowers. The buds are long and pointed. Flowers range from single to very double. Most of those introduced in the last 50 years are high-centred. Blooms are usually borne singly; rarely in a cluster of less than six flowers. The foliage is usually thin and dark green.

Today hybrid teas are the most popular roses, cornering more than 60 per cent of the world's rose market. Most florist roses are hybrid teas. They are elegant plants, perfect in a formal setting, yet comfortable in a quaint cottage garden. Their beauty, fragrance and form is unsurpassed in any other group of roses.

Above: *Electron*

Below: *Balia*

HIGHLY RECOMMENDED HYBRID TEA ROSES

RED
'Chrysler Imperial'
'Olmpiad'
'Precious Platinum'
'Tropicana' ('Super Star')

PINK
'Century Two'
'Dainty Bess'
'Electron' ('Mullard Jubilee')
'Miss All-American Beauty'

WHITE
'Garden Party'
'Pascali'
'Pristine'
'White Knight'

BLEND
'Granada'
'Maria Stern'
'Nantucket'
'Paradise'
'Peace'
'Swarthmore'

MAUVE
'Lady X'

96

FLORIBUNDA ROSES

DT Poulsen, a hybridiser from Denmark, can be credited with creating the first floribundas. His goal was to create a rose that would be hardy in the cold winters of northern Europe, floriferous, consistently recurrent, and require little or no special attention. A logical man, he felt that if he crossed a very hardy rose with a very attractive rose, the resultant rose would have the characteristics of both. He crossed the polyantha 'Orleans Rose' with the hybrid tea 'Red Star', and produced 'Else Poulsen' in 1924. He had created a new group of roses, which he called hybrid polyanthus; others called them Poulsen roses and it was not until the 1950s that these modern roses were finally called floribundas. Initially, the colours were limited to red and pink, and the roses lacked fragrance. Gene Boerner in the United States and Jack Harkness in Britain did much work with floribundas in the years following World War II, developing the characteristics so prized in hybrid tea roses, fragrance, a high-centred bloom, and a range of colours.

Today, floribundas rank second only to hybrid tea roses in their popularity. They fit into any landscape, formal or informal. Grow them into a hedge by planting two staggered rows 38cm (15in) apart, include them in a flower bed for contrast, or plant them by themselves for a splash of colour. Floribundas give a lot of colour for a little effort.

HIGHLY RECOMMENDED FLORIBUNDA ROSES

RED	PINK
'Europeana'	'Cherish'
'Impatient'	'Gene Boerner'
'Lichterloh'	'Sexy Rexy'
'Showbiz'	'Simplicity'

YELLOW	MAUVE
'Sunsprite' ('Korresia')	'Escapade'

WHITE	BLEND
'Evening Star'	'Anabell'
'Iceberg'	'Angel Face'
'Ivory Fashion'	'Apricot Nectar'
	'Sea Pearl'
	'Summer Fashion'

GRANDIFLORA OR FLORIBUNDA HYBRID-TEA TYPE ROSES

Grandifloras are the newest class of rose, created in the United States in 1954 for the rose 'Queen Elizabeth'. The hybrid tea 'Charlotte Armstrong' was the seed parent, with the floribunda 'Floradora' the pollen parent. By Act of Parliament, Queen Elizabeth II gave permission to use her name for this stately rose.

Most grandifloras are the results of crosses with 'Queen Elizabeth' or other offspring of 'Charlotte Armstrong' and 'Floradora'. In the United States, the results of some of these crosses are not considered grandifloras, and are instead classified in the floribunda subclass, 'floribunda, hybrid-tea type'. The British have not recognised grandiflora as a separate class, and place all such roses in that same floribunda subclass.

Grandifloras are crosses between hybrid teas and floribundas, with the resulting roses having the best characteristics of boths types. They bloom continuously through the growing season. They are floriferous, with an abundance of 7.5-13cm (3-5in) double flowers, borne singly or in clusters. The stems are longer than those of floribundas. Unfortunately, they did not inherit the floribundas' hardiness, and do not survive cold winters without good protection. The resemblance to hybrid teas is evident in the buds, flowers, leaves and thorns. The range of colours is extensive, but there are no lavenders and few bicolours. Oddly, grandifloras are taller than either of their parents, growing from 90 to 180cm (3 to 6ft) or taller. 'Queen Elizabeth' is a statuesque 210cm (7ft).

When incorporating grandifloras in the garden, make good use of their height. They are excellent as a background plant, whether in a rose garden or perennial border. They can be used to create good hedges. With their long stems, even on the clustered blooms, they are impressive as cut flowers.

HIGHLY RECOMMENDED GRANDIFLORA ROSES

RED	PINK
'Love'	'Aquarius'
	'Queen Elizabeth'

YELLOW	
'Gold Medal'	ORANGE
'Shining Hours'	'Arizona'
	'New Year'
	'Prominent'
WHITE	'Sundowner'
'White Lightnin''	

Shrubs

Shrubs can provide fragrance in all seasons, even — in mild climates — winter. This list includes the most widely available shrubs prized for their scented flowers and, in some cases, for their aromatic foliage too.

Buddleia (Butterfly bush)

The cultivars of *Buddleia davidii*, justifiably popular for their graceful flower clusters in shades of red, purple, pink and white, also bring superb fragrance to the summer garden. Bushes grow to about 8ft (2.4m) in height and spread.

Chimonanthes (Winter sweet)

This is one of several shrubs that provide sweetly-scented flowers during the winter. *Chimonanthes praecox*, which takes several years to establish, has pale yellow flowers with a purplish centre; *C.p.* 'Luteus' has all-yellow blooms. Both reach a height of about 10ft (3m).

Choisya ternata (Mexican orange blossom)

The common name aptly describes the heady fragrance this shrub offers in spring. Both the white flowers and the glossy, evergreen leaves (when crushed) are fragrant. A superb shrub for a sunny sheltered spot, *Choisya ternata* grows to a height of 6½-10ft (2-3m).

Clethra alnifolia (Sweet pepper bush)

Late summer sees the emergence of slender clusters of creamy white scented 'flowers' on this deciduous shrub, which requires a lime-free soil. Grow *C.a.* 'Paniculata' for the most abundant bloom; up to 7ft (2.1m) tall.

Corylopsis

This easily-grown deciduous shrub provides cowslip-scented, pale yellow flowers in early spring. Best grown on acid or neutral soils, *Corylopsis* generally reach a height of 5-7ft (1.5-2.1m). Recommended species are *C. pauciflora, C. spicata, C. veitchiana* and *C. willmottiae* (up to 10ft [3m] tall).

Cytisus battandieri (Moroccan broom)

For a tang of pineapple, grow this fast-growing tall shrub, preferably against a warm wall. The cone-shaped yellow flowers appear in midsummer.

Daphne

The daphnes are among the most fragrant of shrubs. From late winter until early spring the bare stems of the most popular daphne, *Daphne mezereum*, are clothed in sweetly scented blooms of white, pink or purplish red depending

Daphne eneorum (above left) *and* Daphne odora *'Aureomarginata'* (left) *are both prized for their sweet-smelling flowers.* Nicotiana alata *'Lime Green' (above) is also heavily scented.*

on variety. Also in bloom during winter and early spring is *Daphne odora* 'Aureomarginata', and as spring turns to summer *D. cneorum, D. X burkwoodii* 'Somerset' and *D. retusa* add their scent to the garden air.

Daphnes range in size from 1 to 5ft (30cm to 1.5m), and thrive in a moist but well-drained acid soil.

Genista cinerea

This lovely member of the pea family has profuse clusters of fragrant yellow pea flowers in early to midsummer. It forms a bush up to 10ft (3m) tall and 8ft (2.4m) across.

Hamamelis (Witch hazel)

For fascinating flowers during cold months it is hard to beat this shrub. Its spidery yellow or reddish-yellow blooms are delicately scented, the strap-like petals able to withstand the severest weather. Choose from *H. X. intermedia* 'Jelena' ('Copper Beauty'), yellow-suffused coppery red; *H. millis*, golden yellow; *H. m.* 'Pallida', sulphur yellow. All grow slowly to about 10ft (3m) tall.

Jasminum officinale

In a warm, sheltered site the climber jasmine and its variety 'Affine' ('Grandiflorum') can be relied upon for a crop of sweet-smelling white flowers throughout the summer.

Lavandula

In any discussion of fragrance, the lavender cannot be overlooked. Its familiar silver-grey aromatic foliage and highly scented flowers in blue, violet, white and pink enrich the garden from midsummer until early autumn.

Lonicera (Honeysuckle)

Of the popular climbing honeysuckles, *L. periclymenum* 'Belgica' and 'Serotina' can be recommended for their yellow and purple scented flowers in early and midsummer to autumn respectively. Of the bush varieties, *L. fragrantissima* bears creamy white fragrant blooms from mid-winter until early spring.

Magnolia sieboldii

This magnolia produces a succession of lemon-scented white cup-shaped flowers from late spring until late summer. It forms a shrub up to 10ft (3m) tall.

Mahonia

The mahonias are at their best from midwinter until early spring, sporting bright yellow fragrant flowers in clusters or slender spikes against a foil of glossy evergreen foliage. Choose from these recommended mahonias: *M. aquifolium*, golden yellow, *M. X media*, mimosa yellow; *M. X media* 'Buckland', deep yellow; *M. japonica*, lemon-yellow.

Myrtus communis (Common myrtle)

In a sunny sheltered location, the common myrtle scents the summer air with its creamy white solitary flowers. The evergreen foliage is a dark glossy green, and aromatic when crushed. Bushes grow to a height and spread of 10ft (3m).

Osmanthus

It is impossible to pass close to an osmanthus bush in spring without stopping to savour its rich perfume; the white flower clusters nestling amid the dense evergreen foliage are powerfully fragrant. *O. delavayi* is the

The highly fragrant flowers of Osmanthus (right) and Syringa (left).

most popular species; *O. X burkwoodii* (also known as *Osmarea burkwoodii*) is similar and just as fragrant. Both shrubs grow slowly to over 6½ft (2m) in height.

Rhododendron (Azalea)

The *Occidentale* hybrids of deciduous azaleas sport some superbly fragrant shrubs. The pink-flowered 'Graciosa', and 'Irene Koster', the yellow-opening white 'Bridesmaid', and the pink-flushed white 'Superba'. All bring pastel shades and delicious perfume to the garden in late spring.

Rubus tridel (Benenden)

The adaptable member of the bramble family brings scent into the late spring garden with its large single white flowers, each with a central boss of bold stamens. It grows quickly to a height of 10ft (3m).

Skimmia japonica

Justly prized for its bright crops of autumn and winter berries, this compact evergreen shrub has several forms that bear fragrant spring flowers. Notable among these is *S. j.* 'Fragrans', a male clone that bears dense clusters of white flowers giving off a lily-of-the valley perfume.

Spartium junceum (Spanish Broom)

A long season of honey-scented flowers grows on this hardy deciduous shrub. From early summer until early autumn its erect green stems are smothered with bright yellow fragrant pea-like flowers. Excellent for seashore locations, it can reach up to 10ft (3m).

Syringa vulgaris hybrids (Lilac)

What a rich resource of fragrant shrubs these hybrids represent! All thrive in full sun on a wide range of soils, being particularly suited to chalky soils. Colours range from pure white through creamy-yellow, shades of blue, lilac and red to a rich claret-mauve. Choose from single-flowered cultivars such as 'Souvenir de Louis Spaeth', wine red, and 'Vestale', white, or the double-flowered cultivars such as 'Charles Joly', dark purple-red, or 'Madame Lemoine', creamy yellow opening white. The flowering period lasts for about three weeks between late spring and early summer, depending on the cultivar.

Viburnum

For winter and early spring fragrance, *V. X. bodnantense* and *V. farreri* (*fragrans*) have much to offer. Both grow to 8ft (2.4m) in height and bear clusters of rose-tinted white flowers that can survive fairly cold weather. As spring merges into summer, the pink buds of *V. X burkwoodii* and *V. carlesii* open to reveal light flowerheads of richly scented white flowers.

99

Herbs and vegetables

Vegetables and herbs are not difficult to grow, yet the rewards are great. Growing them together and with the right companions improves the chances of a good crop.

INVASIVE HERBS

Some herbs, mint for example, are very invasive, spreading by underground runners. They make good companions, but their invasiveness restricts their use. However, their rambling tendencies can be curbed if such herbs are planted in a container, for example an old oil drum or old bucket, which has had the bottom removed and then sunk into the earth with its rim level with the ground. Another way is to put the herb in a conventional container and stand it among the other vegetables and herbs.

LIGHT

All plants must have light reaching their leaves in order to produce carbohydrates on which they live. Plants that do not get enough grow spindly and are sickly looking. Be careful when selecting and planting companion plants that they do not exclude light from each other. Most vegetables need full sun. A few, listed here, will tolerate partial shade, however, they must have direct sunlight for part of the day: Asparagus, broccoli, brussel sprout, cabbage, carrot, celeriac, celery, cress, cucumber, garlic, kale, kohlrabi, leek, lettuce, onion, parsley, parnsip, spinach, Swiss chard, turnip.

OTHER COMPANIONS

Not all companion plants are normally grown in the garden. Some fodder crops or even wild plants are useful for fixing nitrogen in the soil. They can be used as green manure or, since they will not overrun the garden, as companion plants among the vegetables. The following are worth considering:

Alfalfa or lucerne *Medicago sativa*
Bird's foot trefoil *Lotus corniculatus*
Lupin *Lupinus* (see right)
Red clover *Trifolium pratense*

Sainfoin *Onobrychis viciifolia*
Vetch *Vicia*
White clover *Trifolium repens*

BENEFICIAL HERBS

Some herbs seem to have a beneficial presence in the garden and go with nearly all other vegetables and herbs. Below are listed a few of these.

Hyssop *Hyssopus officinalis*
Lovage *Levisticum officinalis*
Marjoram *Origanum majorana*

Tarragon *Artemisia dracunculus*
Thyme *Thymus*
Yarrow *Achillea*

Herbs and flowers mix together well in pots (left). Lupins Lupinus *are ideal companion plants for vegetables.*

100

Here is a list of vegetables with what many gardeners believe to be their good and poor companions — other plants which are claimed to be beneficial or detrimental to their growth and well-being. Gardening lore suggests planting them together to enhance their growth or flavour, or to protect them from pests and diseases. Research has proved that some of these claims are justified, others await proof or disproof.

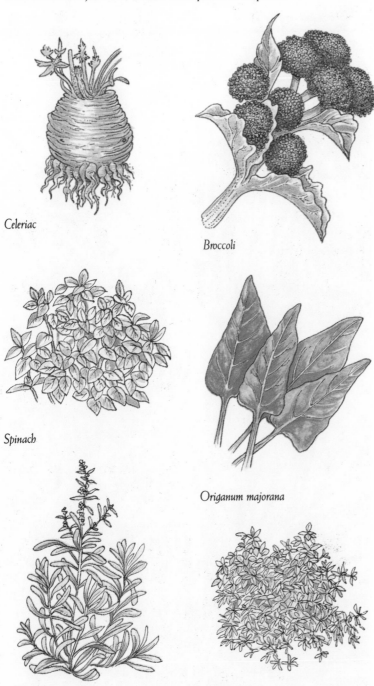

Celeriac

Broccoli

Spinach

Origanum majorana

Artemisia dracunculus

Thymus

Vegetable	Good companions	Poor companions
Asparagus *Asparagus officinalis*	parsley, tomato	onion
Bean *Phaseolus vulgaris* *Vicia faba*	beet, borage, cabbage, carrot, cauliflower, corn, marigold, squash, strawberry, tomato	chive, fennel, garlic, leek
Beet *Beta vulgaris*	cabbage, kohlrabi	runner bean
Broccoli *Brassica oleracea*	bean, celery, chamomile, dill, mint, nasturtium, onion, oregano, potato, sage, rosemary	lettuce, strawberry, tomato
Brussels sprout *Brassica oleracea*	bean, celery, dill, hyssop, mint, nasturtium, potato, sage rosemary	strawberry
Cabbage *Brassica oleracea*	bean, beet, celery, chamomile, dill, hyssop, mint, nasturtium, onion, oregano, potato, sage, rosemary	grape, strawberry, tomato
Carrot *Daucus carota*	bean, leak, onion, pea, radish, rosemary, sage, scorzonera, tomato, wormwood	dill
Cauliflower *Brassica oleracea*	bean, beet, celery, chamomile, dill, hyssop, mint, nasturtium, onion, oregano, potato, sage, radish	strawberry, tomato
Celeriac *Apium graveolens*	bean, cabbage, leek, onion, tomato	
Celery *Apium graveolens*	bean, cabbage, leek, onion, tomato	
Corn *Zea mays*	bean, lupin, melon, pea, squash	
Cucumber *Cucumis sativus*	bean, broccoli, celery, Chinese cabbage, lettuce, pea, radish, tomato	rue, sage
Eggplant *Solanum melongena*	pea, tarragon, thyme	
Horseradish *Armoracia rusticana*	potato	
Kohlrabi *Brassica oleracea*	beet, onion	bean, pepper, tomato
Leek *Allium porrum*	carrot, celeriac, celery	broad bean, broccoli
Lettuce *Lactuca sativa*	beet, cabbage, clover, pea, radish, strawberry	
Melon *Cucumis melo*	corn, peanut, sunflower	
Onion *Allium cepa*	beet, cabbage, carrot, lettuce, potato, strawberry, tomato	bean, pea
Pea *Pisum sativum*	carrot, corn, cucumber, eggplant, lettuce, radish, spinach, tomato, turnip	
Pepper *Capsicum*	basil, carrot, lovage, marjoram, onion, oregano	fennel, kohlrabi
Potato *Solanum tuberosum*	bean, cabbage, corn, lettuce, onion, petunia, marigold, radish	apple, pumpkin, tomato
Pumpkin *Cucurbita moschata*	bean, corn, mint, nasturtium, radish	potato
Radish *Raphanus sativus*	bean, cabbage, cauliflower, cucumber, lettuce, pea, squash, tomato	grape, hyssop
Spinach *oleracea*	cabbage, celery, eggplant, onion, pea, strawberry	
Squash *Cucurbita moschata*	bean, corn, mint, nasturtium, radish	
Summer squash *Cucurbita pepo*	bean, corn, mint, nasturtium, radish	potato
Tomato *Lycopersicon lycopersicum*	asparagus, basil, cabbage, carrot, onion, parsley, pea, sage	fennel, potato
Turnip *Brassica rapa*	pea	
Zucchini *Cucurbita pepo*	bean, corn, mint, nasturtium, radish	potato

101

Herbs and their companions

Herbs can be beneficial to a large range of other herbs and vegetables. Claimed companions improve the performance or taste as well as keep predators away. On the other hand, poor companions can be detrimental to associated plants growing close by. The list below shows a range of herbs and those plants which are said to be their good and bad companions.

Herb	Good companions	Poor companions
Anise *Pimpinella anisum*	bean, coriander	carrot
Basil *Ocimum basilicum*	bean, cabbage, tomato	rue
Borage *Borago officinalis*	strawberry, tomato	
Caraway *Carum carvi*	pea	fennel
Chamomile *Chamaemelum nobile*	cucumber, mint, onion	
Chervil *Anthriscus cerefolium*	carrot, radish	
Chive *Allium schoenoprasum*	carrot, grape, parsley, tomato	bean, pea
Coriander *Coriandrum sativum*	anise, potato	fennel
Dill *Anethum graveolens*	cabbage, lettuce, onion	carrot, tomato
Fennel *Foeniculum vulgare*		bean, caraway, coriander, dill, tomato
Garlic *Allium sativum*	carrot, rose, tomato	bean, pea, strawberry
Hyssop *Hyssopus officinalis*	cabbage, grape, plants in general	radish
Lemon balm *Melissa officinalis*	tomato	
Lovage *Levisticum officinale*	bean	
Marjoram *Origanum majorana*	plants in general	
Mint *Mentha*	cabbage, plants in general	parsley
Oregano *Origanum vulgare*	cabbage, cucumber	
Parsley *Petroselinum crispum*	asparagus, carrot, chive, tomato	mint
Rosemary *Rosmarinus officinalis*	bean, cabbage, carrot	potato
Rue *Ruta graveolens*	rose	basil, cabbage, sage
Sage *Salvia officinalis*	cabbage, carrot, marjoram, strawberry, tomato	cucumber, rue
Savory *Satureja*	bean, onion	
Tansy *Tanacetum vulgare*	blackberry, pepper, potato, raspberry	
Tarragon *Artemisia dracunculus*	plants in general	
Thyme *Thymus*	cabbage, plants in general	
Yarrow *Achillea*	plants in general	

102

Chive (Allium schoenoprasum) *is a very versatile herb, both in the kitchen and in the garden. It is reputed to be good friends with carrots, grapes, parsley, and tomatoes. It is also quite lovely to look at, especially when in flower, and can be used at the front of the flower border.*

Fruit and their companions

As with other plants in the garden there are benefits to be had by carefully mixing fruit crops with other plants. Below are listed those that are claimed to be good companions to fruit.

Also listed are other fruit and vegetables which are said to have a negative effect when grown close to certain fruit crops.

Fruit	Good companions	Poor companions
Apple *Malus pumila*	chive, nasturtium	potato
Blackberry *Rubus*	grape, tansy	
Citrus fruit *Citrus*	coffee, pepper	
Fig *Ficus carica*		rue
Grape *Vitus vinifera*	blackberry, hyssop, legume	cabbage, radish
Mulberry *Morus nigra*	grape	
Nectarine *Prunus persica*	asparagus, corn, grape, onion, strawberry	
Peach *Prunus persica*	asparagus, corn, grape, onion, strawberry	old and new peach trees
Pear *Pyrus communis*	currant	
Quince *Cydonia oblonga*	garlic	
Raspberry *Rubus idaeus*	tansy	blackberry, potato
Strawberry *Fragaria*	bean, borage, lettuce, nectarine, peach, spinach	cabbage, cauliflower, broccoli, Brussels sprout

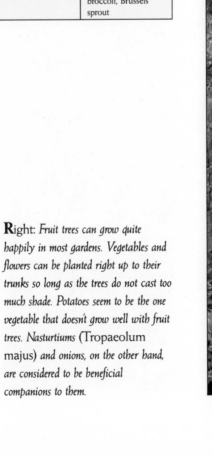

Right: *Fruit trees can grow quite happily in most gardens. Vegetables and flowers can be planted right up to their trunks so long as the trees do not cast too much shade. Potatoes seem to be the one vegetable that doesn't grow well with fruit trees.* Nasturtiums (Tropaeolum majus) *and onions, on the other hand, are considered to be beneficial companions to them.*

Boundaries, backdrops and special features

chapter six

BOUNDARIES, BACKDROPS AND SPECIAL FEATURES

Most of us seek that sense of privacy, even if it is sometimes illusory, which a boundary fence or hedge gives us. It marks our plot out from the others, and forms a framework for the garden. You do not have to be a recluse to want privacy or to define your boundary.

Walls, fences and hedges do more than mark out our territory, however. To a large extent they are the setting, the backdrop, or the stage in which we set our plants. They are part of good landscape design.

There are, of course, times when a visible barrier is *not* the right answer. If the view from your home is a stunning one, the last thing that you'll want to do is block it out. Even so, you'll probably want to keep animals either in or out of your garden, and to have some physical mark of your territory. If you are ambitious, and the site is suitable, you could even make a modest haw-haw; but there are other boundary markers, such as a post-and-chain, which can be small and unobtrusive. Even plastic-coated wire mesh with low-growing shrubs in front can be effective. Whatever the size and shape of your garden, there are good ways and there are bad ways of marking what is, after all, its external skeleton.

Since hedges and screens are a backcloth for many of your plants, and an integral part of any well-designed yard, it would be a mistake to think of them only as boundary markers. *Internal* hedges, or walls, play an important role that should not be overlooked.

A screen, whether it is a hedge, a wall, or a fence, also benefits the plants. It can provide shelter and possibly even a microclimate within the garden — but some provide shelter more efficiently than others.

105

Backdrops can provide more than just privacy. Here the colour of the evergreens within the yard is nicely set off against the darker background.

Fences

A fence is by far the quickest way to screen your yard or mark your boundary. It is obviously more 'instant' than a hedge — which may take several years to grow to the height that you require — and quicker than a brick or block wall to erect.

WOODEN FENCES

Although most fences are close-board or something similar (because these offer privacy), there are many other options well worth considering.

Most fences provide more than merely a screen for people: they offer protection to plants in exposed places and even a framework for suitable climbers (if you provide the necessary additional support).

For complete privacy, a close-boarded fence is the answer. Interwoven fencing is a good screen from a distance, but not peep-proof at close quarters.

POSTS

A fence is only as strong as its supports. A solid fence offers a lot of wind resistance and requires stronger posts than an open fence. Sizes generally vary between 2in × 2½in (50mm × 75mm) and 4in × 6in (100mm × 150mm). You should also allow sufficient depth in the ground; as a guide, a low fence intended to rise 2ft (60cm) above ground needs at least 1ft (30cm) below ground. For a fence 6ft (1.8m) high, there should be at least 2ft 6in (75cm) of post below ground.

The fence manufacturer should adivse on the size of posts required — if in doubt, though, err on the large side even if it means paying a bit more.

All timber posts should be treated with a preservative, preferably pressure or vacuum impregnated by the fencing supplier. If you cut the timber for any reason, this is likely to expose untreated timber in the centre; overcome this by soaking the cut end in a preservative.

Concrete posts solve the problem of rot, but not everyone likes the appearance. In the right setting, however, they can be perfectly acceptable. Most are cast with grooves to take a fencing panel, and this does make erection a little easier.

A less common option is a metal post — again with grooves in to take a fence panel.

You must be careful to order the right type and number of concrete or metal posts — for, as opposed to working with wooden posts, you need to specify what is required in the way of corners, and ends, together with the number of intermediate posts (because of the position of slots for the panels).

CHAIN-LINK AND OTHER WIRE FENCES

The posts at each end of a wire, chain link or chestnut paling fence need struts to take the strain when the wire is pulled tight as the tension is so great.

METAL POST SUPPORTS

If you do not like the idea of digging or boring holes, and perhaps mixing concrete to pack back into them, you could use a metal fixing post instead. There are several kinds, varying in sophistication, but the principle in all is the same.

The metal stake is driven into the ground using a sledge-hammer or club hammer (there is a fitment available to protect the top of the post support while you drive it in).

The advantages of metal supports are that they demand less effort than digging and filling holes, and you do not have to buy, carry, and mix concrete. The posts can be smaller (although the saving on the post does not in itself pay for the cost of the post holder), and do not rot in the ground.

The disadvantages are that you must make sure the post fits, and it is not always easy to drive them in absolutely straight (which is vital). In some circumstances you may find they look obtrusive, even though only a small section is visible at the base of the post.

CONCRETE PANELS

The panels are slotted into the grooves in the concrete posts. Do not do this until the concrete anchoring the posts has set firmly.

The panels sometimes seen around commercial premises are undisguised concrete and hardly attractive. There are finishes available, however, that you might find acceptable as a surround to a patio. Although one side has the traditional finish and the usual concrete strip appearance, the other (ideally 'inside') side has an imitation brick finish. The effect is one of a white brick wall, but you can paint it with any good quality exterior grade emulsion paint to make a potentially exciting backdrop for your plants.

Concrete comes in other disguises too — as simulated stone walls, or in an overlapping 'shiplap' pattern, for instance. It is worth shopping around to see what is locally available.

A word of warning about erecting a concrete fence: the posts must align *exactly*, or you will find it difficult, if not impossible, to slide the inflexible panels into the grooves that should — but do not — correspond.

WIRE MESH

Probably not taken seriously enough as a form of fence, the various wire mesh fences available are not serious contenders for a front yard boundary. Yet they have potential as useful dividers between back yards where you want a fairly open outlook and are not bothered about privacy. They are also useful where the yard borders open countryside, many of them being inconspicuous, especially when shrubs are planted against them.

A wire fence, especially chain-link, can be both strong and cheap. It is also easy to erect (see below), but the job must be done properly if disappointment is not to follow. It is imperative that wire fences are properly strained and kept taut.

Galvanized wire should last for 10 years or more; plastic-coated wire should have an even longer life, and also looks better.

Fences made with concrete panels can provide a durable boundary but may have a rather 'industrial' appearance. Choose panels with a more attractive finish than just plain concrete, a simulated brick or a 'shiplap' pattern for example. Make sure that the posts are correctly aligned before sliding the panels one by one into the preformed grooves.

Tension the top line between the posts and attach the chain-link mesh with twists of tying wire at 15cm (6in) intervals.

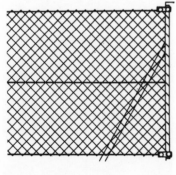

For fences higher than 1.2m (4ft) use three wires to stabilize the mesh between the posts. Attach the mesh to the middle and bottom wires about every 45cm (18in). Brace the end posts with angled struts, ideally concreted into the ground in the same way as the end, corner and intermediate posts.

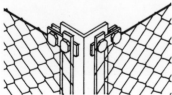

Where the fence changes direction pass stretcher bars through the last row of meshes and bolt these to the metal posts.

ERECTING A WOODEN FENCE

1 Start by marking the line of the intended fence with string stretched between two stakes, and lay the posts in approximately the right positions.

Remember that the distance between the centre of one post and the next is not the length of the fencing panel, but the panel plus post.

2 Make the first hole. You can dig this out with a spade, but a post-hole borer should make easier work of it.

3 Pack bricks or rubble around the base to hold the post upright, and check for plumb in both directions, using a long spirit-level. Once you are confident that it is true, pack more rubble around the base to firm it, and check verticals again.

4 Lay the first panel on the ground butten up to the post as a guide to the correct positioning of the next post. Make the next hole.

5 Insert the second post as the first, but also check that the two are the same height by using a string stretched taut at the final height, or by using a spirit-level on a board spanning the two.

If the fence has rails that have to be jointed to the post, fit the rails into the first post before you position the second (an extra pair of hands really is essential).

6 Fix the panel into position with galvanized nails or screws. You may find it easier to use brackets to fix the panels. It is in fact more convenient to fix these to the posts before you erect them.

7 Always use a line stretched between the ends at the height of the top of the fence, to ensure that the height is even.

8 Try to ensure that the main part of a timber fence does not come into contact with soil. Either use a gravel board (which you can replace more easily if it rots), or rest the fence on a layer of bricks or blocks.

9 Finally, firm the posts again, double-checking that they are vertical. Small posts can be firmed with rammed earth and rubble, but it is generally better to concrete in posts with more than about 3ft (90cm) above ground. If you are setting the posts in concrete, nail temporary struts to keep the post in position until it sets (wait for a few days before removing them).

WARNING: Do not attempt to erect tall or solid fences on a windy day, or if strong winds are forecast.

107

PLANTING NEAR A WALL

The ground near walls and fences is often much drier than the rest of the garden. This means the plants there have to be watered more often than the rest of the garden, and it also means careful planting.

Make the hole about 1ft (30cm) away from the wall. (If you want the plant to go up the fence or wall, you can train it towards it, using a sloping cane if necessary.)

Always incorporate plenty of moisture-holding material, such as peat, well-rotted compost, or manure.

After planting, water well and then mulch the moist ground with damp peat, pulverised bark or compost.

MAKING BOUNDARIES MORE BEAUTIFUL

No matter how tasteful or how well constructed boundary walls and fences are, their appearance can usually be improved by plants.

Low walls and fences of 4ft (1.2m) or less in height do not really call for intensive planting; in any case, climbers are clearly unsuitable for a wall or fence of that height. It is best to make a feature of such a wall or fence rather than try to hide it. (In fact, if you feel that you have to hide a low fence or wall, the chances are you have made the wrong choice in the first place.)

Of course, a previous owner may have committed the error of putting it up, leaving you with a decision either to pull it down and start again, or to make the best of what is there. If you feel that it has to be improved, try to use shrubs, particularly evergreens, to soften the overall effect. Alternatively, low walls can be extended in height with either closeboard or trellis panels, allowing you more privacy, and more scope for planting climbers and wall shrubs.

The sort of plants that you can use to liven up an unexciting fence or wall are:

- climbers;
- all shrubs:
- ordinary shrubs, particularly evergreens; or
- 'architectural' plants.

CLIMBERS

Climbers are generally not the easy solution that they may seem at first thought. Most of them are far more suitable for climbing a house wall or up a specially prepared trellis or other support. Virginia creeper (*Parthenocissus quinquefolia*) and Boston ivy (*Parthenocissus tricuspidata*) can cover a building superbly but are not for garden walls and fences; sweet peas and morning glories (*Ipomoea rubro-caerulea*, syn *I. violacea*) are among the most attractive annual climbers, but neither makes a good screen, nor can they fend for themselves without a suitable support.

There are, however, a few plants that do climb and clothe without much help and with no need to erect netting or trellis for them to grow up. Some ivies are among the most useful, but there are other plants equally so, such as *Polygonum baldschuanicum* and various loniceras (honeysuckles).

Ivies are particularly useful because they are evergreen, and there are many variations in leaf colour and shape. Two large-leaved varieties of outstanding merit are the Persian ivy *Hedera colchica* 'Dentata Variegta', and the Canary Island ivy *H. canariensis* 'Glorie de Marengo', also called 'Variegata'. Both these variegated ivies look interesting all the year round, although the Canary Island ivy may look the worse for wear in very cold areas.

The ordinary *H. helix* vrieties are also suitble, although these tend to look better on walls than on fences. There are dozens of varieties from which to choose.

Another evergreen to consider is the Japanese honeysuckle *Lonicera japonica* 'Aureoreticulata', which has golden reticulation on bright green leaves. It tends to lose leaves in a severe winter.

Deciduous climbers are obviously less desirable, assuming the object is to cover the fence or wall, but there are also some useful plants in this category.

The mile-a-minute, or Russian, vine *(Polygonum baldschuanicum)* is a rampant plant that covers a large area quickly, and crowns the fence or wall with foaming masses of small creamy flowers in late summer and through autumn. Not a particularly pretty plant, it is fine though if you want quick cover.

For a really pretty flowering climber, it is difficult to beat clematis. Some initial support is required, such as netting or a trellis, but then species such as *C. montana* simply romp along the fence. The species is white, but the pink variety 'Rubens' is justifiably more popular.

Garden walls come 'alive' (left and right) *when covered in climbing plants.*

If you are prepared to use a trellis of some kind, the various large-flowered hybrids can make a spectacular show. One of the most popular, 'Nelly Moser', actually does best on a shady fence (its colour is stronger out of sunlight); a useful bonus.

Wisterias must rank among the most desirable of all climbers and wall shrubs, but only a large, tall wall can do them justice. If your wall is suitable, and you have the patience to wait for a few years to see it at its fully glory, a wisteria can be very rewarding.

For an annual climber that covers a fence quickly, try the Japanese hop, *Humulus japonicus*. The variety 'Variegatus' is particularly decorative.

These are many other climbers that you could try, including honeysuckle.

WALL SHRUBS

Although most wall shrubs grow equally well in the open, they usually have some feature or 'habit' that makes them specially suitable for growing against a structure such as a wall. Some, for example, have become known as wall shrubs because they are not particularly hardy and tend to grow better with the protection offered by a wall.

Pyracanthas come high on the list of desirable plants because, apart from summer foliage (and some small white flowers), there is the bonus of autumn and winter berries.

'ORDINARY' SHRUBS

There are so many shrubs that it is always difficult to single out a few. But the shortlist can be confined to plants that are:

- evergreen;
- able to grow well against a fence or wall;
- widely available; and that
- make a good screen/provide good cover.

High on the list must be variegated hollies *Elaegnus pungens* 'Maculata', and *Viburnum tinus*. Many conifers provide year-round cover and interest, of course, but their shape tends to be more upright and less bushy than those mentioned.

'ARCHITECTURAL' PLANTS

You do not have to have a densely planted area to offset the boredom of a long wall or fence. Often, one or two really striking plants can enliven the scene and act as focal points.

A large clump of phormium, a single yucca, or a large castor oil plant *(Fatsia japonica)* may be all that is needed.

109

The pink-and-white blooms of Clematis *'Nelly Moser'* (right) flourish on a wall. Climbing plants create a 'vertical' aspect to the yard (above).

Living screens

For sheer impact, there is no substitute for the living boundary or screen formed by a hedge, even though it needs regular maintenance.

Apart from the regular trimming or pruning that is necessary with all hedges, there is one other big drawback: waiting for results.

Yet despite the extra work involved, a hedge is much preferred by many gardeners, for, besides marking the boundary, a hedge can, by illusion, extend it; it can blur the boundary even while defining it.

Often treated as a background against which to set other plants, a hedge can also be something beautiful in its own right. There are some spectacular flowering hedges to consider, and certainly many more pleasing evergreens than privet. Many of the most useful hedging plants are described on the following pages.

BIG IS NOT NECESSARILY BEST

Because it is natural to want to see results quickly, there is the temptation to buy tall hedging plants. Resist it. They often take several seasons to become established and to start growing again, and frequently they lack the dense base that can be achieved by planting small and clipping early.

Small plants are cheaper, as well as better, in the long run.

To speed your hedging along, it is better to put money and effort into preparing the ground well.

DECIDING WHAT YOU WANT

It is worth being quite clear what you want from your hedge — a screen, something to keep animals in or out, a barrier to muffle sound from a busy road, or a decorative feature that contributes its own quota of beauty to the grden. The possible requirements are numerous.

The Table opposite should enable you to find a hedge that suits your needs, whether you want a formal evergreen screen or an informal flowering hedge.

Planting distances differ according to whether you require a screen or a hedge. Distances between plants for a screen are greater, for the plants themselves are to become bigger; close spacing keeps the plants more compact for a low hedge. Recommended spacings for each plant are given on the appropriate page. Also in the Table, the likely number of necessary cuts in a year will help you to decide whether a particular hedge is too labour-intensive for you.

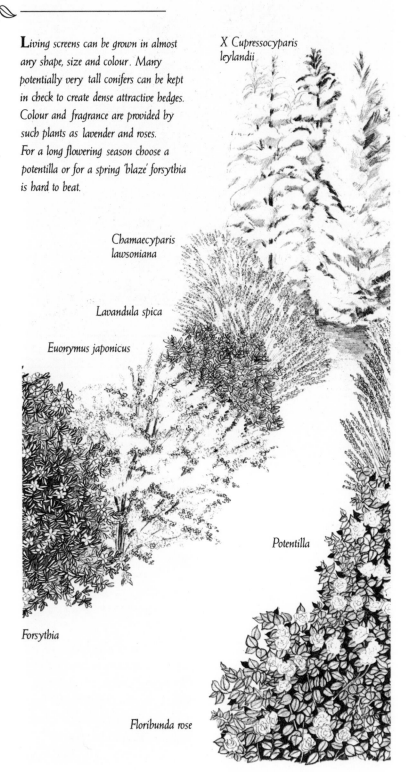

Living screens can be grown in almost any shape, size and colour. Many potentially very tall conifers can be kept in check to create dense attractive hedges. Colour and fragrance are provided by such plants as lavender and roses. For a long flowering season choose a potentilla or for a spring 'blaze' forsythia is hard to beat.

X Cupressocyparis leylandii

Chamaecyparis lawsoniana

Lavandula spica

Euonymus japonicus

Potentilla

Forsythia

Floribunda rose

HEDGING PLANTS

Name	Evergreen/deciduous	Recommended height	Formal/informal	Main features	Cuts/year
Berberis darwinii	evergreen	4-6ft (1.2-1.8m)	formal/informal	foliage/flowers	one
Berberis x stenophylla	evergreen	6ft (1.8m)	informal	flowers	one
Berberis thunbergii	deciduous	1½-6ft[1] (0.4-1.8m[1])	formal/informal	foliage	one/two
Buxus sempervirens	evergreen	1-4ft (0.3-1.2m[1])	formal	foliage	one/two
Carpinus betulus	deciduous[2]	5-8ft (1.5-2.4m)	formal	foliage	one
Chamaecyparis lawsoniana	evergreen (conifer)	5-8ft (1.5-2.4m)	formal	foliage	one
Cotoneaster lacteus	evergreen	6-8ft (1.8-2.4m)	informal	foliage/berries	one
Crataegus monogyna	deciduous	5-8ft (1.5-2.4m)	formal	foliage	one/two
X Cupressocyparis leylandii	evergreen (conifer)	10-15ft (3-4.5m)	formal	foliage	one
Cupressus macrocarpa	evergreen (conifer)	8-10ft (2.4-5m)	formal	foliage	one
Elaeagnus x ebbingei	evergreen	4-6ft (1.2-1.8m)	formal	foliage	one
Euonymus japonicus	evergreen	5-6ft (1.5-1.8m)	formal	foliage	one
Fagus sylvatica	deciduous[2]	5-8ft (1.5-2.4m)	formal	foliage	one
'Flamboyant'	deciduous	8-10ft (2.4-3m)	formal	foliage	one
Forsythia	deciduous	4-6ft (1.2-1.8m)	informal	flowers	one
Griselinia Littoralis	evergreen	5-7ft (1.5-2.1m)	formal	foliage	one
Ilex aquifolium	evergreen	5-6ft (1.5-1.8m)	formal	foliage	one
Lavandula spica	evergreen	1-4ft[1] (0.3-1.2m[1])	informal	foliage/flowers	one
Ligustrum ovalifolium	semi-evergreen	4-6ft (1.2-1.8m)	formal	foliage	six
Lonicera nitida	evergreen	2-4ft (0.6-1.2m)	formal	foliage	six
Potentilla	deciduous	3-4ft (1-1.2m)	formal/informal	flowers	one
Prunus ceracifera 'Nigra'	deciduous	5-8ft (1.5-2.4m)	formal/informal	foliage	one
Prunus x cistena	deciduous	4-5ft (1.2-1.5m)	informal	foliage	one
Prunus laurocerasus	evergreen	5-6ft (1.5-1.8m)	formal	foliage	one
Rosa	deciduous	3-6ft (1-1.8m)	informal	flowers	one
Rosmarinus	evergreen	4-5ft (1.2-1.5m)	informal	foliage/flowers	one
Spiraea x arguta	deciduous	4-5ft (1.2-1.5m)	informal	flowers	one
Taxus baccata	evergreen	3-6ft (0.9-1.8m)	formal	foliage	one
Thuya plicata	evergreen (conifer)	5-8ft (1.5-2.4m)	formal	foliage	one

[1] Depends on variety   [2] Old leaves remain throughout winter

WHAT IS A HEDGING PLANT?

Some of the plants grown as hedges could reach 30ft (9m) or more if grown as individual plants. Others could make specimen shrubs if grown in isolation. What makes them into a hedge is the close spacing (which restricts their growth and modifies their habit), coupled with clipping and pruning.

The dramatic difference between a beech tree and a beech hedge should be sufficient to demonstrate how even a seemingly unpromising plant can be tamed and trained into a first-class hedge. Do not rule a plant out simply because you do not normally associate it with your idea of a traditional hedge. On the other hand, be cautious with plants that you do not know will work; not every plant responds.

Hedges make a fine backdrop for many plants, but unfortunately they also cause problems for plants close to them. There is a potential shade problem, the ground near the base is always very dry because the soil is largely protected from driving rain, and the soil is also likely to be impoverished.

Whatever is planted close to a hedge has to compete for light, moisture and food.

As a very rough guide, anything that you plant within a distance of half of the height of the hedge is likely to suffer unless you choose particularly tolerant plants. So a 6ft (1.8m) hedge could cause problems for a distance of about 3ft (90cm). If the hedge backs a large border, you probably need a path at the back anyway in order to be able to trim the hedge, and in these circumstances a 4ft (1.2m) hedge is likely to cause fewest problems.

The main difficulty arises with narrow beds between lawn and hedge. It is those borders narrow enough to be reached over to trim the hedge that are the most difficult in which to grow plants.

Nature has adapted plants to grow in even the most adverse spots, however, and some of the possible candidates are listed below. But because most of them are fairly tough does not mean that you can neglect them — they do need special care while they are becoming established.

Always water the plants regularly and thoroughly until they are established. Even if they tolerate dry soil normally, give them an extra chance to start with.

Be prepared to feed the plants, at least perennials, for the first year. Foliar feeding has the advantage of feeding the plants without encouraging the hedge to compete.

Because the plants likely to succeed near hedges, range from shrubs to annuals, they have here been grouped under type. But do not be afraid to mix them — there is nothing wrong mixing shrubs and herbaceous perennials, nor annuals with perennials. Often, however, it is best to keep to one or two plants in a small bed for real impact.

112

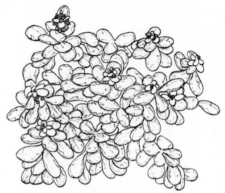

Bergenia cordifolia (left) *is excellent for spring colour in the shade of a hedge.*

Herbaceous perennials
Ajuga reptans: *Bugle*
Excellent as a ground cover plant. There are several good varieties, all of them suitable. Most of these ground-hugging plants have attractive coloured and variegated leaves. They have the considerable merit of being evergreen. Small spikes of blue flowers appear in late spring and early summer, but its main use is as a foliage ground cover.

Anemone x hybrida:
Japanese anemone
Useful if you want a late-flowering herbaceous plant. The usually white or pink flowers (it depends on variety) are carried on stems about 60-90cm (2-3ft) tall in late summer to midautumn.

Bergenia
Another useful evergreen ground cover, but with striking flowers in spring. The large, round leaves often take on a reddish-purple hue in winter. Most varieties have pink flowers; the height seldom rises to more than 30cm (1ft).

Epimedium perralderianum
Although almost evergreen, the leaves usually look the worse for wear by the end of winter. The bronze-yellow flowers in mid- to late spring are not particularly conspicuous, but it is a useful if slow-growing plant. The height is of about 30cm (1ft).

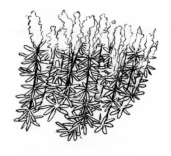

Euphorbia: *Spurge*

There are many different spurges, but E. robbiae is one of the most suitable for this situation. Its habit is always interesting with rosettes of dark green leaves, over which yellowish-green flowers are carried in early to midsummer. Its height is of about 45cm (1½ft). E. wulfenii is also a possible candidate, but is a much bolder plant, reaching 1.2m (4ft).

Lamium maculatum

Another low-growing carpeting plant. There are several varieties, with either pink or white flowers in midspring to early summer. It is grown mainly as a foliage plant, however; the leaves are usually marbled or splashed with white.

Liriope muscari

An established clump of this distinctive plant is always interesting when in flower in late summer to midautumn. Its foliage is evergreen and rush-like, with blue spires of flowers resembling a grape hyacinth. Its height is of about 30cm (1ft).

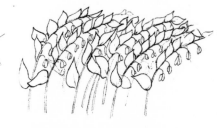

Polygonatum x hybridum:
Solomon's Seal
Frequently sold as P. multiflorum, but useful whatever its name. The greenish-white bell flowers hang down from arching stems in late spring and early summer. The height is of about 75cm (2½ft).

Pulmonaria

Can be used as a ground cover, or as isolated 'clumps' — either way, a desirable plant. There are several species and varieties available, generally with spotted or mottled leaves, and with pink, violet, and blue flowers in mid- to late spring.

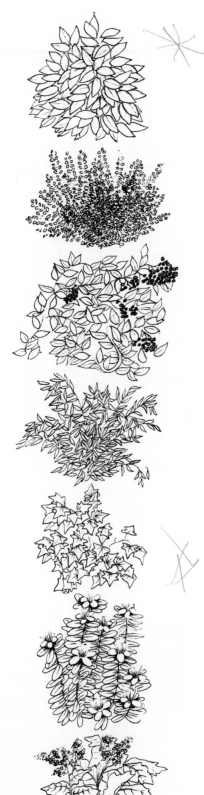

Shrubs

Aucuba japonica

Only suitable near a large hedge, otherwise probably too big.

Berberis

Dwarf kinds can be used, or larger ones if the hedge is substantial in size.

Cotoneaster

A diverse family, some species of which make small trees, others ground-hugging carpeters. For planting in a small bed near a hedge, a dwarf kind such as C. dammeri or C. salicifolius 'Repens' is probably best. Both these are evergreen.

Danae racemosa:
Alexandrian laurel.
Not a spectacular plant, but a useful evergreen with glossy green leaves and orange berries, appreciated most in winter.

Hedera: *Ivy*

Ivies are very versatile. In addition to the uses described elsewhere in this book, they make a fine ground cover for difficult sites.

Hypericum calycinum:
Rose of Sharon
A tough plant that completely takes over its bed in time. The evergreen leaves give year-round cover (although they can look tatty in winter and may drop), but it is worth growing just for its vibrant display of large yellow flowers from early summer to early autumn. Height: 30-45cm (1-1½ft). Its leaves take on red and purple tints in winter.

Mahonia aquifolium:
Holly-leafed berberis
An evergreen shrub growing 60-120cm (2-4ft). Its leaves take on red and purple tints in winter.

113

Planting and training

PLANTING A HEDGE

Every hedge is intended on planting to remain in place for a long time, so there is only one chance to prepare the ground properly. It is easy to be tempted to take short cuts, but thorough preparation helps the hedge to become established more rapidly.

Prepare the ground in advance by digging two spits deep (a spit is the depth of a spade blade), and incorporate as much well-rotted manure or compost as can be spared. Level the ground and rake in a general fertilizer at about 4oz per sq yd (140g per sq m) before planting your selected bushes.

Excavate holes at the spacing recommended for the hedge, large enough to take the rootball, and for the roots to be spread out if the plants are bare-root.

Always firm the soil around the plants, and water thoroughly so that the roots get a good start in their new home.

Container-grown trees can be planted at any time, provided the ground is not frozen or waterlogged, but bare-rooted and balled plants are generally best planted from midautumn to early spring. Mid- to late autumn is a good time for deciduous hedges, but evergreens are better planted in spring — mid- to late spring is perfectly satisfactory — so that they are not exposed to water loss from the leaves before the soil has had a chance to warm up enough for the roots to grow.

There should be no need to stake your hedge, but if the site is very exposed it is a good idea to provide a temporary screen or fence. If this is too much for the horticultural budget, stretch strings or wires between stakes to support the intervening plants.

AFTER PLANTING

Water your hedge if the weather is dry, at least until established — especially if you want your hedge to grow quickly while it is young. Soak the ground thoroughly rather than sprinkling the surface, even if it means doing so less often.

Feed it with a foliar feed regularly for the first year. This may seem an extravagance for a hedge — it is certainly not essential — but even if you never feed it again, it is worth a little extra effort to get the hedge moving as quickly as possible.

Prune early. Shaping and forming your hedge can begin as soon as you have planted it.

Cut back straggly stems, and even upward growth if you want a row of even plants. (The only exceptions are plants, such as tall conifers, that you want to grow up as a *high* screen.)

TALL WINDBREAKS AND SCREENS

For a tall windbreak or screen, some of the plants listed on pages 106-7 are suitable, but you must plant them further apart. Bear in mind that such tall screens are really suitable only for a fairly large garden.

Shaping hedges for decorative effect is normally associated with stately homes, although they can also have a place in modest gardens.

114

Topiary, the art of pruning and shaping
hedging plants into sculptural features to
decorate the garden, has been a
traditional pursuit for centuries. Early
training may involve the use of wire to
hold growing stems in the required shapes.
With expert trimming and meticulous
attention to detail, fantastic shapes can be
achieved with plants such as privet and
yew. These privet peacocks (left) perch
atop crisply clipped blocks formed from
the same plant.

Paving

The wealth of paving materials available from gardening and DIY
centres can make their selection difficult. However, choosing on a basis
of cost and any existing materials may help, and the breakdown of
materials below should also prove a useful starting point.

NATURAL STONE
This tends to be expensive and also involves considerable transportation
costs. In an area where the natural rock is suitable for paving, however,
use of stone may well be more suitable than other paving types.

Paving stone comes in different shapes, which include random
pieces — irregular shapes and thicknesses; dressed pieces — rectangular
shapes; or sawn pieces — rectangular with smooth surfaces. A variety of
colours and shades is available, depending on the type of stone selected.

Dressed stone is easiest to lay successfully and is more polished in
appearance than random stone, but using random stone in areas where
curves feature strongly saves a good deal of cutting. It lends itself well to
less formal situations. Sawn stone tends to be too finished for garden
paving, and is, perhaps, better suited to interior use.

Where available, reclaimed, second-hand stone has the advantage
of being weathered and therefore lends character and age to a newly-
paved garden.

CONCRETE
Either laid as required or used as pre-formed slabs, concrete plays a
great part in many gardens. The multitude of finishes that can now be
obtained makes it increasingly useful. Similar sized paving slabs can
form a regular pattern, or a number of different sizes combined give a
more complex arrangement. A good effect can be produced by laying
slabs within 'tramlines': various sizes of slabs are used but laid within set
lines running along or across the garden. This increases the apparent
visual length or width of the garden.

'In situ' concrete is more commonly used for utility areas. The
aggregate can be exposed, or it can be given a brushed finish for texture.
The appearance of squares or rectangles of concrete is much improved
by bordering them with bricks or other small unit pavings; these can be
used to create a strong ground pattern where this is desired.

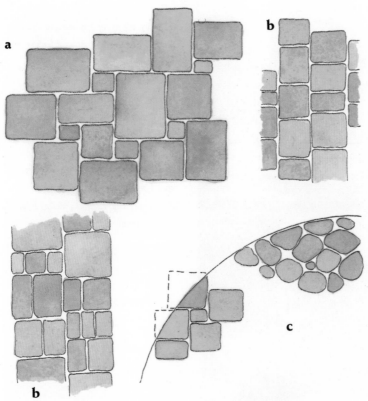

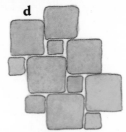

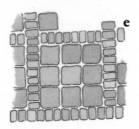

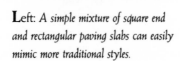

Above: *Paving may be laid in many different styles. A few are shown here: a) large slabs of natural stone traditionally laid around small 'key' stones; b) another traditional style of laying various-sized slabs of stone in even bands or 'tramlines'; c) random stone may be laid with ease around curves while rectangular slabs would require cutting; d) using two or more sizes of concrete paving slabs can result in attractive patterns; e) square paving slabs may be laid within a pattern of brick to heighten visual interest*

Left: *A simple mixture of square end and rectangular paving slabs can easily mimic more traditional styles.*

BRICK

Brick is a very pleasing medium to work with, as its small size makes it suitable for irregular shapes and angles, and its usually warm colour can be used to contrast and complement other paving and building materials. If selected to match the house, the bricks will have a unifying effect, visually tying the house and its surroundings together.

Bricks that are to be used as paving should be selected for their ability to withstand frost if your area is prone to frost; soft bricks will soon have their face shattered by the repeated action of freezing and thawing, leaving an uneven, unattractive and possibly unsafe surface. Recently the production of special clay paving blocks which do not shatter has boomed, and there is now a complete range of colours with complementary kerbing blocks and matching walling bricks available. These clay paviors have the additional benefit of greater strength than ordinary bricks, and may be used as a flexible paving (that is laid without a rigid base) for both driveways and patios.

SMALL UNIT PAVING

This includes bricks and the smallest of the pre-cast concrete pavings, but also takes in items such as granite setts and cobbles which are increasing in popularity. Their diminutive size makes them extremely suitable for the small site, and allows them to be laid in radial as well as rectilinear patterns.

Used on their own, setts and cobbles give an interesting but uniform surface which acts as a good foil for planting, etc. Alternatively, they may be mixed or contrasted with larger paving types to create bold patterns.

The mellow tones of natural stone (above) blend easily with the colours of the garden. The laying pattern is a traditional 'tram-line' style.

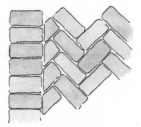

Above: *45° herringbone (bricks laid flat at 45° to edging).*

Above: *90° herringbone (bricks laid flat at 90° to edging).*

Above: *Basketweave (bricks laid flat).*

Above: *Basketweave (bricks laid on edge).*

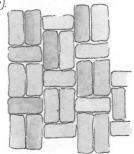

Above: *Running basketweave (bonding gives greater sense of direction).*

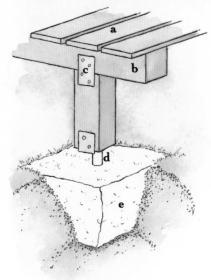

Above: *The combination of concrete slabs with other paving types such as brick and gravel allows many interesting variations.*

Above: *Tiny carpeting plants thrive in niches between the paving and increase the variations in texture in the brick and stone.*

TIMBER

Although timber can be successfully used as a paving when the area is only used occasionally, its main drawback is its slippery nature when wet. This increases as a layer of algae and moss slowly builds up on the surface, so it is not sensible to use wood for main paths and thoroughfares.

By its very nature, timber is in keeping with woodland situations and can be used to help re-create similar effects in the yard. Heavy timbers such as railway sleepers make useful steps, or they can be set in the ground as stepping stones or continuous paving. Rounds cut from

117

Above: *Squares of timber decking set as stepping stones over gravel. The ridged timber surface will give good grip even when it is wet.*

Left: *Timber decking should be supported clear of the ground by strong joists and with sufficient air gaps to allow rapid drying. Timber posts should be set clear off the ground by a metal bracket set in a substantial concrete footing.*
Key: a) timber decking with air gaps; b) joists; c) metal tie; d) post supported clear of the ground; e) concrete foundation.

tree trunks can be set on sand to provide an effective surface. The gaps should be filled in with smaller rounds, gravel, or wood and bark chippings to make the area easier to use.

Wood and bark chippings are now commonly used as a planting mulch, but are also useful as loose surfacing on paths, edged by cordwood or edging board pegged in position.

Timber decking can produce a clean, striking surface. Supported above the ground on joists, the timber dries quickly to leave a dry and safe surface. Such treatment is suited to leisure areas around swimming pools, etc, where the drainage/air gaps are unlikely to be a problem and where a softer, more flexible surface might be preferred over stone or concrete.

GRAVEL

Gravel and stone chippings are often seen simply as a cheaper alternative to other paving surfaces, while, in fact, they can be admirable materials in their own right. Retained with an edging of brick, stone or timber, they can fit into any shape (which is very useful for small areas) and provide a good backing for foliage or tubs. Plants can be selectively planted through the gravel to give a more informal feel in desired areas.

It must be remembered that each of the different paving types requires a foundation or base. These will vary widely depending on the situation of the yard and relative use the area is likely to receive. However, careful inspection of the photographs and illustrations in this section, which show a wide variety of paving types, will help to establish the various situations in which they could be best used. Advice on laying the appropriate foundations can be obtained from suppliers or manufacturers, whose brochures often include instructions for use and installation.

Gravel is useful both as a paving and a mulch, flowing easily around obstructions and plants (above). Tulipa richardii is a useful dwarf species tulip.

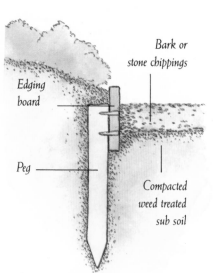

Above: *Treated timber boards provide a suitable edging for areas of gravel, or timber or bark chippings. Secure fixing to a stout timber peg provides stability.*

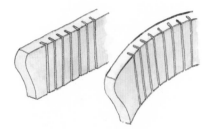

Above: *Make a series of vertical saw cuts part-way through the board to bend it around quite a tight radius.*

Walls

Constructed from natural stone, concrete or bricks, walls make the strongest and most imposing boundaries and divisions in the yard. As they are permanent in nature, they will in time lend the area a sense of continuity and coherence.

NATURAL STONE

As with paving, natural stone is found in a random or dressed state, depending on the finish required. Random stone may be used on its own, or 'dry' (unbonded), or with mortar to bond the pieces together. Dry stone walls are very attractive but difficult to construct properly or with any degree of stability, and require a lot of work and skill. Building the wall with a suitable batter on each side makes a safer structure and is easier to construct — as long as you have the patience.

Dry stone walling is particularly suitable for low retaining walls, and if soil is compacted into the gaps, small alpine plants can be rooted through. Stability is provided by a wide concrete or stone foundation, by building the wall to a batter, and by inserting occasional long stones to tie the wall back into the mass of soil.

Walls built with mortar are much easier to construct, although the mortar can detract from the appearance of the stone. Stones of different sizes will give a random wall, or the stones can be sorted into roughly equal thicknesses and laid in level courses. Dressed stone is laid in even layers to produce a coursed wall, although 'jump' blocks several courses high may be incorporated.

Both types of wall will require a coping, which usually consists of large flat stones and serves to waterproof the wall.

BRICKS AND BLOCKS

Concrete or reconstituted stone blocks are more commonly available than those of natural stone. All walls of these materials should be based on a firm concrete foundation and built in a suitable bonding pattern (as illustrated) so that the vertical joints do not coincide. If the bonds of a particular decorative pattern coincide, strips of reinforcing mesh should be set into and along the horizontal mortar bed at regular intervals to aid stability.

Concrete blocks tend to be plain to look at, but can be rendered to provide a good surface for painting, or used as a strong backing to which a facing of brick or natural stone can be fixed with mortar and metal ties. The latter is a practical construction for retaining walls, where only one face is visible.

Reconstituted stone is, by and large, a poor alternative to natural

The inherent beauty of natural stone is exhibited clearly in this dry stone wall (above). The cushion-forming Sempervivum *amongst other plants, has been grown in a tiny niche to provide further appeal.*

119

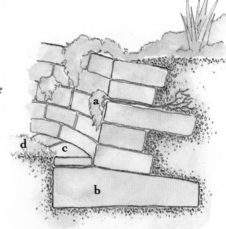

Right: *A dry stone retaining wall should be built to a backward leaning batter with occasional long stones to tie back into the body of soil. A simple stone edge will make the area much easier to mow.*
Key: a) plants growing through wall (positioned during construction); b) concrete foundation; c) stone mowing edge; d) lawn.

Above: *Bricks of varying colours may be used to highlight the bonding pattern. Here red and grey bricks are laid in Flemish bond.*

Above: *A 'half brick' wall (10cm/4in wide) built in stretcher bond, showing how a pier should be bonded in.*

Above: *A 21.5cm (8½in) wide, or single brick wall constructed in Flemish bond with alternate headers (small face) and stretchers (long face) in each course.*

The combination of brickwork with stone copings, pier caps and finials can make for a particularly fine wall (above).

Above: *A simple coping of bricks laid on edge gives a clean, functional finish. Metal ties prevent the end brick being knocked off.*

Above: *The addition of a double tile creasing below the brick on edge will further weatherproof the wall and add detail.*

Above: *Flat or ridged copings may be made from stone or precast concrete. Narrow grooves cut in the underside will ensure any water falling on the coping drips clear of the brickwork.*

stone. But it can be used to reasonable effect where cream and beige tones are required to match paving stones, or as a contrast to dark foliage and timber.

Brick is perhaps the most flexible of building materials. It works well

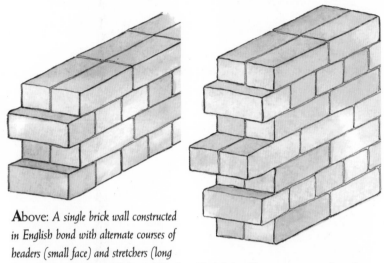

Above: *A single brick wall constructed in English bond with alternate courses of headers (small face) and stretchers (long face). English Garden Wall bond differs from English bond by extra courses of stretchers between the header courses.*

for either very plain and simple walls, which are a backcloth to the garden, or for more detailed work, as a feature in its own right, which may use specially shaped bullnose, plinth or cant bricks. Such bricks, however, are expensive and should be used sparingly: railings, wrought iron work, and stone finials and copings can also all be combined with the brickwork. Such a wall would provide an imposing entrance to a larger or period house, but should not be over-stated.

The width of all walls should be proportioned to their height, and additional strengthening piers installed as necessary. Brick walls less than a brick thick (21.5cm/8½in) tend to look flimsy and are unsatisfactory unless particularly small. Brickwork that is (21.5 (8½in) wide is generally suitable for walls up to 6ft (1.8m) high, but should be strengthened with piers for greater heights. In any case, piers will add interesting details to even the smallest of walls and should always be used to provide suitable end stops to a length of brickwork. Remember also to allow expansion joints in walls over 11 yards (approximately 10m) in length.

Retaining walls will need to be thicker than free-standing walls to withstand the force of soil bearing down on them. Their strength can be increased by digging deeper foundations, with steel strengthening bars, and by constructing the wall to a batter. Professional advice should be sought in cases where the soil height retained is over 3ft (1m).

Steps

Although often thought of as a nuisance, steps have enormous potential to create interest in the yard, with an endless variety of materials and styles which can be used. While a yard with a gentle but appreciable slope provides the most suitable site for steps, even a flat site has one or two possibilities.

By cutting and filling an area of land, different levels are produced and a step or two can be installed. By raising an area of paving a step will automatically be created, breaking up the expanse of hard surfacing and making a smaller, more intimate area.

Steps need to be easly negotiable, and so the risers and treads must be of suitable size. Risers taller than 18cm (7in) become an effort to climb, while treads narrower than 1ft (30cm) are difficult to descend with ease. Where different levels mean a steep flight of steps, a handrail provides a sense of security. A riser of around 15cm (6in) combined with a 45cm (18in) tread gives a broad step of pleasing proportions and one that can be constructed easily from modern paving materials.

Steps onto a main thoroughfare should be straight and functional, but those elsewhere in the yard can be more decorative, with curves and circles. Changes in direction provide a welcome break from a long flight

Above: *The clean, crisp lines of steps made from concrete paving slabs are softened by the trailing growth of ivy.*

Above: *The timber and gravel steps have been laid to make a graceful curve.*

of steps, and a collection of pots would help to soften the hard, architectural lines of the steps.

Spectacular effects can come from combining steps with other features such as sculpture and water, thus making a point of real emphasis. Careful planting can add yet another dimension by softening, enclosing, and adding colour and life.

Above: A large, flat expanse of paving does little to excite visually. Even by putting in just a small raised area interest is immediately created.

122

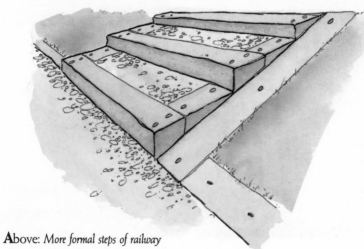

Above: More formal steps of railway sleepers and gravel ascend a grassy bank. The use of additional sleepers as a mowing edge adds a pleasing detail and helps maintenance.

Above: By offsetting stone steps and allowing the planting to encroach, a completely informal arrangement is produced.

Ponds

Water, both still and moving, has enormous potential to improve a backyard. The construction, shape and style of pond will all greatly influence the final atmosphere in the garden.

The effect of ice on the construction of a pool is of paramount importance if you live in a frost-prone area. During the winter months even a thin layer of ice can exert tremendous pressure on the pool sides, causing inferior constructions to crack and therefore to leak. Reinforced concrete in particular produces a rigid pool which requires attention and strengthening to the top section of the pool (where the ice will form in winter), whether the pool is built above ground level or not.

Among the most suitable flexible liners is Butyl rubber, increasingly popular for its long life and easy installation. Ice presents less of a problem to flexible liners, although if a pool is raised it may need the added strength of reinforced concrete to help the surrounding walls withstand any sideways pressure.

Water height fluctuates with evaporation and the operation of waterfalls and fountains, and so the top edge of liner or concrete is often exposed. To overcome this, a stone or brick edge overhang will camouflage the exposed strip and water's edge with an area of deep shadow. Suitable marginal planting can achieve the same result.

Above: *A creative and varied use of plants, in terms of height, colour and texture, leads the eye to the pond.*

The use of any water features must be governed by the overall feel of the garden. A formal layout may suggest a central pool with fountain, whereas a rock garden and waterfall would be better suited to a more natural and informal layout, particularly where a change in levels is already present. Rectangular raised pools with a bubble or geyser fountain and simple fall between two levels would look more in keeping with a modern, geometric layout, as would a large, shallow reflecting pool.

Even the smallest gardens need not be without the pleasure of sound and movement that water gives. A simple wall-mounted mask fountain spurting into a stone trough takes up little space and can provide all the qualities desired. It could also be used as an incidental feature in a larger landscape.

The combining of sculpture, plants and water needs careful consideration. Plants with lush foliage look luxuriant beside a pool, and upright strap-like leaves will help to balance its strong horizontal nature. Remember also the mirror-like quality of water; this should be reflected in the choice of plants placed around the pool. The sculptural element of stone can be very useful, the simple lines of water-worn rocks and cobbles providing the perfect complement to a smooth, untroubled pool.

124

Above: *18 × 24in (45 × 60cm) paving slabs together with a brick-on-edge riser make an easily constructed, well proportioned set of steps.*

Above: *Steps using bricks on edge as the tread. The curved edges of bullnosed bricks make for a softer look. Both flights of steps will need a fairly substantial concrete footing to ensure they remain stable.*

Above: *The combination of a flight of steps and water feature can be particularly attractive.*

Right: *The simple movement of water brings light and life to a shady corner.*

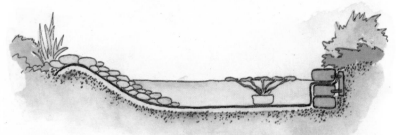

Above: *Two more unusual ways of disguising butyl rubber liner involve the construction of a gently shelving cobble beach or taking the liner up behind a railway tie. The tie would be firmly fixed to other ties with battens or secured to pegs.*

Rock gardens and screes

For a rock garden to have any real effect, it must imitate an alpine scree or rock escarpment as closely as possible. Rocks should be sorted into various sizes, using the largest at the base and smaller ones higher up. Only a small proportion of the rock should be exposed, with the remainder being buried in soil. The rock strata should be aligned in a single plane to give the effect of a natural outcrop. Smaller rocks can be carefully placed immediately next to each other to take on the appearance of a single larger piece if this effect is required.

In yards without natural slopes, the back of the rock garden may be supported by a brick or concrete block retaining wall. Such an arrangement must be heavily planted, however, and the rock garden kept low to prevent it seeming out of place.

The scree garden takes its name from the bank of loose chippings found at the base of a rock face, and is easier to reproduce in a back yard. A small raised bed surfaced with a mulch of stone chippings and the occasional embedded rock is the ideal habitat for many alpines and dwarf conifers and shrubs. A sunny situation and suitable drainage is needed, though. A scree garden can exist simply in a large bowl or stone trough which incorporates plants and rocks of similar scale.

A *miniature scree garden can be constructed in a large sink or pot (above) which makes a good setting for the beauty of alpine plants.*

Right: *A framework of black-painted metal provides interesting support for plants, and the bold dark leaves of* Ligularia *provide an impressive contrast.*

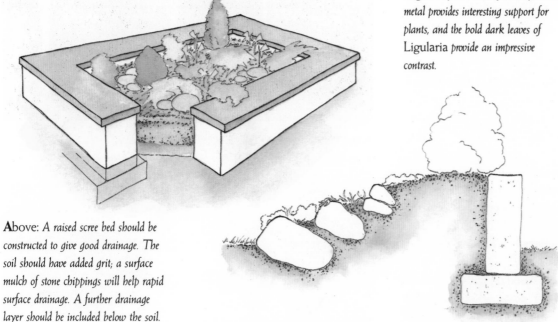

Above: *A raised scree bed should be constructed to give good drainage. The soil should have added grit; a surface mulch of stone chippings will help rapid surface drainage. A further drainage layer should be included below the soil.*

Above: *When a rock garden is not built on a natural slope, the drop behind should be screened by larger plants. Most of the rock will remain hidden, although smaller rocks may be placed together to make them look stronger.*

Trellis work

Trellis gives immediate height to any landscape design, and is the perfect support for climbing plants such as clematis or roses. It works well as a screen as it interrupts a view without completely hemming a yard in. Foliage-covered trellis is particularly useful for internal divisions in the yard, allowing occasional glimpses through to provide interest.

Traditionally constructed in squares or diamonds, trellis needs to be fairly substantial to be of any long-term use in the garden. Maintenance is difficult, if not impossible, once climbers are heavily entwined, and small timbers would quickly deteriorate thanks to rain and wind.

White-painted trellis stands out, but should not be overused as it has a tendency to make the yard seem smaller. Conversely, a dark-stained trellis will provide a mellow, sombre framework for climbers which will merge more naturally with the surrounding planting.

Panels with curved and shaped tops can transform a plain trellis screen, and decoration of the posts with finials will create a distinctive style. Special 'perspective panels' (which can be bought ready made) can also be incorporated in a screen or against a wall to open up an apparent alley or vista, particularly when used in conjunction with a mirror.

The look of a trellised yard can be completed with a range of matching artefacts such as obelisks or spheres.

Pergolas

In a similar way to trellis, a pergola — an arbour or garden walk arched with climbing plants — gives instant height to a yard, and in a small space utilizes the area above ground, thereby increasing the scope for plant growth.

Once the planting is established, the pergola gives a dappled shade beneath providing an enclosed and protected area. The transition from an open terrace to a path straddled and shaded by a pergola leading to an open lawn is one of the strongest, most enticing ways of guiding people out into a yard.

The pergola straddling a path can act as a frame for a suitable ornament or piece of planting. A simple seat backed by dark planting would give an ideal goal to head towards.

Pergolas also make an ideal transition from the dark of the house to the brightness of the garden. A simple covering could be used to create a loggia effect, giving protection on a cool or breezy night.

The pergola's screening properties prevent the eye straying upwards to overbearing buildings, keeping it settled down amongst the surrounding garden. If space is limited, a 'single bar' pergola constructed along the boundary or across the yard will give additional height and pleasantly enclose the environment. Its height can be adjusted to screen a line of windows or nearby telephone cables.

The construction of pergolas is generally based on timber, although steel or concrete may be used with timber posts or brick piers as support. Heavier timber is better for a solid, sturdy-looking construction and of course lasts longer. The shade and support that the pergola offers will depend on the number and frequency of crossbars installed, and the spacing between climber-bearing posts. Plastic-coated or galvanised

A *more elegant pergola with cast iron pillars and a timber beam.*

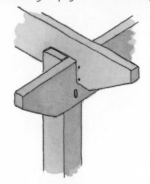

Above: *The posts, beams and crossbeams must be securely fixed to provide strength and stability.*

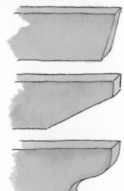

Above: *Simple finishes for pergola beams and cross beams.*

126

wires stapled across the crossbars will provide additional support for climbers where necessary.

Any further finishes will obviously be selected to blend with the general style of the yard. Attendant climbers may be chosen to give a single period of massed display, or as often preferred in a small yard, as an ongoing show of flower and leaf colour.

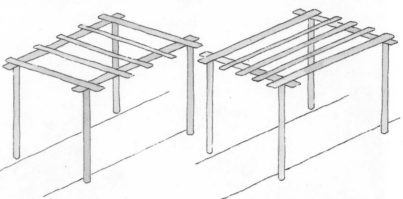

Left: *A sturdy pergola with brick piers and weathered hardwood beams and crossbeams. The generous proportions allow easy movement beneath.*

Above, left and right: *Simply altering the direction of the cross beams can give a tremendous sense of direction.*

127

Garden ornament

Just how much ornament is included in the yard relies heavily on personal tastes, as does the choice of ornament itself. Statues, sculpture, pots and tubs will all attract the eye, and so could be used with care to create specific points of interest. Pots and tubs will help to break and punctuate a paved terrace and are particularly useful close to the house where they can be watered frequently with ease.

Sculpture and statues combine well with water. A smaller piece used as a distant attraction needs a similarly scaled enclosure, such as a small niche. The possibilities are limited only by imagination and it is worth looking out for special additions for your yard. Simplicity of form is often the best thing to aim for.

Above: *Concrete sheep add relief and humour to a shaded lawn.*

Old *chimney pots* (left) *are harder to come by as they become more fashionable. Filled with ivy-leaved geraniums, lobelia and* Tagetes *they make a colourful display.*

Boundaries, backdrops and special features

Garden design styles

chapter seven

GARDEN DESIGN STYLES

Planting design is far more than just using pretty flowers, glorious autumn tints, seasonal effects or fashionable new hybrids. It includes these elements, but in a context that is much wider and more appropriate to the garden in question. Equally, hard landscape design is not simply a facility for the display of objects, and it is quite definitely not about dotting baroque cupids, ivy-clad rustic birdbaths or gnome-like concrete horrors around the garden. But how should you decide which elements of planting or decoration preserve a place in your yard? This chapter aims to deal with this question by looking at several specific styles of landscape feature: foliage, city, wild, edible, flower and formal.

129

The seclusion offered by a terrace is for many the ultimate achievement in garden design. The textured surfaces of foliage and paving form a room, defining space in a way which is both versatile and informal. The atmosphere is evocative of long summer days and warm sultry nights when outdoor living comes into its own.

The foliage landscape

Colour in planting design is most frequently associated with flowers — their brilliant hues and delicate shapes are seen as the epitome of beauty and grace. Although it would be difficult to ignore their charm, it pays to look beyond the transient flashes of inspiration. Foliage, particularly evergreen foliage, creates a permanent feature in the landscape but often attractive colour is revealed in deciduous species in the darkest months of winter. Herbaceous plants show dramatic growth over short periods of time, expressed chiefly in foliage bursting fresh from the earth.

Foliage does more, then, than simply enhance the flowers it frames. It enriches the landscape with architectural shapes and forms, interesting colour variations and a variety of textures.

FOLIAGE FORMS

Foliage is found in so many guises as to make generalization difficult. It is easiest to consider foliage in terms first of screening or background scenery and then in terms of specific accent or specimen planting.

In the former category is a vast number of species with inconspicuous or neutral leaves, which can be used to screen or to create privacy. They also provide structure or a background wash of colour or texture against which more flamboyant material is displayed to dramatic effect. Control and understatement form the essence of good design in this respect for, as with flowers, too much decoration, colour

or pattern simply confuses. The great herbaceous borders of the traditional English garden were all framed by the smooth dark velvet-green of yew hedging.

In the other category, accent plants demand attention. These are the jewels of foliage planting whose qualities and characteristics are dynamic, bold and theatrical. The grass-like texture of bamboo (*Miscanthus* or *Arundinaria*), the sword-shaped leaves of New Zealand flax (*Phormium tenax*), the glossy heart-shaped spread of the fatsia leaf (*Fatsia japonica*) and the gigantic veined and fleshy splendour of *Gunnera manicata* indicate the variety and range of plant material available. The art of using these plants well lies in the careful positioning of specimen plants against a neutral backdrop.

Alternatively, foliage plants can be massed together in stands of the same species. Where space permits create patterns and textures in bold swathes but in small areas, combine a number of individual plants with differing leaf characteristics in small informal groups. Foliage can contrast in terms of shape, texture and colour or associations of plants may be developed which share a common characteristic, such as leaf colour. The same association, if successful, could be repeated throughout a yard (depending on its size) to introduce a feeling of continuity and rhythm. In affect you are sculpting with plant material, working in three dimensions with foliage, light and space.

130

Right: *The rigid geometry of topiary relies on the fine textures of box* (Buxus sempervirens) *for edging and yews* (Taxus baccata) *for the main structure. Contained within are themed borders of foliage or flower colour which contrast well with the dark dense hedging.*

Right: *The qualities of decorative foliage are often expressed in waterside planting, where large leaves and spiky rushes seem to embody the concept of water itself. Here the overhanging canopy filters and dissipates the sunlight, producing strong patterns and a multitude of shapes and colours.*

Garden design styles

SEASONAL ATTRIBUTES

The seasons affect plant associations. The changes are unavoidable and challenging, but also most welcome. Spring brings fresh new growth and a sense of excitement and anticipation, changing and maturing the planting design. Summer develops the foliage, and the bright sunshine plays light against shadow. Luxuriant growth revels in warmth and deep, cool greens relax the mind.

The more golden light and deeper shade of autumn complement new colours in the dying foliage. Gardeners are often tempted to clear and tidy their gardens too quickly at this time but the lingering coppers and golds of strewn leaves provide the last links with summer and dead foliage has a sweetness of its own.

As autumn turns to winter, the foliage recedes and the framework of the plant itself is introduced. Here the texture of bark or the colour of stems become the focal points in planting design, complemented by the tracery of the branches. Fiery crimsons of dogwood *(Cornus)*, delicate purples of willows *(Salix)* and papery layers of birch *(Betula)* or maple *(Acer)* bark are some of the options available to the designer. The cinnamon trunk of the strawberry tree *(Arbutus unedo)* or the fabulous tracery of the Indian bean tree *(Catalpa bignonioides)* are elements often forgotten in landscape design. Remnants of berries echo the rich colours of winter and seem particularly attractive against stark branches.

Evergreen plant material provides continuity through these seasons and also complements the naked branches of deciduous plants. It is important to think across the full spectrum of evergreen material. Although conifers, so widely used, have much to offer in form and texture broad-leaved evergreens provide a valuable alternative. The evergreen or holly oak *(Quercus ilex)* is dark and majestic, ivy *(Hedera)* climbs or covers the ground in a multitude of varieties and cabbage palms *(Cordyline australis)* offer an exotic quality.

The blue-grey leaves of the *Eucalyptus* characterize an unusual evergreen species which can be grown as a shrub or a tree depending on the species, and are valuable in theme planting where foliage colour is as important as flower. The magical quality of white or silver plant associations is so over-used as to be almost a designer cliché but the frosted, mystical charm of such planting is difficult to ignore. Alternatively fiery combinations of reds, purples and yellows provide drama and excitement.

Playing with coloured foliage, as with texture and shape, is rather like trying to find the correct sequence for a combination lock by trial and error. Many combinations are possible and every so often you succeed in cracking the code. The effect can be inspirational, but lasting beauty and a sense of balance are usually achieved through control and restraint in choosing plant material and simplicity and caution in arranging shapes and forms.

132

The curving path becomes lost in a deep border of foliage colour and contrast with climbers, conifers and ground-cover clothing almost every surface. The fallen tree leads the way alongside the path, decorated with Hedera helix *and* Viola X wittrockiana.

Today a large proportion of any country's population resides in urban areas. Towns and cities offer many attractions, but from a landscape design viewpoint, the possibilities and options appear limited. The restricted space, disturbing background or neighbourhood noise, the lack of privacy and the problem of pollution all mean that the creation of a small oasis of peace and greenery is difficult, if not impossible, to achieve. In fact, there are many design options available and the challenge of a city property has produced some of the most imaginative design solutions in gardening.

PLANTING

Although it is possible to design a yard or terrace that is wholly reliant on hard materials for effect, in an urban space this would be a mistake. The over-riding impression of most towns and cities is their hard, man-made environment from which the green space or rural idyll provides a much sought-after relief. The soft lines and patterns of plant material, by changing with the seasons, keep us in touch with nature, help us to relax the busy mind and provide a distraction or inspire a hobby.

Compost-filled containers or pots provide a growing medium that will support an abundance of plant material. Generally, the larger the pot, the more vigorous and healthy the plant, or the greater the variety of material capable of cultivation. The most important point is the container's ability to retain enough moisture within the soil to support plant life, without needing to be topped up daily. Ameliorants within the compost can help with this. Otherwise periods of absence, on holidays in particular, can thwart your efforts.

Terracotta and other clay pots, although attractive, do absorb the available moisture quickly and the soil is left dry and cracked. PVC or fibreglass containers retain moisture much more efficiently, though excess water must be allowed to drain away.

It is a good idea to use the cheaper or more functional PVC containers for lining much more attractive clay containers, a solution offering the best compromise between looks and efficiency. Alternatively, dense planting in containers with additional annual or seasonal planting, will cover even more unsightly pots successfully so that they become almost invisible.

Irrigation tanks can be fitted to larger containers with a filler pipe connected to the surface. Liquid fertilizer and water can be poured into the tank, which then releases the moisture and nutrients into the soil by capillary action. Alternatively, automatic drip-feed irrigation systems can be installed around the planted area.

133

This compact roof-top garden uses timber both for decorative effect and to increase privacy. The pergola construction allows climbing foliage to drape and cover from above. Moveable containers introduce summer or exotic bedding species, which may be taken indoors or into a conservatory over the winter period.

Garden design styles

PLANTING CONTAINERS

Small herbs for scent, or textural grasses and ground-covers, can be accommodated easily in relatively small pots, perhaps 15-30cm (6-12in) deep. Annuals and colourful bedding plants can be grown in similar depths. It is best to plant one species as a mass in one container, or different species with the same colour range or theme and to introduce bold splashes of colour rather than use just one or two plants.

Larger shrubs or spreading ground-covers and climbing plants need containers of 45-75cm (18-30in) deep to sustain their demand for moisture without constantly suffering from drought. The extra depth also means greater stability through the rot system. Greater diameters are the result of greater depth in a container and the restriction of space may dictate the sparing use of containers such as these.

Small trees may also be accommodated but you need at least 90cm (3ft) or more of soil to grow them successfully. The same proportions should be adhered to with built-in containers. Often the structural brickwork can absorb the available moisture or the proximity of buildings may mean that little natural rainfall ever feeds the planting.

The plant material itself can also be manipulated to suit the style of the garden. The more informal arrangements can abound with colour and variety of texture, erupting like a controlled explosion of green foliage, decorative stems and colourful flowers. Perennials, such as rhododendron, sumac, laurel, *Fatsia* or *Cotoneaster*, can provide the main structure. Spikes of iris, New Zealand flax *(Phormium tenax)* and cabbage palm *(Cordyline australis)* provide vertical interest or specimens, whilst intense autumn colour is provided by Japanese maple *(Acer palmatum)*, the smoke tree *(Cotinus coggygria)* or Chinese witch-hazel *(Hamamelis)*.

Pots of Pelargonium, tobacco plant *(Nicotiana)*, mint *(Mentha)*, miniature rose *(Rosa)*, pinks *(Dianthus)* and *Fuchsia* can provide a broad spectrum of summer colour and scents with daffodil *(Narcissus)*, hyacinth, crocus, *Muscari* and *Primula* producing softer shades in spring.

For shaded areas, try *Hosta, Fatsia*, ivy *(Hedera)* and ferns. The climbing hydrangea *(Hydrangea petiolaris)* is useful for brightening cold dark walls.

SPACE AND ILLUSION

The eye can be deceived by playing with perspective, by emphasizing converging lines in planting borders, using large-leaved plants adjacent to the house or in the foreground and small-leaved plants in the distance or towards the end of the yard. Whites, greys and blues appear distant and red or yellow appear stronger and closer.

Ornament or sculpture can be used as a focal point to draw the eye into the imagined distance, whilst trellis can frame or direct the eye. *Trompe l'oeil* can deceive with the illusion of space or activity beyond the garden. Mirrors can also be used to reflect the surrounding boscage and hint at a space beyond.

PRIVACY AND SHELTER

Privacy may be difficult to achieve in a space that is overlooked by neighbouring houses on all sides. Screening with climber-covered trellis may help in proximity to the house. Otherwise, pergolas when clothed with climbing plants can promote an overhead canopy under which you can entertain, dine or simply relax with a good book.

Take care when planting climbers. The immediate vicinity of walls and buildings is usually very dry. Plant at least 45cm (18in) away from the structure to allow the roots to seek moisture successfully. Climbers can be pruned and trimmed into shape as an alternative to rampant uncontrolled growth. Pyracantha is particularly useful in this respect as it can be closely trimmed and shaped. It also flowers profusely and produces rich red or orange berries in autumn. Virginia creeper also provides a vivid display of fiery red leaves that drop to reveal a delicate tracery against the stone or brickwork.

135

Opposite: *This garden illustrates the value of bold foliage planting to create an atmosphere of seclusion. The use of different-sized pots together with the bright red parasol add drama and colour, and the impression of sunlit space beyond the terrace is very strong.*

Above: *The timber decking helps to relate the hard materials of the house to the densely planted garden. The walls play an important part in this softening effect, supporting climbing plants such as* Clematis, Hedera *and* Parthenocissus. *The planting drops vertically down to ground level to create depth and height, and the variegated leaf of* Hedera helix *"Glacier" breaks the monotony of green.*

The wild landscape

As human pressures destroy the landscape around us the idea of a wild landscape, in which plants and animals are shielded from the ravages of progress, grows in popularity and value. The idea is not new.

William Robinson and Gertrude Jekyll were responsible at the turn of the century for stimulating moves away from rigid planting plans and formal designs. Their use of native and special plants in woodlands and flowering borders created a novel aura of disorder, impressionistic mixes of colour and exuberant nature.

Although their work was inspiring and influential, the wild landscapes that have developed recently are quite different — flowering meadows, dark, still, ponds with floating lilies and spiky rushes, damp bogs with golden marsh marigolds and quiet woodlands with bustling verges and clearings. These elements all, of course, occur naturally and even if you think they are impossible to recreate, the opposite is true.

Ecologists would argue that intensively mown lawns are sterile and unimaginative compared with the alternative of a colourful, easily maintained, species-rich environment, otherwise known as a meadow.

The associations of grasses and flowerng plants give the verges their romantic connotations. The picture of poppies swaying in corn fields and verges (not strictly meadows) is evocative of warm hazy summer days, their vivid scarlet and dusty gold sympathetic to the sultry atmosphere. Snakeshead fritillary lends a more sinister beauty to the water meadow with its quivering snake-like flowers. These decorative blooms are set amidst the fine emerald spikes of grasses, expressing the movement of the wind waving their delicate seed-heads.

A meadow can be recreated on the scale of the back yard, without the well-manicured lawn being squeezed out altogether. The mowing regime adopted can allow fine ornamental turf to co-exist alongside longer grass verges containing the meadow species. Borders, pathways and lawn areas are easily created, harsh lines are eliminated and the effect is subtle but effective. Strimming machines allow you to cut the grass to any height but the timing of the cut is important.

Daffodils and other spring bulbs rejuvenate by drawing strength from their leaves, which should not be cut back for some time after flowering. Late spring and early summer flowers must be allowed to finish their flowering cycle so that those that set seed may do so, thus ensuring continuity for the next season. The same applies to late summer flowers.

136

Right: A complex arrangement of colour and texture introduce a wild character to this mass of planting. Lysimachia and Lilium boast vivid colour against the finer variegated texture of Phalaris arundinacea "Picta".

Right: Delicate poppy heads decorate the European countryside with fluttering crimson petals, often waving in the golden haze of cornfields, as if in some impressionist painting. As seeds are brought to the surface they explode and grow, eventually producing lantern-like heads in late summer.

Garden design styles

WOODLAND EDGE

Many of the species associated with meadows and grassland adapt to the fringes of woodland, scrub and hedgerows or field boundaries. The intermingling of field and woodland plants provides a species-rich community which crosses the boundary between full and deep shade.

Here tiny mounds of spring primroses *(Primula vulgaris)* are followed by towering spikes of pink-freckled foxglove *(Digitalis purpurea)*. Flowering thorn species *(Crataegus)* and viburnums tangle with scrambling roses, honeysuckle *(Lonicera)* and clematis, their simple flowers providing elegant alternatives to often over-embellished garden varieties.

Groups of small trees, appropriate to the back yard scale, such as birch *(Betula)* or alder *(Alnus)* offer spring catkins and flickering summer shade. If space allows, a small thicket can provide a woodland effect. This transition zone between field and wood can be easily compressed into a community of plants only 5-10cm (2-4in) across.

WATER

The inclusion of water in the wild landscape is essential. Even the smallest pool is capable of supporting plants from a variety of water habitas. Water lilies *(Nymphaea)* float serenely on the surface of a pond while their roots plummet to invisible depths below. Marginal plants such as iris, water mint *(Mentha aquatica)*, and water forget-me-not *(Myosotis palustris)* escape from the pond bed. The marsh marigold *(Caltha palustris)* or ragged robin brighten rank bog planting before dry land is regained.

Butyl liners or prefabricated pond liners are relatively cheap and are ideal for sealing porous ground to allow water to collect to form small pools. It is surprising how quickly such man-made elements are colonized by flora and fauna to provide one of the most satisfying and interesting of ecosystems.

WILD ANIMALS

The creation of wild habitats should attract wildlife immediatèly. Indigenous plants provide basic foodstuffs — berries, nectar, seeds and nuts — creating the shelter and protection necessary for nesting or burrowing animals.

For most property owners it is exciting and fulfilling to provide such shelter for a variety of birds and mammals, bringing us closer to nature. Wildlife activity identifies the passage of the seasons as birds return to nest, ground hogs sniff and poke for food after their long hibernation and the air is filled with the buzzing drone of bees or the brilliant flashes of darting dragonflies enjoying the warmth of the summer sun. Decaying vegetation or wood in discreet piles will encourage insect life which in turn attracts birds.

Allowing the odd nettle patch to thrive or introducing buddleia, brambles, viburnum, mint and lavender into the borders will attract butterflies and bees. Although native species are attractive to and valuable for wildlife, exotic annuals and shrubs will not detract from the wild quality of the yard if used sympathetically. The tobacco plant provides a sweet fragrance unmatched on warm evenings.

An exuberant mix of foliage pattern and filigree light and shade makes this woodland floor rich in colour and texture. Fine grasses, ferns and shrubs cover the ground in an ad hoc mixture, whilst light penetrates the canopy in camouflage shapes.

The edible garden

Fruit and vegetable plots have a utilitarian character that often relegates them to a small patch in the garden at the furthest point from the house. Here, alongside compost heaps, stores of timber and disused machinery, the rows of plants produce their crops. But food production in the back yard does not need to be like this. In the wider definition of edible plants all kinds of fruiting, culinary, vegetable and seed-bearing species may be included. Many of these plants are highly decorative and colourful, more than capable of standing alongside more widely accepted flowering or foliage plants.

Even a complete yard could be devoted to edible plants and achieve decorative effect. Many of the more ornate plants are already in common use. The globe artichoke (*Cynara scolymus*) can easily be incorporated into a herbaceous border, as it grows about 1.8m (6ft) tall, with grey-green floral bracts and attractive thistle-like flowers. The heads are edible in the bud stage and the leaves can be used like celery.

Some culinary herbs such as dill (*Peucedanum graveolens*) and fennel (*Foeniculum vulgare*) possess fine feathery leaves and large umbelliferous flowers. Together with angelica (*Angelica archangelica*), they provide height and foliage interest. Marjoram (*Origanum vulgare*) and thyme (*Allium schoenoprasum*) give vertical interest in clumps of rich green with the bonus of delicate purple flowers.

Many knot gardens were traditionally devoted to herbs. From medieval times, monasteries would possess a herb garden, usually simply laid out, where the culinary and medicinal plants were grown. In the Renaissance, these gardens became highly elaborate with grand geometric beds, edged with clipped box (*Buxus sempervirens*), creating formal parterres. Decorative plants and coloured gravels usually filled out the pattern.

Nowadays herbs are usually grown in a much less formal manner, often in free-standing pots. The containers can be arranged in informal groups to take advantage of the sunniest positions or to stand close to the kitchen for easy access when cooking. The idea of low hedging separating plant material can still be applied to the contemporary garden to create controlled colour schemes for borders or terraces. The idea might also be adopted in the vegetable garden to create sections for specific plants. Indeed, the old-fashioned *potager* consisting of formal, neatly arranged beds for herbs and vegetables are still viable today. Some kind of logic and order is required in fruit and vegetable cultivation. From a functional aspect crop rotation, easy access and plot-size are all important considerations when planning a vegetable garden.

DECORATIVE EDIBLE PLANTS

Each vegetable has an inherent decorative property, whether the tubular vertical leaves of the onion (*Allium cepa*), or the feathery plumes of carrot (*Daucus carota*). Use these textures in rows and stripes for strong abstract pattern in a variety of shades from palest green to deepest blue.

Trellis or framework can support beans (*Phaseolus coccineus*) with their decorative orange-red flowers. The frames can be made in a variety of shapes to enclose or screen sections of the garden.

Fruit lends itself to similar training methods with espaliers, fans or cordons tied back to fine wire supports. Their decorative charm is enhanced by delicate blossom in spring and blush-tinted fruits in late summer or early autumn. These growing methods are economical in terms of ground coverage and resultant high cropping, although many free-standing miniature fruit trees are now available if you prefer.

The protection of a south-facing wall in colder climates can be used to support the fine branches of peaches and nectarines (*Prunus*). Their downy flesh against the terracotta of old brick or whitewashed surfaces produces a splendid combination of colour and texture. The more alluring charm of the fig (*Ficus carica*) with its decorative and unusual leaf can also be displayed to good effect against a wall, although as a free-standing courtyard specimen it looks even better. Equally attractive are the sinuous branches of the vine (*Vitis vinifera*), curling out along horizontal supports, garlanded with crenated leaves and blessed with lightly bloomed branches of purple or green-white grapes. Many of

139

Rows of different vegetables produces stripes of textured green, like some abstract painting or collage. This kind of decoration is incidental to the production of crops which demands neatness and order, but in a large kitchen garden, for instance, the effect can be very dramatic.

the vine species are used as decorative plants regardless of their fruiting capacity, which comes as an added bonus. Their large leaves are handsome and colour extremely well in autumn.

Ground covering plants such as strawberry and marjoram would grow together with carrots or peas *(Pisum sativum)*, sprinkled between with flowering plants such as delphinium *(Delphinium consolida)*, lupin *(Lupinus polyphyllus)* and hollyhock *(Althea rosea)*. The primrose *(Primula vulgaris)*, heartsease *(Viola tricolor)* and daffodil *(Narcissus pseudonarcissus)* would also decorate the garden. Flowers rich in nectar would be included to feed the bees to produce honey.

Many of the idyllic scenes of cottage gardens can be reproduced in the contemporary garden with improved varieties and more colourful species. Vivid purple or russet-fringed cabbages, such as "Sekito", an ornamental variety, or "Ruby Red", can decorate the border, surrounded by decorative herbs such as bronze fennel *(Foeniculum vulgare* "Giant Bronze")*, purple sage *(Salvia officinalis* "Purpurascens")* or the silver curry plant *(Helichrysum angustifolium)*.

The combinations of edible species interplanted with delicate roses, herbs and soft fruits are the true prizes of the edible garden, providing treats for the eye as well as the palate.

In planning for produce, take time to consider your requirements. Think of the edible species as alternative options to the standard range of flowering plants or decorative shrubs. They possess similar textural foliage or colour properties. Many are compatible with most other garden plants, and have the extra qualities that excite our taste buds and decorate our plates. Little in life is quite fulfilling, or tastes quite as good, as growing your own.

140

Left: *This recreation of a cottage garden mixes herbs, vegetables, fruit and flowers in decorative combinations. As a working garden, many would prefer a more ordered approach which can look sterile in comparison, but many combinations of these plants are possible.*

Right: *This simple herb garden uses the plants around the main entrance. The sunny location will produce strong scents and rigorous growth. Incorporte the herbs in pots too, which may be arranged or rearranged at will. Herbs such as thyme* (Thymus), *mint* (Mentha) *or chamomile* (Anthemis) *may be introduced to invade paved areas, softening the harsh lines and filling cracks with foliage.*

Garden design styles

Garden design styles

Flowers are at the forefront of most gardeners' minds. Perhaps it is their purity of colour which attracts us, their abstract simplicity or their impressionistic sweeps of colour seen from a distance, catching the eye or presenting an image of romantic charm. In seeking to capture these snap-shots of nature in our gardens, we sometimes lose the freshness and naive charm of nature's creations and substitute them with gaudy, ostentatious alternatives.

Ideally, you should use flowers as sparingly or carefully as you would use decoration in your home. Too much information in pattern, colour and shape can lead to a tangled, incoherent mess. Value flowers, treasure their specific qualities and set them like jewels in a frame, contrasted with neutral foliage to enhance and accentuate their worth.

COLOUR

Flower colour can be manipulated by the gardener to produce co-ordinated, sophisticated colour schemes, mixing colours within a range to provide harmonious sweeps from white to pink, pink to red, red to orange and so on. Alternatively, a single colour may be adopted as a theme where flowers are restricted to monochromatic white, quiet pastels or hot oranges and yellows. Gertrude Jekyll and Vita Sackville-West both brought this style to perfection.

Alternatively, use strength of flower colour to produce abstract shapes or masses in fiery red, brilliant yellow or vivid blue. Foliage helps to emphasize shape or provide atmosphere with spires of cordyline (*Cordyline australis*), yucca (*Yucca gloriosa*) or bamboo (*Arundinaria japonica*).

Colour-themed garden borders are difficult to achieve and require a great deal of planning. Whilst a number of different flowers may sit happily within a colour range, the various species used may not flower in the sequence intended; equally they may all flower at once. Foliage characteristics then play a more important role, and have little in common with the intended scheme.

It is important to understand about colour harmonies and contrasts. Contrasting colours are opposites in the spectrum, so red opposes green and yellow opposes purple. To achieve harmony, these opposites need to balance each other within a particular colour scheme.

Pastel colours tinted with white achieve a harmonious range more easily. Few colour clashes or contrasts are possible within this range as the purity and strength are absent. The proportions or amounts of colour used may also achieve a kind of harmony or balance. When organizing a colour theme border it is important to remember that warmer colours such as reds, oranges and yellows appear to advance towards you and appear closer than blues, greens and violets, which tend to recede into the distance.

If planning a single-colour-themed border, do not exclude all other colours. A white garden can include other tones, perhaps yellow and

143

Left: *The flower beds of* Lilium regale, Allium giganteum *and* Verbascum olympicum *all share a certain light-reflecting quality. The sulphur-yellow and rich purple of* Verbascum *and* Allium *respectively are echoed in the huge trumpet-like flowers of* Lilium, *which blows its powerful scent around the garden.*

Above: *This narrow pathway is almost hidden by overwhelming borders of flowers. The hot pinks of roses and scarlets of poppies are balanced by the cooler white of* Chrysanthemum *and the tall spikes of pale pink foxgloves (*Digitalis*). The path could be a little wider to match the line of the steps though some of the overgrown charm would be lost.*

certainly green in small amounts. In the words of Gertrude Jekyll, "a blue garden may be hungering for a group of white lilies or for something of the palest lemon yellow, but it is not allowed to have it because it is a blue garden…my own idea is that it should be beautiful first and then just as blue as may be expected with its best possible beauty."

DECORATIVE FLOWER FORMS

We appreciate flowers particularly for their decorative qualities. Their intricate patterns and exquisite forms express purity, perfection and beauty.

Highly structured flowers, such as lily *(Lilium)*, day lily *(Hemerocallis)*, rose *(Rosa)* and paeony *(Paeonia)* are feats of architectural design in miniature. They possess exotic qualities and compete successfully with even the fabulous tropical species such as passion flower *(Passiflora caerulea)* and bird of paradise *(Strelitzia reginae)*.

More simple arrangements of petals, usually single flowers, are often overlooked as horticulturalists seek ever more decorative flowers. The purity and simplicity of the Himalayan blue poppy *(Meconopsis betonicifolia)*, tree mallow *(Lavatera arborea)*, quince *(Chaenomeles speciosa or C. X superba)* and camellia are valuable additions to many borders.

Some trees produce quite stunning flowers, apart from the heavy pink clusters of the much-favoured flowering cherry. The tulip tree *(Liriodendron tulipifera)*, famed for its unusual leaf, is covered in yellow-green flowers in high summer. Cream candlestick flowers stand erect all over the horse chestnut *(Aesculus hippocastanum)* in late spring and its graceful, drooping white bracts give *Davidia involucrata* its common names of pocket handkerchief tree or dove tree.

The golden rain of laburnum *(Laburnum X watereri "Vossii")* brings sunlit yellow into the garden with its long drooping racemes of flowers. It is possible to train laburnum against a wall or over a pergola or archway.

Trees or large flowering shrubs should be used to introduce structure to the flowering border. They have a mass and solidity which holds together the often disparate shapes of flowering plants.

As an alternative backdrop use climbers such as wisteria *(Wisteria sinensis)*, clematis *(Clematis)*, rose *(Rosa)*, climbing hydrangea *(Hydrangea petiolaris)* and canary creeper *(Tropaeolum peregrinum)*.

Unusual flowers should be used sparingly to avoid the curiosity factor. It pays to think of flowering plants as the essential fabric of the garden rather than as a collection of ornaments. One or two exotic specimens among more mundane species will add to their effect and increase their value.

Fatsia japonica produces globular bream-green umbels to match the summer heads of angelica *(Angelica archangelica)*. Verbascum spires flash

with sulphurous yellow flowers almost hidden in grey woolly leaves, tiny gypsophila flowers *(Gypsophila paniculata)* float cloud-like amongst the undergrowth and feathery astilbe or rodgersia complement it with pinks and creamy whites. Schizophragma *(Schizophragma integrifolia)* suspends graceful teardrops from its climbing branches whilst below the elegant arum lily *(Zantedeschia aethiopica)* is difficult to surpass.

Enjoy the design possibilities presented by flower gardening. The cottage garden look may be regarded as a relatively easy option where wonderful combinations of flowers are the result of happy accident. The cottage garden, often perceived as the epitome of the flower garden also contained fruit and vegetables as it had to be functional.

The rose garden is one of the most popular images of flower gardening and certainly the profusion and quality of flower of any rose is difficult to match. Display the flowers against dark foliage backgrounds for the best contrast. This also helps to disguise the awkward shape of the shrubs, which often become leggy or disfigured by pruning. Using groundcover beneath the plants is another option. Grow roses for scent and colour, rather than as a horticultural exercise which often results in patchy colour from individual plants or flowers.

144

The formal garden

Formality in the garden can be interpreted in many ways. Formal gardens can take many different forms: grand avenue, parterres, knot gardens, vistas and geometric pools come instantly to mind.

Many of the great gardens of the world are formal, among them those of the Alhambra, Versailles and Hampton Court. In terms of style, the gardens at Hidcote Manor or at Sissinghurst can still be described as formal, yet their character is quite different. What all these gardens have in common is scale. They occupy large areas or depend on long vistas for effect.

SHAPE AND PATTERN

Formality in garden or landscape design is symbolic of man's domination over nature and his environment. It communicates order and organization impressing man's achievement upon us.

The French and Italian influence on garden design brought formal layout to a high art form of geometric balance in Western classicism. The main elements were enclosed, directional avenues, large open spaces, parterres, water in cascades, canals or ornamental pools and, where possible, grand staircases. The European gardens of Versailles, Karlsruhe and Potsdam embody this style and are truly grand in scale and imagination.

Symmetry is important to these layouts, introducing balance and harmony. These formidable plans usually emanated from, or revolved around, a residence, usually a formal palace, château or castle. The formal lines of the garden related to the built form and the façades, creating a plinth or setting for the property and translating its vertical form into horizontal decoration.

Away from the terrace, planting should be restricted to foliage plants, shrubs and trees. Little colour is evident traditionally and the herbaceous borders of the English style are something of a compromise.

The dynamic forms and colour schemes of herbaceous planting do not fit in with true formality and symmetry although the material may well be arranged within a formal bed, against clipped hedges or even balanced with other borders. Their beauty lies in dramatic foliage and romantic combinations of flower and colour.

Near the house the treatment was mainly hard becoming softer, though still controlled and moulded into the far distance. These elements still exist in contemporary garden design. The main feature in the majority of gardens is the house, with formal geometric shapes and façades. Somehow those patterns and forms must be reconciled to the garden surrounding the property, which is soft and organic in character.

The terrace or entertaining area of the garden is still one of the main features of the modern garden and here formal elements can be freely introduced. Paving patterns take scale, proportion and geometry from the property creating a transition zone between house and garden where hard surfaces meet and inter-relate with soft plant material. Symmetrical arrangements are well suited to this section of the garden creating strong axes from window views along the terrace and out into the garden beyond. Pots, ornaments or statuary may channel the eye into the chosen vista, which might end with specimen planting, water or sculpture.

FORMAL PLANTING

Planting should be retained in geometric beds, usually in a formal style, perhaps using roses or lavender, with clipped box hedging. The creation of vistas works by continuing views along pre-determined routes. Clipped hedging such as yews *(Texus baccata)*, beech *(Fagus sylvatica)*, hornbean *(Carpinus betulus)* or holly *(Ilex aquifolium)* identifies space with architectural precision. Tapestry hedges mixing various species are useful for introducing colour and texture, contrasting the copper leaves of beech against the velvet green of yew.

Figurative or geometric topiary is only one step away. Exciting

The formal lawn is characteristic of English style. Trimmed to perfection close to the house, the lawn often slips into wild verges or woodland at some distance, or a haw-haw allows a continuous view into parkland beyond.

145

forms and shapes can be incorporated into hedging, and topiary is seen at its best when the dark leafy forms are contrasted with terrace paving or with the smooth green sward of a formal lawn.

The lawn beneath or around the formal elements should be mown to a smooth texture, restricted to bold rectangular shapes and used as a foil for the architecture, ornament and formal planting.

Take care when choosing ornament or statuary; there are many inadequate artefacts now available. Sundials, bird baths, vases and cherubs are mass-produced in poor imitations of stone. These elements are often too small in scale to act as a focus of attention. Even in restricted space aim for bold and dramatic elements, choose terracotta or stone pots of some magnitude, overflowing with exuberant plant material, or use specimen plants or a water feature. Experiment with asymmetry contrasted with symmetry. Contemporary sculpture is often set off well in a formal landscape. It proclaims its presence and strength against a rigid framework. Sculpture is complemented by mobile reflections in the rippling mirrored surface of water.

Pots containing clipped bay (*Laurus nobilis*) or box (*Buxus semper virens*) may be arranged formally in quite tiny spaces and *trompe l'oeil* can create classical vistas on bare walls. Furniture should be rigid and strong, such as timber benches in weathered hardwood or painted softwoods. White or elegant aquamarine are the favourite colour options. Fixed seating works well here to take advantage of particular views or focal points.

Generally the formal garden is regarded as a maintenance liability. Hedges must be pristinely trimmed, decorative bedding effects are changed seasonally, lawns need regular mowing and frequently planted rose beds need a great deal of pruning. These gardens certainly need man's intervention if they are to succeed. Much of the work though is associated with scale: once the scale is reduced, their work requirement is not necessarily greater than any other garden style.

Left: *The exotic spendour of the Alhambra uses water as a major influence. Reflective pools or elegant fountains have a cooling effect using light, sound or moving pattern alongside dark foliage.*

Right: *This small courtyard-style garden is carefully planted with a range of muted evergreens, permitting the paving patterns and the contrived effect of trompe l'oeil to dominate the design. The rich honey colour of the stone contrasts well with terracotta, and is repeated in the containers and brickwork. The gravel dressing and the dark green bench complete a harmonious combination.*

Garden design styles

Small gardens and difficult sites

chapter eight

SMALL GARDENS AND DIFFICULT SITES

Site problems, of one kind or another, are evident on every property. Areas where, for whatever reason, plants are difficult to grow, can rapidly develop into eyesores, harbouring pests and weeds which may threaten the rest of the garden. Careful selection of plants can go a long way toward overcoming the problems presented by awkward locations. Many plants are specifically adapted to conditions that are generally inhospitable; others can be used to disguise unattractive features or brighten a dull corner.

From the gardener's point of view, the amount of time and effort that can be spared for working in the yard are just as important determining factors. Here, again, selecting the right plants and careful design consideration can help to create a landscape which is labour-saving as well as attractive.

149

A *small sand pit set in an area of hard paving* (opposite) *goes a long way to satisfy a child's need for active play and can fit neatly into the overall scheme.*

Design basics

A basic comprehension of landscape design leads to making better decisions concerning both the retention of existing features and in the creation of any new layout. The principal areas of concern are discussed below.

BALANCE

Using three-dimensional drawings, any design can be reduced to a series of voids and masses which helps to check whether a layout is balanced or not. A yard which is unbalanced, particularly along the main viewing axis (usually from the house), will have an unsettled feel to it. The aim in balancing is to achieve an effect where the sum of the masses on each side of the yard is not too dissimilar from that on the other.

The main masses to be considered are buildings and plants, particularly trees and larger, screening plants. An unsightly building on the boundary of a yard will not only need screening but may also require balancing, as the combined effect of a building with a screening planting will be particularly pronounced. Too many points of interest in a small area of the yard will also lead to imbalance. Each major feature should be given its own space, which will not only give it greater impact, but help in the design as a whole.

STRONG LINES AND PERSPECTIVE

The intelligent use of perspective has an important role to play in landscape design. The human eye can be easily deceived or misled in what it sees, and lines running along the site (i.e. away from the house) will tend to lengthen it, while those running across the property will make it appear wider. The lines could be details in the paving, the sides of a path or even the edges of a lawn; they can be used to alter the visual shape of a plot.

Whereas in a large yard perspective will be naturally apparent, in a smaller space this may disappear. However, converging lines will help to force a perspective length, whereas diverging lines will have the opposite, shortening effect. The positioning of features such as paths, pergolas and walls can therefore be used to great effect, and should be undertaken with care. Careful placing of coarser textures — plants with larger leaves, stones or large paving slabs — near the main view point and fine foliage, pea shingle and smaller unit paving further away will deceive the eye. By giving the eye the necessary visual stimuli — in this case, that things in the distance are smaller — the brain can be led to believe that a true perspective exists.

'Atmospheric perspective' can also be used in this situation, and is best described as a watering down of colour as it recedes into the distance: the same effect that gives mountains their blue-grey colour

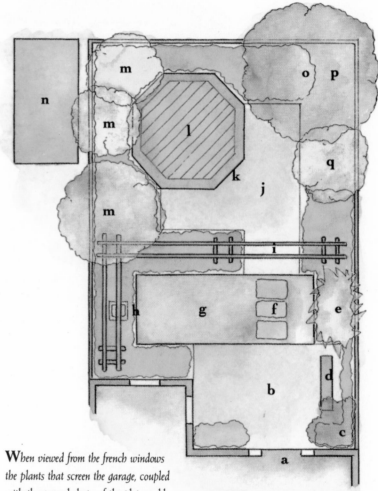

When viewed from the french windows the plants that screen the garage, coupled with the general shape of the plot, could easily unbalance the design. The use of a large tree, bold foliage and a bench to the right of the main viewing axis brings the yard into balance.

KEY: a) french windows; b) paved patio; c) large over-hanging shrub; d) bench; e) large bamboo; f) stepping stones; g) reflecting pool; h) statue/ornament; i) pergola with brick piers; j) paving; k) step up; l) timber-decked sitting area; m) screening tree and shrubs; n) garage; o) large tree; p) compost and storage; q) screening shrub.

150

when viewed from afar. Pastel shades and foliage with a grey or blue hue will bring the feeling of atmospheric perspective into the yard. The opposite foreshortening effect of bright colours applies too, even in a large yard.

TEXTURE

Variety in paving types and leaf size used in the yard will heighten visual interest: everything has a texture, be it in the fine appearance of gravel and closely mown lawn or the boldness of *Bergenia* leaves and cobbles.

The balance of fine and bold textures — and all the stages in between — is a matter of personal taste, but as a rule the bolder textures of cobbles, large foliage types, etc, should be used sparingly. Larger

The straight lines of the path and the repetition of metal arches gives great perspective depth to the view (above) and draws the onlooker into the yard.

Left: A more open but equally good effect is created by this straight gravel path and narrow borders of lavender and bedding plants.

152

Above: *The fine appearance of gravel acts as an excellent foil for the brick-paved circles and paths and the stylish timber seats. The gravel here has been bonded in resin to give a stable surface which can be washed or brushed clean.*

Right: *The tightly clipped foliage of a dwarf box hedge (Buxus sempervirens 'Suffruticosa') would be considered a fine texture until compared with the closely mown lawn. The strong lines running across the view have a foreshortening effect.*

components used to excess can lead to a disturbing imbalance.

Different effects can be created by blending or contrasting various textures, some of which will be quite marked. Coarse textures contrasted against fine — such as bold foliage types against grass or railway sleepers against gravel — can be used to attract and hold the eye successfully. Smooth and fine surfaces, such as paving, grass and gravel, should normally be used as the main surfacing, as they provide an even and unobtrusive background for other, coarser, textures.

Every element used in a garden has to be considered in the context of texture. A paving slab with its smooth surface, for example, would normally be considered a fine texture, but when contrasted with brick or other paving materials, its large size would make it appear coarse. Such anomalies can only add further interest and a case can often be made for breaking the rules.

FRAMING AND SCREENING

If a site is fortunate enough to have a pleasant view, this can be incorporated into the overall design, effectively enlarging the yard. Particularly strong and interesting items such as a distant church spire or a large tree can even be framed to form the main focal point.

Others may wish to screen out or obscure their surroundings. Screening is most commonly provided by planting, fences and walls, although overhead structures also have a part to play. In many small yards, screens are often placed around the edges, but an object nearer the onlooker will screen a larger area than one further away. It might therefore be better to bring the screening into the garden in many cases. A large plant in a tub on the terrace might screen as much as a tree

153

Above: *Alternative panels of insitu concrete and granite setts give textural interest to this bold, sweeping path. The finely cut leaves of bordering geraniums complement the effect.*

Right: *The strongly weeping nature of Betula pendula 'Youngii' (Young's weeping birch) tends to hold the eye down near the ground, a useful ploy when space for screening is limited.*

154

The tall bank and planting of rhododendrons (above) successfully screens the surroundings and helps to focus the eye on the small informal pool below.

An ugly building which overlooks the yard from beyond the perimeter (far left) may be screened just as well by a smaller object or plant placed nearer the viewpoint (centre) as by a much larger object or plant placed further away (left).

placed near the boundary.

If adequate screening is impossible, a strong ground pattern may help to hold the eye within the boundaries. Plants and particularly trees of a weeping nature help, as the eye is liable to follow the line of the tree and so to be returned to ground level.

Just as items beyond the boundaries can be framed, so can objects within the yard. This too can be used to detract from unattractive surroundings.

INTRIGUE

Visual interest is one of the main goals in designing a small area and this can be heightened by creating intrigue. Spacial division, in the form of screens and visual blocks, will accentuate various parts of the yard and so prevent the whole scene being absorbed at once. The scale of division will largely depend on the size of plot, but even a small area hidden from direct view will go a long way towards maximizing interest.

COLOUR

The use of colour in the garden depends on the quality of light as well as individual hues. Although bright colours stand out, they need a high intensity of light to show the true depth of colour. Pale colours, particularly blues, will tend to be washed out by strong sunlight, so a partly shaded position is better for them. Pastel shades have a receding effect in contrast to bright colours, and in general will combine more easily to form an area over which the eye can flow uninterrupted.

Combining colours satisfactorily is a difficult task. Single borders or even whole gardens can be planned on a single colour theme with, for example, a yellow border which encompasses a full range of flowers from rich golds through lime greens to creamy whites. The flowers would be set against a varied backdrop of green, golden and variegated foliage, with touches of grey to add further depth.

The colour of building and paving materials is just as important as that of plants. Mellow stone colours provide the best foil for plants.

The peephole through a garden (left) allows only a restricted view and encourages further exploration.

155

A very open garden (top) holds few surprises and can be taken in almost at a glance. By partly screening an area (above) interest is immediately created without losing the feeling of space.

Unless it is intended to stand out, timber work should be stained dark although lighter colours will tone down as they weather. Green as a stain, paint or stone colouring should generally be avoided. If an object or structure is to be highlighted, white is often the most appropriate colour as it is bright but also combines well with other hues and shades in the garden.

MATERIALS

The selection of paving and walling types is often a daunting prospect. Choose those which are in keeping with the house — after all, it is the largest and most influential part of the setting. Where bricks are to be used they should match the house wherever possible, and when in doubt the simplest materials are likely to be the best. One or two materials used in repetition throughout the design will have a unifying effect, linking the various elements of the yard.

Above: *The bright foliage of massed* Coleus *plants mingle easily together as the colours all come from the limited yellow to red range of the spectrum.*

An elegant white-painted seat makes a commanding focal point.

A *pink grey border (above) give a variation of hues that lead the eye gently along the border.*

Left: *The enormous conifers give the house a quaint appeal.*

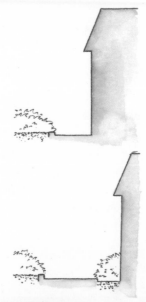

Above: *A narrow terrace is overpowered by the house. Widening the paved area and adding planting by the house gives a far more satisfactory result.*

157

The use of climbers such as Clematis montana rubens *(below) will soften the hard lines of the house.*

The pre-cast concrete paving slab in its vast array of shapes and finishes has been used in the design of many modern yards. But in smaller areas, more expensive, high-quality materials, such as natural stone paving, might be a possible alternative.

SCALE AND PROPORTION

The need for scale in a yard is overwhelming, or one element could easily overpower the others, causing visual disturbance. Similarly too many small features cluttered into a large yard give a 'bitty' and confused look. Architectural features such as paving, paths and walls must be in proportion to the house, and the planting should be in scale with both these and the overall design. These rules extend down to the more intricate levels of pattern and texture. Particular skill must be employed if a tiny garden is to be successfully combined with a large multi-storied house.

In most cases where there is space, a large building will need large-scale planting to merge it into the landscape. Comparatively small

buildings could be dwarfed by a large tree and bold planting, for example, or smaller trees and planting can make it appear larger and more impressive.

One of the most successful ploys in a small garden is to make it appear as the only visible part of a larger estate: mirrors can be used here, apparently opening up whole new vistas and sections of garden. Obscuring the boundaries of a garden with a band of planting and shadows will also immediately disguise its size, making it easier to merge with the house.

The scale of planting not only depends on the size of individual plants, but also on their shape and on the groups in which they are massed. Although of only medium height, the 'Indian Bean Tree', *Catalpa bignonioides*, branches strongly and has stout twigs and enormous leaves and so appears very large in scale. Similarly, where a large scale is necessary, it may be modified by using a big tree with fine tracery and small leaves.

LINKING THE GARDEN AND HOUSE

The house and garden can be closely linked by extending perpendicular lines from points around the house, such as from the corners of walls and the edges of doors and windows. Planting around the foundations of the house and using climbers trained up the walls will help to reduce the sudden junction of vertical and horizontal planes. By softening the hard architectural lines, the house will merge more easily into the garden environment.

WATER

The tranquility of water always makes a commanding feature and, when used properly, brings the landscape life and poetry. Still water will give beautiful reflections, adding an extra dimension to the garden and making a busy space look larger and more relaxed. Care must be taken in providing the correct conditions to prevent stagnation, however, so as to avoid the dead plants and undesirable insects that will result.

The dominating effect of water makes its scale and positioning of utmost importance. It can be sited either as a focal point or as a surprise

Left: *By working outwards from the lines and angles of a house, the building and garden can be successfully combined. The colours of weathered railway sleepers and terracotta tiles tone well with the house bricks.*

This narrow watercourse and rock garden (right) has been excellently constructed to mimic a natural stream.

Far right: *A simple fountain playing over a rock and shallow pool brings this small Japanese garden to life.*

158

element, but it should not be placed where it will detract from a view or another feature of the garden.

As water will fill any given shape it lends itself to both formal and informal gardens, and works particularly well with other landscaping features such as sculpture, lighting or natural stone in the form of cobble beaches or in a 'natural' rock garden. So its uses can be very varied, of a style to suit almost every taste.

Water can be a real liability when children are in the garden, however. But careful consideration of the design can avoid danger. A raised pool, for example, will help keep children out of the water, and by supporting a sturdy metal grid on bricks just below the surface of the water or part-filling the pool with broken stone or cobbles, the depth of the water can be reduced. These solutions retain the aesthetic appeal that fencing or netting over the pool certainly would not.

One final important point to note is the colour of the pool lining. Black is most often recommended, as it provides a good background, lending the pool depth, and interferes far less with reflections than the blue or beige of cheaper liners or the grey of concrete.

159

Difficult sites

SHADE

Most ornamental garden plants are grown for their flowers, and many of these need actual sunlight, not just daylight. But a surprising number will either flower in shade or need shade in order to flower. Shade varies in degree, too; it can be light or dappled, where light filters through small trees, shrubs or fencing; or it can be deep and permanent. The soil in shady areas is often responsible for lack of growth. It can either be wet and badly aerated or dry, because tree roots suck up the moisture or the canopy is too heavy to allow rain to penetrate. The soil must be carefully examined first, then suitable material added to supply humus and grit for drainage, or nutrients if it is sandy. Digging alone will improve matters in most cases; if tree roots are an obstruction use a handfork and deal with a pocket of soil at a time.

Plants suitable for growing in shady conditions		
Ajuga reptans	Deutzia	Lysimachia
Aquilegia	Endymion	Narcissus
Japanese anemone	Ferns	Polygonatum
Bergenia	Hedera spp	Primula
Camellia	Helleborus	Rhododendron
Cyclamen	Heuchera	Vinca
Decentra spectabilis	Hosta	
Digitalis	Lilium	

Above *and right: Foxgloves are easily grown plants, and are naturally found in areas of light woodland, where there is some shade during the day. They self-seed, and there are many hybrids in various shades of pink, purple, cream and yellow.*

Lysimachia punctata *also enjoys shade as well as moisture, and can be situated in borders or by water (far left). Lysimachia nummularia (top left) is a particularly useful species as it will also thrive in dry sites. The hosta is another ideal plant for the shady spots (left and above). They are noted for their mass of attractive foliage as well as their tubular flowers.*

160

DAMP OR WET SOIL

Bog or water-loving plants require this type of soil, but excess moisture will have to be removed if other plants are expected to grow. One method of improving conditions is to dig down to a depth of one or two spits and mix grit into all levels of the soil; or dig a trench 12-18in (30-45cm) deep and either half fill it with brushwood, replacing the topsoil, or quarter fill it with rubble, quarter with brushwood and the remaining half with topsoil. Use tile-drains, if all else fails. Imported soil can be used to build raised beds or, if there is a sunny place, a rock garden could be built.

Plants suitable for growing in damp or wet soil

Alnus	Hosta	Primula
Japanese anemone	Iris	Pulmonaria
Astilbe	Lysimachia	Rodgersia
Caltha	Mimulus	Salix
Hermerocallis	Polyanthus	

If you are faced with a damp patch of garden, marsh marigolds are the ideal plants to grow. Caltha palustris is able to thrive in water, 6in (15cm) deep, and flowers profusely in shades of golden-yellow in midspring (left). Primula denticulata, or the drumstick primula, is another border plant, which thrives in damp, waterlogged conditions (above). It flowers throughout the spring in purplish colours. The monkey flower also grows naturally in boggy conditions. Mimulus luteus is a useful species as it grows as a mat-like cover, producing attractive yellow flowers, often with red markings (above right).

161

Above: Rodgersia pinnata 'Superba' is a useful plant as it may be grown satisfactorily in any damp site, such as by a stream or pool. Large bronze-purple leaves and pink flowers are produced in midsummer and the genus was originally a native of China and Japan.

DRY SOIL

Dry patches can occur anywhere in the garden: in open sunny positions, under trees and especially at the foot of walls facing the sun. To moisten the soil, work in organic material in early spring and again in early summer, which will act as a sponge and help retain the water. This should be followed by a heavy mulch of the same material, which must be placed on moist soil to trap the moisture and keep in the soil warmth. If no vegetative mulch is possible, stones used as a continuous covering will keep the soil moist; so will a black plastic sheet, straw or sawdust. Supply nutrients little and often, and make watering these areas a priority in drought; keep a good stock of watering equipment handy, and arrange for at least one standpoint in the garden.

Plants suitable for growing in dry soil

Achillea	Genista	Salvia
Allium spp	Geranium	Santolina
Alyssum	Helianthemum	Sedum spp
Artemisia	Iberis	Sempervivum
Campanula	Lavandula	Tulipa
Cistus	Phlomis	Verbascum
Cytisus	Potentilla	Veronica
Eschscholzia		

Potentilla fruticosa 'Katherine Dykes' grows to a height of 4ft (1.2m) and requires a dry sunny position (above). Achillea filipendulina is a suitable plant for rock gardens (top right).

162

Above: Alliums are easy to grow, and are often found growing wild in temperate regions. They are bulbous plants, preferring a sandy soil and sunny position. Some have a distinctive onion smell.

Sedums are ideal wall plants with their unusually shaped leaves and flowers (right). They flourish in dry conditions and can survive well in prolonged droughts. Another such plant is the rosette-shaped houseleek (Sempervivum) (left). The curved leaves are often purple-tipped.

ACID SOIL

Fortunately the majority of plants will thrive in any soil regardless of its pH level, but there is a small group which can only be grown easily in acid soil. It is possible, however, to grow any of these in a lime-containing soil, if the soil is suitably prepared. Either dig out a pit and fill it with specially mixed compost whose reaction is acid, or water plants annually with sequestered (chelated) iron, magnesium and manganese formulated in one product. Otherwise, the pH level of the soil can be gradually altered with rotted organic matter, acidic fertilizers, and flowers of sulphur, but this is a slow method and in the case of the sulphur, fraught with danger, as the chemical balance of the soil can be detrimentally altered.

The majority of calcifuges (lime-hating) plants are shrubby; virtually all conifers grow much better in acid conditions. However, some plants are border-line calcifuges, such as camellia, enkianthus, fothergilla, magnolia and mahonia, and, although they will grow in neutral soils, they will do better if helped with leaf-mould or a similar material. Hydrangeas will need acid or alkaline soil depending on the flower colour.

Plants suitable for growing in acid soil		
Calluna	Fothergilla	Magnolia
Camellia	Gentiana	Mahonia
Chimonanthus	Hamamelis	Pieris
Dabeocia	Lilium	Rhododendron
Erica	Lithospermum	Vaccinium
Ferns	Lupinus	

Rhododendrons (left) *will not grow well in alkaline soil and will even struggle in a neutral one. An acid-reacting soil is essential, preferably containing leaf-mould, to produce a longer-living and more floriferous shrub. Pieris formosa 'Forestii' (above) is another acid-loving plant. Its young leaves are coloured brilliant red, providing contrast with its sprays of white lily-of-the-valley-type flowers. In suitable conditions it will grow to at least 15ft (4.5m).*

163

WIND

Wind can be a serious problem, and gardens that are exposed need to have screening and protecting plants put in as a major priority, otherwise nothing will grow satisfactorily. The problem is doubled in coastal gardens where salt is carried on the wind, but fortunately there are barrier plants which do not burn brown in a salty gale. Shrubs and trees which will provide good dense screens are advisable.

Plants suitable for growing as windbreaks

Aucuba japonica	*Deutzia escallonia*	*Pinus mugo*
Arundinaria japonica	*Euonymus japonicus*	*Pinus nigra*
Berberis darwinii	*Fagus sylvatica*	*Prunus laurocerasus*
Berberis stenophylla	*Hippophae rhamnoides*	*Primus spinosa*
Chamaecyparis	Ilex	Pyracantha
Corylus avellana	*Ligustrum ovalifolium*	Tamarix
Crataegus oxyacantha	*Lonicera nitida*	*Ulex europaeus*
Cupressocyparis leylandii	*Picea spp*	Viburnum

164

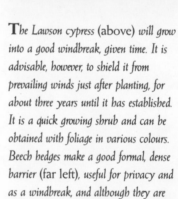

The Lawson cypress (above) will grow into a good windbreak, given time. It is advisable, however, to shield it from prevailing winds just after planting, for about three years until it has established. It is a quick growing shrub and can be obtained with foliage in various colours. Beech hedges make a good formal, dense barrier (far left), useful for privacy and as a windbreak, and although they are deciduous shrubs, they retain their green-coloured leaves in winter, when they change to russet-brown. In very exposed positions, they should be shielded for their first two years. Berberis (left and below) is a prolific flowering shrub, with berries and prickly, sometimes evergreen leaves. It is an excellent informal hedge.

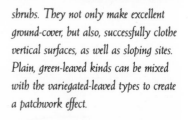

Parthenocissus henryana (left) is a form of Virginia creeper, but with dark green leaves marked with silver and pink. It is particularly effective if it is planted against a sheltered wall. It is a deciduous shrub and climbs by sticky tendrils. The ivies (above) are extremely useful shrubs. They not only make excellent ground-cover, but also, successfully clothe vertical surfaces, as well as sloping sites. Plain, green-leaved kinds can be mixed with the variegated-leaved types to create a patchwork effect.

STEEP SLOPES OR BANKS

The problem here is threefold: which species to grow on such a site, how to make it ornamental and how to retain the soil. Furthermore, since the angle is difficult to stand on, the plants should not need much care and attention. A laborious and expensive alternative to plants is to terrace the site and build retaining walls, but this may not be practicable. Trailing or creeping plants are good; there are some tough, low-growing species, too, which need little care and will bind the soil.

Plants suitable for growing on steep banks		
Ajuga reptans	Erica	Lamium maculatum
Bergenia	Fragaria indica	Lonicera japonica halliana
Calluna vulgaris	Genista lydia	Saxifraga x urbium
Campanula portenschlagiana	Hebe pinguifolia	Sedum spurium
Campanula poscharskyana	Hedera	Thymus serpyllum
Cerastium tomentosum	Helianthemum	Vinca major
Cotoneaster dammeri	Hypericum calycinum	Vinca minor
Cotoneaster horizontalis	Juniperus horizontalis	Viola odorata
Cytisus x kewensis	Lamiastrum galeobdonon	

Cerastium tomentosum (below left) will help to hold crumbling banks together, and provide an attractive silvery effect all year. However, it is inclined to spread, so should be sited with care. The periwinkle (above left) will grow in sun or shade, although preferring sun. Its stems root as they grow along the ground, and it provides good, labour-free cover on any sloping site. Deadnettles (above) also cover the ground well and need no attention.

GLOSSARY OF TERMS

A

Acid soil Soil with little or no lime content, having a pH level of 6.5 or less.

Aeration The process of airing the soil — by spiking a lawn with a fork, for example.

Air plants Also known as epiphytes, plants that physically grow on other plants, often trees, but are not dependent on them for nourishment.

Algae Primitive organisms, found growing in damp places as green powder or strands.

Alkaline soil Soil with a high lime content, having a pH value of more than 7.4. Some plants will not grow in alkaline soils.

Alleopathy The process whereby a plant restricts the growth or development of other plants around it by releasing toxic chemicals.

Alternative hosts Also referred to as decoy plants, these are plants that are used to attract insect pests away from the principal crop.

Annual A plant whose life cycle is completed in a year or less, usually from spring to autumn, but also from autumn to late summer.

Apex The top of a plant.

Apical bud A bud at the end of a stem.

B

Bark ringing The removal of a narrow ring of bark from the tree trunk.

Bedding A system of planting that uses tender herbaceous plants, grown with protection while young and then planted out in summer.

Biennial A plant that takes two growing seasons to complete its life cycle, from germination to death after flowering.

Biennial bearing When a plant produces a very heavy crop one year and little or none the next.

Beneficial insects Those insects that are helpful to the gardener because they pollinate plants or prey on pests.

Branch bark ridge A ridge that can be seen at the junction of the branch and the trunk of most trees.

Broadcasting The scattering of seed over an area, as opposed to sowing it in drills.

Botrytis A common fungal disease also called grey mould; its scientific name is *Botrytis cinerea*.

Bud An embryonic shoot or flower, often with protective outer scales; potential fruit or flower-buds are round and fat; vegetative buds are long, thin and pointed.

Bulb A plant organ in which the leaf bases have been modified and swollen with food; it is, in effect, a bud.

Bush A low, dense shrub or fruit plant.

C

Calcifuge A plant that dislikes alkaline soil, rhododendron, for example.

Callus The tissue formed by a plant at a wound, which covers and protects it; in trees it is overlaid with bark.

Candle Extension growth of pine branches.

Central leader The main stem.

Chlorophyll The green colouring matter found in the leaves and other parts of plants; iron is an integral part of it.

Chlorosis Yellowing of leaves. If lime-induced, this discoloration appears in the younger leaves first, at the shoot tips, and means that the iron needed to produce chlorophyll is not being absorbed by the plant roots because the plant is a lime-hater.

Climbing plants Tall, spindly plants that need the support of other plants, a fence or trellis.

Clone A group of identical plants that have been vegetatively propagated from the same source.

Companion plants Plants that relate in a positive way to their neighbouring plants.

Compost Organic material like garden and kitchen wastes that has decomposed to form a nutrient-rich humus.

Conifer Mainly cone-bearing plants, usually evergreen.

Cordon A plant trained as a single stem. (There are also double and triple cordons.)

Corm An underground plant organ, in which the modified and compressed stem becomes thickened and acts as a food store.

Cover crops Crops that are planted to protect the ground between the harvest of one main crop and the sowing of the next.

Crotch The angle between two branches.

Crown The arrangement of branches at the top of a stem.

Cultivar A variety of a plant originating in cultivation as opposed to in the wild.

Cutting A piece of stem cut away from a plant to be rooted in order to produce a new plant.

Cutting, hardwood or ripe A length of stem about 10in (25cm) long, cut from the end of a current season's shoot in autumn, when it is brown or mature for most of its length.

Cutting, root A piece of root, 2-4in (5-10cm) long, used to increase herbaceous perennials. These cuttings are taken in winter.

Cutting, semi-hardwood or half-ripe The end 3-6in (7-15cm) of a young shoot, cut off when it is turning brown at its base, but it is still green at the tip; it is taken from mid- to late summer.

Cutting, soft or tip The tip or soft, green end of a new shoot which is cut off, 3-4in (7-10cm) long, from spring to mid-summer.

D

Deadheading The removal of flower heads immediately after they have died, to prevent the plant wasting its energy on seed formation.

Deciduous A woody plant that sheds its leaves naturally during autumn.

Dehorning Severe shortening of a branch.

Dioecious Having male and female flowers of separate plants. Both male and female plants are required for pollination.

Division Method of propagation in which the plant is split into several parts so that each part can grow into a separate new plant.

Dormancy A period when a plant or a seed is inactive and waiting for some stimulus to start it into growth.

Double digging Breaking up the soil to the depth of two spades.

Drills Shallow trenches drawn out for sowing seeds.

E

Earthing up The drawing up of earth around a plant. Especially done to potatoes and celery.

Epiphytes See Air plants.

Evergreen A shrub or tree that retains its leaves all year, although not every leaf is everlasting — some leaves are shed all year.

Extension growth New growth arising from the previous season's shoots.

F

Fallow Ground which has been dug and left unplanted, partly to revitalize it, and partly to allow weed seeds to germinate so that the seedlings can be destroyed before planting or sowing cultivated plants.

Fan A plant trained so that the branches radiate fan-wise from the trunk.

Farmyard manure Manure produced by cattle, horses, chickens, etc. For safe use in the garden it must be well-rotted or composted thoroughly.

Fastigiate Having branches that grow almost vertically, parallel to the trunk, having a columnar outline.

Fertilizer A plant food in concentrated form, either powder or granular, containing one or more mineral nutrients such as calcium or iron.

Fimbriate Fringed, used to describe flower-petal margins.

Firm wood Branches and shoots with tough rind.

Floribunda Roses also known as cluster-flowered bush roses. A rose plant with flowers in trusses, clusters or many stems.

Flush cut A cut that is made close and flush with another part of the plant.

Focal point A point to which the eye is drawn.

Foliar Leafy, used to describe sprays containing nutrients, which are applied to leaves as a method of 'instant' feeding.

Frame A 'box' placed on the ground with sides made of brick or wood, and the lid of glass with a wooden framework. A frame is used for protecting tender plants in cold weather, bringing on rooted cuttings and seedlings, and for growing tropical plants, especially fruit, in temperate climates.

Framework The main branch skeleton of a plant.

Friable soil Soil that is crumbly in texture.

Frost hollows An area where the cold air that causes frosts gathers. Also known as frost pockets.

Fungus An organism separate from a plant or animal, which does not contain chlorophyll and needs organic matter to supply its food; yeast is a fungus.

Fungicide A substance that is used to control or eradicate fungal diseases infecting plants, usually a chemical.

G

Genus A grouping of plants having similar characteristics. It is subdivided into species and is represented by the first element in a botanical name.

Germination The first stage in the development and growth of a seed.

Glaucous Covered in a bluish bloom.

Green Manure Plants grown so that they can then be dug directly into the soil, while they are still green, in order to enrich it.

Ground Cover Plants grown not necessarily for their harvest but to cover large areas of soil when the garden or field is idle. They are often planted to keep weeds down and prevent soil erosion.

Gummosis An exudation of a gumlike substance from cherry and plum trees.

H

Half-standard A tree or shrub with a clear stem or trunk that is three to four feet tall, which is shorter than that of a standard.

Head The uppermost part of a plant, the branches above the trunk, or stem. Also known as the crown.

Herbicides Chemicals used to kill off vegetation, in particular weeds.

Hosts Plants that attract insects because they are a good source of nectar, pollen, or other food.

Humus A brown-black substance, which can absorb a lot of moisture; it is formed from the rotting remains of organic matter, whether animal or vegetable; its presence is essential for the maintenance of a good soil structure.

Hybrid A plant created by crossing two dissimilar parent plants.

Hybrid tea Roses also known as large-flowered bush roses. A rose with shapely buds which develop into large- or medium-sized flowers.

I

Insecticides Chemicals used to combat insect pests.

Intercropping Growing two or more crops together to make the best use of the ground available or because of the mutual benefit they afford each other. Also known as interplanting.

J

Jardin potager A French kitchen garden, usually with the vegetables planted decoratively, often within low hedge borders.

L

Lateral A shoot growing from a main stem.

Layer A method of plant increase in which a slanting cut is made partially through a low-growing, one-year-old stem on the underside, opposite a leaf joint. The stem is pinned down onto the soil and the cut is covered with more soil. This is performed in spring or summer, when roots will form at the injury.

Leader The main stem of a plant.

Leafmould Partially decayed leaves, useful for incorporating into the soil as humus.

Leguminous plants Plants belonging to the pea family. Valuable for their ability to fix nitrogen from the air into the soil, thereby making it available to other plants.

Lime A word describing several forms of calcium, such as calcium carbonate (chalk), but strictly calcium oxide (quicklime). It is used to decrease the acidity of the soil.

M

Maiden A young tree with only one-year-old growth above ground.

Manure Animal excreta mixed with bed-litter such as straw, sawdust, or wood shavings.

Mature wood Growth that has completed its extension longitudinally.

Monocrops Crops of a single variety filling the whole of the garden or plot.

Mulch A cover of organic material placed around the plant primarily to help retain moisture in the soil and to restrict the growth of weeds.

N

Neutral soil Soil that is neither acid nor alkaline, having a pH of 7.0.

New wood Growth made during the current season.

Nicking Cutting into the rind below a bud.

Notching The removal of a small wedge of bark above a bud.

O

Offset A young plant produced from, and next to, a parent plant; bulbs are typical examples.

Old wood Growth made before the current season.

On year The year when fruit is produced by a plant subject to biennial bearing.

Open centre A plant trained so that the centre of the head is devoid of branches.

P

Parasites Plants that grow on other plants on which they are dependent for food and support.

Perennial, herbaceous A plant with soft tissues, not bark or woody stems. It lives from year to year, and often dies down in autumn to ground level, although this does not apply to all species. The term generally refers to the flowering plants used in beds and borders.

Pesticide A substance used for controlling or eradicating organisms that prey upon plants, such as insects, fungal diseases, bacteria, snails and slugs, or small mammals.

pH A scale from 1.0–14.0 for measuring the acidity or alkalinity of the soil. Neutral is 7.0; anything below this point is acid and above is alkaline. Each figure needs to be multiplied by 10 to give the actual increase of acid or alkaline content in the soil.

Photosynthesis The process in plants whereby the green parts manufacture oxygen and carbohydrates in the presence of sunlight, from the water and carbon dioxide of the atmosphere.

Pinch To remove a portion of stem with finger and thumb.

Plant association The way plants relate to other plants.

Pollarding Cutting tree branches back hard. It is often carried out on plants with colourful bark such as *Salix* (willow).

Pollination The fertilization of a flower by the transfer of pollen from male to female parts.

Predators Insects that eat other insects.

Pruning The removal of shoots or branches from a plant in order to maintain its healthy growth, encourage flowering/fruiting, and keep its size under control without stunting it.

Propagation The means of increasing the numbers of a plant.

Prostrate Close to the ground, low growing.

Pyramid A plant with branches growing over the length of the main stem, with the lower branches longer than those above.

R

Renewal pruning A method of pruning which encourages new growth to replace that which has borne fruit.

Reversion A shoot with totally green leaves growing from a plant that normally has other than green leaves. Also a virus disease of blackcurrants.

Rhizome A stem which grows underground and extends horizontally, sending up shoots. It is often fleshy and serves as a storage organ; pieces that break off will root and produce new plants.

Root stock The underground part of a plant that gives rise to the shoot.

Rotation of crops The yearly movement of crops from one place in the garden to another to make the best use of the ground and to reduce the incidence of pests and diseases.

S

Saprophytes Plants that live on the dead remains of other plants.

Sequestrene A metal compound of such a type that the metal behaves in a different way to normal, and becomes available in chalky soils to plant roots, where it would otherwise be 'locked up'.

Shrub A plant with many woody stems radiating from one point on the plant at soil level.

Soft wood Young stems devoid of tough stems or bark.

Soil erosion The washing or blowing away of soil by winds, rains, and floods.

Soil sickness A disease caused by repeatedly growing the same crop in the same soil.

Species An individual or closely related group of plants within a genus.

Spur A short, jointed twig containing fruit buds.

Spur system A collection of spurs on a branch.

Standard A tree or shrub with a clear stem or trunk that is almost five to six feet tall. (See half-standard.)

Stopping The removal of the growing point of a plant.

Stub A portion of stem or branch that has been left after pruning.

Sub-lateral A shoot growing from a lateral.

Successional cropping The planting of a new crop as soon as one is harvested so that the ground is always in use.

Successional planting The positioning of plants in a garden so that one takes its place visually as the other dies back.

Sucker A shoot produced from the rootstock of a plant, as in roses; many suckers will take over the top part of the plant, but can be useful and form a method of increase, as in the stag's-horn sumach.

T

Tap root The main root of a plant.

Tender Plants unable to withstand frosts.

Thinning The process of reducing the number of seedlings in a row so that the remaining ones have room to grow.

Tie down A method of training roses so that the stems are trained close to the ground on horizontal wires, or by being pegged down.

Tie in To tie to a support.

Tip bearer A plant that produces fruit buds at the end of shoots.

Tilth The physical condition of the surface of the soil. A fine tilth is needed for sowing seeds.

Topdressing An application of material to the soil or compost surface close to plants; it may be fertilizer or the replacement of the top few inches of compost in a container.

Truss A compound stalk with flowers or fruit.

Tuber A storage organ, either stem or root, swollen with plant food and carrying the plant through its dormant period.

U

Union The junction between shoot and root.

V

Variety Any distinct form of species or hybrid.

Vegetative propagation Propagation by methods other than seed. Produces a plant identical to its parent.

W

Water shoot Vigorous growths often arising from around pruning cuts.

171

INDEX

—◦—

174

175

176

ACKNOWLEDGEMENTS

The publishers wish to thank the following for supplying the photographs used in this book:
A-Z Collection pp 9 (t, br), 10 (r), 16, 25; Agriframes Ltd p 129; Juan Baxter p 78 (br); Ann Berry pp 78 (l), 79 (tl, bl), 80 (tl, r), 81, 83 (bl, r), 85; Ann Bonar p 10 (tl); Alastair Campbell p 22 (tl); Paul Collins pp 120 (t), 122, 127, 131 (t); Priscilla Connell p 80 (tl); Andrew Crace Designs p 120 (b); Hank Dijkman pp 149, 150; Liz Eddison pp 120 (l, r), 121 (l), 124 (t), 126, 152 (b), 156 (t), 157 (t, b); John Glover p 139; Carole Hellman pp 149, 150; Marijke Heuff p 136; Patrick Johns pp 123, 125 (b); Edward Kinsey pp 20 (b), 27; John A Lyons p 80 (bl); Robert B Lyons pp 78 (tr) 79 (r), 80 (tl), 83 (tl), 84; A Peter Margosian p 82; Maggie Oster pp 86-91; Anthony Paul p 136; Jerry Pavia p 47; Jenny Plumley p 83 (bl); Birmid Qualcast Ltd p 29 (l); The Harry Smith Horticultural Photographic Collection pp 8, 9 (l), 10 (bl), 11, 12, 29 (r), 30-1, 36, 41, 44, 46-9; Spectrum Colour Library pp 13, 18 (t), 32, 34-5; Ron Sutherland (Mien Ruys Design) pp 121, 135, 137, 138, 146; Brigitte Thomas pp 132, 140-2, 143-5, 148; Cathy Wilkinson Barash pp 92-5, 98-101; Steven Wooster p 131 (b); Kate Zari p 134. Other photographs were supplied by Gillian Becket, Eric Crichton, Daansmit, Bob Gibbons Photography, Richard and Sally Greenhill, Jerry Harpur, Neill Holmes, Arthur Hellyer, Ian Howes, Patrick Johns, Tom Leighton, National Vegetable Research Station, Photobank, The Plant Photo Library (Susan Roth), Harry Smith Photography Collection, Photos Horticultural (Michael Warren) and Dennis Woodland. Key: t — top; b — bottom; l — left; r — right.